# DESCRIBING AND EXPLAINING GRAMMAR AND VOCABULARY IN ELT

## WITHDRAWAL

Language description plays an important role in language learning/teaching because it often determines what specific language forms, features, and usages are taught and how. A good understanding of language description is vital for language teachers and material writers and should constitute an important part of their knowledge. This book provides a balanced treatment of both theory and practice. It focuses on some of the most important and challenging grammar and vocabulary usage questions. Using these questions as examples, it shows how theory can inform practice and how grammar and vocabulary description and explanation can be made more effective and engaging.

Part I describes and evaluates the key linguistic theories on language description and teaching. Chapters in this section conclude with questions for consideration and discussion. Part II discusses and gives specific examples of how challenging grammar and vocabulary issues can be more effectively described and explained; each chapter focuses on one or more specific grammar and vocabulary issue. These chapters conclude with suggested teaching activities. The book also contains an annotated list of useful free online resources (online corpora and websites) for grammar and vocabulary learning/teaching and a glossary of important terms in language description and teaching.

**Dilin Liu** is Professor of Applied Linguistics/TESOL, Department of English, The University of Alabama, USA.

ESL & Applied Linguistics Professional Series
Eli Hinkel, Series Editor

Visit www.routledge.com/education for additional information on titles in the ESL & Applied Linguistics Professional Series

# DESCRIBING AND EXPLAINING GRAMMAR AND VOCABULARY IN ELT

## Key Theories and Effective Practices

*Dilin Liu*

Routledge
Taylor & Francis Group

NEW YORK AND LONDON

First published 2014
by Routledge
711 Third Avenue, New York, NY 10017

Simultaneously published in the UK
by Routledge
2 Park Square, Milton Park, Abingdon, Oxon OX14 4RN

Routledge is an imprint of the Taylor & Francis Group, an informa business

Library of Congress Cataloguing in Publication Data

Liu, Dilin.
    Describing and explaining grammar and vocabulary in ELT: key theories and effective practices/
By Dilin Liu.
        pages cm.—(ESL & Applied Linguistics Professional Series)
    Includes bibliographical references and index.
    ISBN 978-0-415-63608-7—ISBN 978-0-415-63609-4—ISBN 978-0-203-08560-8
    1. English language—Study and teaching—Foreign speakers.   2. English language—Grammar—
Study and teaching.   3. Vocabulary—Study and teaching. I. Title.

PE1128.A2L5334 2013
428.0071—dc23

                                                                                    2013004263

ISBN: 978-0-415-63608-7(hbk)
ISBN: 978-0-415-63609-4 (pbk)
ISBN: 978-0-203-08560-8 (ebk)

Typeset in Bembo Std
by MPS Limited, Chennai, India
www.adi-mps.com

Printed and Bound in the United States of America
by Edwards Brothers Malloy

To Yun and Jiajia (Julianne)

# CONTENTS

# LIST OF TABLES

# PREFACE

This book is based on my many years of reading and research on the learning and teaching of English grammar and vocabulary, arguably the two most important aspects of language. As an ESL learner, teacher, and teacher educator, I have always been interested in not only how the English language works (especially its grammar and vocabulary) but also why it works the way it does. At the same time, I have been equally interested in how to best describe and teach English grammar and vocabulary usages, especially those that are difficult for students to understand and challenging for teachers to explain. In fact, many of the grammar and vocabulary usage questions I have explored were first raised by my students and colleagues. The search for answers to these questions has involved extensive reading and research (including many corpus-based studies). In the process, I have learned not only a lot about the English language but also about the importance and challenges of grammar and vocabulary description and explanation for teachers in general. The latter understanding has been the motivation for writing this book, which is intended to provide language teachers (including pre-service teacher trainees) and material writers with a solid understanding of grammar and vocabulary description and explanation both in theory and practice.

Grammar and vocabulary description refers to the analysis and description of how the lexical and syntactical components of a language work together to convey meanings. It constitutes an essential part of language description (which includes, in addition, the analysis of phonology, a part of language that this book does not cover, except for a brief mention in Chapter 6). Historically, language description has focused exclusively on grammar. Yet, contemporary linguistic theories and research have shown that grammar and vocabulary are not two distinct domains but the two ends of one continuum (an issue that will be addressed in Chapter 1). This new understanding has led to the inclusion of both grammar and vocabulary in this book. The title of this book also contains the term *explaining* in addition to *describing*. The reason for doing so is that while both terms have essentially the same meaning in this context—presenting how a given language feature/usage works, explanation often covers not only how it works but also why it works the way it does. In teaching a language usage, an explanation is often needed on top of a simple description.

It is also important to note that description and explanation constitute only one part or phase of the complex process of grammar and vocabulary learning/teaching. Besides description and explanation, the process of grammar and vocabulary learning/teaching also involves practice, reinforcement, and actual use. This book covers only description and explanation. Therefore, it is not a comprehensive book on English grammar and vocabulary and their teaching. It does not cover all of the grammatical and vocabulary aspects and issues in English. Instead, the book focuses on some of the most important and challenging grammar and vocabulary usage questions. With these challenging questions as examples, the book attempts to show how theory can inform practice and how grammar and vocabulary description and explanation can be made more effective and engaging.

## Content and Organization

This book consists of an introduction (Chapter 1) and two parts. The introduction describes the purview, importance, and principles of language description. Part I (Chapters 2–5) describes and evaluates the key linguistic theories on language description and teaching, with Chapter 2 on prescriptive, structural, and generative linguistics; Chapter 3 on sociolinguistics and systemic functional linguistics; Chapter 4 on Cognitive Linguistics; and Chapter 5 on corpus linguistics. Each chapter in this part begins with an overview of the linguistic theory(ies) in question followed by a discussion of their impact on language description and teaching. Each chapter (including also Chapter 1) ends with questions for consideration and discussion.

Part II (Chapters 6–14) discusses with specific examples how challenging grammar and vocabulary issues can be more effectively described and explained, with each chapter focusing on one or more specific grammar and vocabulary issues, such as English tenses/aspects, articles, and word collocations. Each chapter in this part typically begins with a description of the grammar/vocabulary features/issues being addressed. It is followed by a discussion of the established useful practices in teaching the given grammar/vocabulary feature/issue, a discussion that is based on a survey of seven existing ESL student grammar textbook series and the observations of classroom teaching as well as my own teaching experience. Then the chapter moves on to a section titled "Explaining/teaching challenging issues with new insights," which provides explanation and teaching practices that are informed by the most recent theories and research findings. The information in this section is based on published studies including those by the author. The main purpose of the section is to show how to apply new research and theory to enhance language description and explanation. The chapters in Part II end with some suggested teaching activities. These activities are meant only as snapshots of the types of activities teachers can use in explaining/teaching the grammar/vocabulary features in question.

There are some minor variations in the format in a few of the chapters, including Chapters 6, 7, 11, and 14. Chapters 6 and 7 differ from the rest of the chapters in this part of the book in that they offer a general coverage of the basic issues involved in vocabulary description (Chapter 6) and sentence structure description (Chapter 7). Chapters 11 and 14 are unique in that they each cover multiple, although related, topics, with Chapter 11 on *object placement, subject/object deletion*, and the *passive voice*, and Chapter 14 on *idioms, phrasal verbs*, and *formulae/lexical bundles*. In Chapters 11 and 14, no description of "established useful practices" is given due both to lack of space and the fact that some of the topics have not received much coverage in English language teaching so far.

The book includes an annotated list of some useful free online resources (online corpora and websites) for grammar and vocabulary learning and teaching, as well as a list for glossary of special terms.

Finally, this book may be used as a textbook for a pedagogical grammar, vocabulary teaching, or material development course, a self-study text, or a reference book. However it is used, I hope readers will find its information useful in their language teaching.

# ACKNOWLEDGMENTS

First, I would like to acknowledge the valuable information and inspiration about grammar/vocabulary and grammar/vocabulary teaching that I have gained in my career from many of my students as well as many colleagues in the field. Their information and inspiration have motivated and contributed greatly to this book. A special acknowledgment should go to my renowned colleagues: Marianne Celce-Murcia, Diane Larsen-Freeman, Paul Nation, and Andrea Tyler, whom I have had the honor of working with on one or more occasions (conference session and/or book projects) and whose work has influenced me and this book tremendously.

Then, I would like to thank Eli Hinkel, editor of the ESL and Applied Linguistics Professional Series (to which this book belongs), for her invaluable advice and suggestions over the course of the development of the book. I would also like to thank Professor Penny Ur of Oranim Academic College of Education, Israel, and an anonymous reviewer for reviewing the proposal for this book and the sample chapters. Their comments and suggestions have significantly enhanced the quality of the book. I also need to express my deep gratitude to Naomi Silverman, publisher at Routledge, for her encouragement and clear directions in the preparation of the manuscript. Finally, I would like to thank my graduate assistant Josh Weathersby for proofreading the manuscript. Of course, I alone am responsible for whatever errors and shortcomings remain.

# 1

# LANGUAGE DESCRIPTION

## Purview, importance, and principles

## 1.1 Introduction

As mentioned in the Preface, grammar and vocabulary description (including explanation) is an essential part of **language description**—the analysis and description of how a language works (i.e., how its lexical, morphological, and syntactical components combine to convey meanings).[1] Historically, language description has focused almost exclusively on grammar, a practice rooted in the long tradition of treating grammar and vocabulary as two separate domains, with the former dealing strictly with the study of language rules and the latter referring simply to the individual words in a language. In language teaching, this separation has often been shown by the fact that there are textbooks and classes devoted exclusively to one or the other (especially to grammar). However, contemporary linguistic research findings from functional, Cognitive, and corpus linguistics have seriously challenged this rigid separation of the two. It has been found that grammar and vocabulary are actually two inherently connected parts of one entity or the two ends of one continuum because "a grammatical structure may be lexically restricted" (Francis, 1993, p. 104) and, conversely, lexical items are not only grammatically confined (i.e., confined to certain grammatical structures) but also grammatical in nature themselves because the choice of a lexical item often has implication for the sentence structure it appears in (Biber, Conrad, & Reppen, 1998; Biber, Johansson, Leech, Conrad, & Finegan, 1999; Hunston & Francis, 2000). As a result of this new finding, many linguists and applied linguists have argued for the integration of grammar and vocabulary in the study of language and have adopted the term **lexicogrammar** to describe this integration (e.g., Halliday, 1994; Hunston & Francis, 2000). This book adopts this approach to language description by covering both grammar and vocabulary. Given this fact and the fact that the term "language description" may not be clear enough about what it means or what it actually covers, the book is thus entitled *Describing and explaining grammar and vocabulary in ELT*. However, for the sake of simplicity, "language description" rather than "grammar and vocabulary description" will be used most of the time hereafter in this book.

Language description plays a very important role in language learning and teaching because language teaching materials and the language features taught in class are often based on the language descriptions provided by linguists. Of course, language teachers and material writers usually do not present to learners verbatim the descriptions provided by linguists because such descriptions are not intended for language learners. They generally have to make selections, adaptations, and/ or simplifications of such descriptions in order to make the information accessible and helpful to language learners. As a result, what is presented to the language learners is what I would like to call *pedagogical language description*, which is tailored to help learners better understand and grasp a language as well as to help teachers master the language analysis skills necessary for successful language teaching. Thus, one noticeable difference between pedagogical language description and general language description is that the former uses less technical terminology. Pedagogical language description constitutes a crucial part of **pedagogical grammar** because a key function of pedagogical grammar is to offer a description and analysis of the grammar of a language for the purpose of teaching/learning that language (Liu, 2012b). In practical terms, pedagogical language description refers to the presentation of grammar and vocabulary usage information to learners to help them grasp the grammar and vocabulary being taught. This book deals mainly with pedagogical language description. However, for the sake of simplicity, the adjective *pedagogical* will not be used in the remainder of the book unless needed for clarity.

## 1.2 The purview of language description

The purview of language description, which refers to the range of issues covered in its description, has changed along with the development in linguistic theories. This is because language description has historically been influenced, as expected, by the dominant linguistic theories and approaches, such as **prescriptive** and **structural grammar/linguistics** (or **prescriptivism** and **structuralism**) in the first half of the twentieth century, **generative grammar/linguistics** (or **generativism**) in the late 1950s through the early 1970s, and the more recent **systemic functional linguistics**, **Cognitive Linguistics**, and **corpus linguistics**.[2] As a result, the approaches to language description as well as the descriptions of some specific language features and rules have changed, sometimes significantly, from one period of time to another and varied from one reference/ textbook to another. Along with these changes, the scope of grammar/vocabulary description has expanded. A detailed discussion of many of the changes that have helped with the expansion of the scope of linguistic description will be presented in the remainder of the book, but a brief mention of them is necessary here to help 1) delineate the characteristics of language description under each major linguistic theory and 2) chart the expansion of the scope of the description.

When prescriptive grammar was prevalent, the focus of language description was on defining correct forms and usages in language. Even some common usages were described as being incorrect. I remember seeing the use of "their" with a singular antecedent included as an error (e.g., *Everyone should do their best*) in the error finding section of the TOEFL test I took in the early 1980s. I also remember spending a lot of time both in and out of class studying prescriptive rules in order to catch such so-called "errors" that we now understand as common and acceptable usages.

The stress on correctness in form advocated by prescriptive grammar was also noticeable in structural and generative grammars, two linguistic theories that were interested mostly in formal structural issues such as phonology, morphology, and syntax, overlooking questions of meaning and use (pragmatics). For example, in the language descriptions used in the audiolingual approach, an approach heavily influenced by structural and behavioral linguistic theories represented by Bloomfield (1933) and Skinner (1957), language is presented essentially as a system of rules or patterns of form that can be manipulated to produce grammatical sentences and can be learned via various pattern drills or habit formation (an issue that will be discussed in detail in the next chapter). This type of language description and teaching practice does not pay much attention to how language learners should use/choose specific linguistic forms to convey their meanings in real life situations. Therefore, as Holme notes (2009, p. 1), the drills based on structural and behavioral linguistic theories and descriptions often resulted in the learner "forever producing versions of a structure that represented meanings they might never use."

Similarly, in the language descriptions based on the generative linguistic theory of Chomsky (1957, 1965), language is also treated as a manipulatable system of rules, but it is presented as a much more abstract system. Furthermore, human knowledge of language rules is considered essentially innate in the form of **Universal Grammar** (UG) and is activated by minimal language input. The activation may involve the setting of some language-specific parameters (rules) of the UG. In this theory, language production or use is mainly a generation of surface sentence structures from deep structures via transformational rules.

These language descriptions and the traditional linguistic theories (structuralism and generativism) on which they were based "all failed," as Roulet (1975, p. 75) pointed out more than three decades ago, "to provide information on the use of language as an instrument of communication" because most of what these theories and descriptions did was (pp. 75–76):

(a)  to describe only the system and not the use of the language;
(b)  to treat only the structure of the sentence and neglect communicative units such as *text* and *dialogue*;
(c)  to study systematically the referential function of language, neglecting other functions (such as interpersonal and relational/textual functions);
(d)  to study only one variety of the language, itself considered as homogeneous and representative and to pay no attention to other varieties which are part of the verbal repertoire of the linguistic community.

Before I move on to the changes that contemporary linguistic theories have brought to language description, it is necessary to note that traditional descriptions have the advantage of being simple and straightforward and hence "relatively easy for teachers and students to use," a point that Willis (2003, p. 111) made in his discussion of the traditional description of the use of the present and the past tenses. However, this advantage is often gained at the expense of accuracy and adequacy in language description. Of course, given the limited class time and other constraining factors in language teaching, it is often very difficult to find the appropriate compromise or balance between accuracy and adequacy on the one hand and simplicity and comprehensibility on the other, an issue I will return to below in Section 1.3 of this chapter.

The emergence of Halliday's systemic functional linguistics (1973, 1994) as well as the work of sociolinguists such as Hymes (1971) and other functional linguists (Givón, 1984; Hopper, 1987) had a significant impact on language description. Systemic functional linguistics views language as a system of choices (rather than rules) available to and made by language users in interactions in various social contexts; hence, function and use are the foundations, rather than secondary or subsidiary issues, of its linguistic analysis and description. Thanks to the influence of functional linguistics as well as the growth of globalism and as a reaction against the meaning-impoverished traditional teaching methodologies of grammar-translation and audiolingualism, issues of meaning and use (pragmatics) have, since the 1970s, become an important part of language description in some grammar books for language teachers (e.g., Celce-Murcia & Larsen-Freeman, 1999) and also in some textbooks for language learners (e.g., Larsen-Freeman's textbook series *Grammar dimensions: Form, meaning, and use*, 1993). Another important influence of functional linguistics on language description is its treatment of lexis and grammar as the two ends of one continuum, rather than two separate domains, a point already noted earlier. This collapsing of the rigid traditional separation of lexis and grammar has since been further supported and strengthened by Cognitive Linguistics and corpus linguistics, two new contemporary linguistic theories/approaches that have introduced some significant changes in language description and further expanded its scope.[3]

Like functional linguistics, Cognitive Linguistics attaches great importance to meaning and function in its approach to language. In this sense, Cognitive Linguistics may be considered a further development of functional linguistics, but it differs significantly from the latter in that it considers cognition key in the understanding and use of language. It is also important to note that, although a theory interested in the role of mind in language, Cognitive Linguistics differs drastically from generative linguistics in that it rejects the claim of the existence of an autonomous linguistic faculty or the innateness of language. The influence of Cognitive Linguistics on linguistic description arises largely from its following three key theories. The first is the theory of language as a symbolic system composed of **symbolic units** i.e., form–meaning pairings that can be as small as phonemes and as large as complete clauses or sentences (e.g., the plural *s* and the entire utterance *What's up?* as a greeting). With language being symbolic, Cognitive Linguistics focuses on human experience (especially embodied experience) and conceptualization in language use and meaning. The second key theory of Cognitive Linguistics is that meaning is fundamental to language as it permeates every aspect of language, including grammatical structures. The third key theory is that language is not innate but usage-based. (These key theories will be examined in detail in Chapter 4.)

Based on the aforementioned theories, language usages are motivated rather than arbitrary, which will be shown with examples in Chapter 4. This understanding would in turn make language learning more interesting and effective. Langacker (2008b) summarizes the point this way:

> The basic point is that conventional usage almost always has conceptual motivation. Though it has to be learned, it represents a particular way of construing the situation described. With proper instruction, the learning of a usage is thus a matter of grasping the semantic "spin" it imposes, a far more interesting and enjoyable process than sheer memorization.
>
> *(pp. 72–73)*

Similarly, as Pütz, Niemeier, and Dirven (2001, p. xv) point out,

> CL [Cognitive Linguistics] offers ways and means to facilitate foreign language learning because it enables us to point out the motivation behind every aspect of language. Language thus becomes explainable, and once learners see the way or ways a language works, they may start constructing and reconstructing their own hypotheses about the language they are learning.

In fact, as will be shown in the rest of the book, there have been quite a few studies that have produced interesting cognitive analysis-based descriptions of linguistic units and empirical evidence that these new descriptions are more effective than their counterpart traditional descriptions.

As for corpus linguistics and its influence on language description, it should be first noted that it is a usage-based approach just like Cognitive Linguistics but it differs from the latter in that it is an entirely data-driven approach that makes extensive use of advanced computer searching technology and large amounts of natural language data. The relationship between the two theories/approaches is an interesting and complex one. While they differ on the surface, with corpus linguistics being a study of the external aspect of language (i.e., language data) and Cognitive Linguistics focusing on the inner workings of language (the human mind), the two share three important commonalities: 1) both are usage-based with a focus on actual language data rather than intuitive judgment in their linguistic analysis; 2) both embrace a lexicogrammatical view of language; and 3) both are meaning-centered. Corpus linguistics offers Cognitive Linguistics "the kind of data that are at the heart of Cognitive Linguistics" (Gries, 2008, p. 412) while Cognitive Linguistics is able to provide corpus linguistics explanations for the motivations for the usages identified in the language data (Leech, 1992, 2000). As a result, corpus linguistics has produced many interesting research findings that have influenced language description, as will be shown Chapter 5.

Clearly, with the emergence of new linguistic theories and new understandings of language, the scope of language description has expanded from dealing with only traditional elements such as phonology, morphology, and syntax to covering important language use and functional issues such as discourse, texts, pragmatics, rhetorical styles, and register. The new theories have led to calls for treating and teaching grammar/language as a dynamic system (Larsen-Freeman, 2003; Larsen-Freeman & Cameron, 2008) and for other new perspectives and approaches (Hinkel & Fotos, 2002; Liu & Master, 2003). Moreover, research guided by the new theories has challenged and collapsed the traditional, rigid division between lexis and grammar. The new understandings of and approaches to language have resulted in more accurate, interesting, and useful pedagogical language descriptions, as will be shown in Part II of the book.

However, it is very important to point out that no single linguistic theory alone is adequate for developing effective and useful pedagogical language description, no matter how contemporary and sound the theory is. The reason that we should not try to base our grammar and vocabulary descriptions on one single theory is threefold. First, the purpose of pedagogical language description, as noted earlier, is to help language learners better grasp grammar and vocabulary usages, so, in designing and giving grammar and vocabulary descriptions, there are many factors we need to take into consideration (such as learner age and learning purpose), and some important principles we should follow (such as clarity and simplicity—issues that will be discussed in detail below in Section 1.4). Second, every linguistic theory may have its own particular weakness, especially from a language learning/teaching perspective. A theory can be sound and comprehensive but it may be too complex and/or too abstract in some of its concepts or procedures of analysis. Third, there is no consensus among researchers that any particularly linguistic theory is more advantageous than others when applied in grammar teaching (Hudson, 2001).

## 1.3 The importance of language description

The importance of language description in language learning and teaching is twofold. First, besides factors such as learner needs and the degree of usefulness of language items, language description greatly influences what language structures and usages are taught and how they are taught. This is because language lessons and teaching materials such as textbooks are often based on the language descriptions provided by linguists with a particular theoretical background. For instance, a textbook which used linguistic descriptions based on structural linguistic theories and was published before corpora were widely used would often focus mostly on grammatical units and rules and present them largely in isolation (i.e., without adequate contextual information illustrating them as choices for effective communication) by using many made-up sentences, rather than authentic ones taken or adapted from corpus data. On the other hand, a textbook based on systemic functional linguistic descriptions and published after corpus linguistics became popular tends to (1) focus on language (lexicogrammatical) units as part of a system or systemic resources that people use for communicative functions and (2) present them in meaningful contexts, employing corpus-based materials, e.g., Celce-Murcia & Sokolik's (2007–2009) *Grammar connection 1–5 series*.

Second, knowledge of sound language description is crucial for successful language teaching because, as Routlet (1975) noted more than 30 years ago, such knowledge "necessarily makes the teacher more aware of the language structures to be taught, thus improving the quality of the linguistic content of his language teaching course" (p. 69). A solid understanding of the language structures or systems is necessary for language teachers because, as Andrews (2007) puts it, "these systems are at the heart of the language acquisition process and must therefore form the core of any teacher's language awareness" and the possession of this awareness "is an essential attribute of any competent L2 teacher" (p. ix). For example, in order to help English-language students learn the correct use of the present perfect tense/aspect, the teacher has to be able to give an adequate description of, among other things, how to express actions and events in the present perfect form (i.e., how to form the tense/aspect) and when the present perfect should be used. To be able to give this description, the teacher must first learn to critically evaluate the existing linguistic descriptions available. As Pütz et al. (2001) point out, "applied work [referring to language teaching] must be based upon the best possible descriptive work" and "the applied linguist must approach descriptive work with a strong critical mind" (pp. xv–xvi). To be able to critically evaluate the existing linguistic descriptions, teachers should possess 1) a basic knowledge of the key linguistic theories that govern the existing linguistic descriptions); 2) a solid grasp of sound language learning theories and effective teaching practices; and 3) a clear understanding of their students, including their background and needs. The understanding of the latter is necessary because it enables teachers to provide helpful language descriptions tailored to their students' needs, especially those needs related to the differences in typology between their L1 and L2, an issue that will be discussed in the next section and later throughout Part II. Only after doing a critical examination can teachers identify the best linguistic descriptions and then turn them into useful pedagogical descriptions for their students.

The need for teachers to have a basic knowledge of the key linguistic theories, especially the most current ones, is also motivated by the fact that language descriptions often change along with the dominant linguistic theories. Dirven (2001, p. 3) makes this point very clearly when he writes,

> it is not sufficient to use some or other descriptive analysis of a grammar segment, but the applied linguist must be informed about the continued evolutions in the field and base his programming of learning problems on the best, even if they are the latest, descriptive proposals.

Many examples in the chapters in Part II of the book will show how new linguistic research findings make language description more accurate and informative and how knowledge of the new research findings can enable teachers to make their teaching more effective and engaging. Of course, having a solid knowledge of linguistic theories is not enough. Teachers should also know the general principles of language description, an issue we now turn to.

## 1.4 Principles for language description

As is the case with language teaching in general (or with doing anything for that matter), there are sound principles to follow in language description. A few scholars have written specifically about this issue (Roulet, 1975; Swan, 1994; Yule, 1998 about grammar description; Nation, 2001, pp. 60–113 about vocabulary description) and a few others have touched on it (Hughes & McCarthy, 1998). Swan's discussion about grammar description/explanation and Nation's points about vocabulary description/explanation appear to be the most thorough, informative, and concise. In fact, a few of the key principles they offered were identical. We will focus on Swan's but will add Nation's points where appropriate. Swan offered six principles for pedagogical grammatical description/explanation (1994, pp. 46–51):

1.  Truth: rules should be true.
2.  Demarcation: a pedagogic rule should show clearly what are the limits on the use of a given form.
3.  Clarity: rules should be clear.
4.  Simplicity: a pedagogic rule should be simple.
5.  Conceptual parsimony: an explanation must make use of the conceptual framework available to the learner.
6.  Relevance: a rule should answer the question (and only the question that the student's English is 'asking').

The first principle, the "truth" principle, may be better labeled the "accuracy" principle because truth is a quite loaded term often associated with value judgment and subjectivity. Furthermore, when we say language descriptions should be true, we really mean that they should be accurate based on how language is actually used. Regardless of what we choose to call it, there are two issues related to this principle that we should be aware of. First, the issue of accuracy in language description is not always clear-cut, both because language is dynamic (i.e., it often changes over time) and because observation and interpretation are always involved in language description. Another issue with this principle is that in order to be completely accurate, a description may end up being too complex, thereby conflicting with the other principles, especially those of clarity and simplicity. However, when all principles are factored into the equation, a language description should be as accurate as possible. It is also important to remember that in order to provide accurate language description, a teacher or material writer "must of course try to suppress his or her own prescriptive prejudices and resistance to language change" (Swan, 1994, p. 46). Thanks to the accessibility of large corpora today, it is much easier now than before for teachers and material writers to check how language is actually used and, in turn, recognize their prejudice and embrace language change.

Swan's principle of demarcation can and should be combined with the third principle, the clarity principle, because what Swan defines as demarcation—the limits on the use of a given form/rule—is truly a clarity issue as it essentially deals with when and where the language form/rule is used and when and where it cannot/should not be used. The importance of the clarity principle in language description is self-evident: the description of any language item/rule must be clear in order for learners to understand it. Fuzzy, ambiguous, or obscure descriptions will only confuse learners. The fourth principle, the simplicity principle, is also of great importance because it is much easier for language learners to understand and use a simple description than a complex or convoluted one. It is important to note that the two most important principles that Nation (2001, p. 90) offers for vocabulary explanation are also clarity and simplicity. For the simplicity principle, there is a challenge: simplicity may sometimes come at the expense of accuracy and/or clarity. For example, with regard to the very complex system of English articles, no simple description seems really possible that can accurately and clearly explain how the *a/the* articles are used. In fact, even the established definite/indefinite distinction between *a* and *the* is not a truly or completely correct one, a point that will be discussed in Chapter 9. However, we can and should certainly strive for grammar and vocabulary descriptions that are simultaneously accurate, clear, and simple. Swan (1994, p. 50) cites, as a good example of such effort, Alexander's (1988) description of the use of the present perfect:

> We often think that there are endless rules for this tense. In fact, there can be boiled down to just two simple precepts:
>
> 1.  To describe actions beginning in the past and continuing up to the present moment (and possibly into the future): *I've planted fourteen rose bushes so far this morning.*

2. To refer to actions occurring or not occurring at an unspecified time in the past with some kind of connection to the present: *Have you passed your driving test?*

Every use of the present perfect (for example with *since, for,* and so on) will fit into one of these rules.

Of course, this description can be further strengthened with insights gained from research in systemic functional linguistics and Cognitive Linguistics, an issue that will be explored in Chapter 8.

Swan's fifth principle, conceptual parsimony, means that in giving a language description, we must take into consideration learners' conceptual and background knowledge. Specifically, we should use terms/concepts that learners already know and avoid those learners are unfamiliar with. For example, if our students have not learned what the subjunctive mood is, we should describe clauses in the subjunctive mood simply as conditional clauses, not subjunctive sentences. Swan's last principle, relevance, suggests that in giving a language description, we should take into consideration learners' L1 because it is often a source of interference in L2 learning. Targeting the source of a learner's potential difficulty can make a given language description more relevant and effective. An example Swan gives is that while ESL learners of different L1s may show the same problem of failing to provide the plural *-s* in plural nouns, the source of the problem may vary from one L1 to another. For instance, both Chinese and Persian ESL learners may produce the incorrect utterance "my two brother," but the L1 features responsible for the missing plural *-s* are different: Chinese does not inflect for number in nouns at all; Persian, on the other hand, inflects for number but it uses the singular form for nouns modified by numerical determiners (perhaps due to the fact that the numerical number such as 2 or 3 already clearly indicate plurality). Thus, the description for the English plural inflection rule for the speakers of the two different languages may need to vary, with the description for Chinese students focusing on the need of nouns to inflect for number in general and the one for Persian students stressing the need to use the plural form for nouns modified by a numerical determiner.

It is important to note that Swan's last two principles may better be considered factors that need to be taken into consideration in language description rather than principles per se. This is because while accuracy, clarity, and simplicity are clearly what we strive for in language description, learners' background knowledge and L1 are really factors we must consider in giving a description. In fact, there are also other factors that we need to consider in language description such as learner factors of age, learning style, and proficiency level, as well as time factors, i.e., how much class instruction time is available. For young learners, grammar description should be kept at a minimum and should be as simple as possible and aided by extensive use of visuals. The same is also generally true for beginning/low level and holistic learners regardless of their age. For these learners, simplicity and clarity should be the priority. Even a little sacrifice of accuracy is occasionally justified. For example, in teaching use of the count vs. the non-count nouns, we can first give them an overgeneralized rule: count nouns are things that one can count while non-count nouns are those one cannot count. As the learners' English proficiency increases, the more adequate Cognitive Linguistics-inspired "bounded/ unbounded" or "object vs. unindividuated substance" distinction method (which will be discussed in detail in Chapter 6) should be introduced to help learners eventually gain a complete and accurate understanding of the rule. Such a practice also conforms to the incremental process of language learning. In contrast to the practices for teaching the aforementioned types of learners, for advanced adult learners, especially those with an analytical style or with strong analytical skills, teachers may provide more detailed and thorough explanations and can involve the use of some technical linguistic terms or meta-language.

There is one other issue that we should bear in mind when developing grammar and vocabulary descriptions, a point already mentioned above in Section 1.1: do not rely on one single linguistic theory. One may even consider this point a principle to follow because sound grammar and vocabulary descriptions are usually developed by drawing from more than one theory. A good example can be found in what Celce-Murcia and Larsen-Freeman (1999) have done in their grammar book for language teachers. In their book, they employ an integrative descriptive approach to grammar, making appropriate use of almost all of the major linguistic theories in its linguistic analysis, including structural, generative, and functional linguistics. For example, it uses basically phrasal structural rules in the analysis of basic sentence structures (a practice of both structuralism and generativism), but it includes discourse analysis in its analysis and description of the use of the sentence structures and other structural features, especially the English article and tense/aspect systems.

In short, following sound principles can make our language description more helpful and effective. While there may be other principles for us to include, *accuracy*, *clarity*, and *simplicity* are what I would consider the most important key principles for language description. It is also important to remember that there are also many factors that must be considered, including those related to individual learners' knowledge and background. It is important that language teachers and material writers understand and follow these principles and take into consideration the various pertinent factors in their own teaching context.

## Questions for consideration and/or discussion

1. Based on your learning and/or teaching experience, how important is grammar and vocabulary description? Give a few examples to support your answer.
2. What is your view regarding whether grammar and vocabulary are two separate domains and why?
3. This chapter has mentioned various issues that language description may cover, such as morphological and syntactic rules, discourse analysis, semantics,

sociolinguistic/pragmatic rules, and the influence of conceptualization and construal on language usages. Based on your experience and understanding, do you think some of the issues are more important than the others? Why?

4. Based on your language learning and/or teaching experience, which of the various linguistic theories and approaches to language description mentioned in the chapter have exhibited the greatest influence on the teaching materials and the ways grammar and vocabulary are presented? Give specific examples to support your answer.

5. Of the principles for grammar/vocabulary description, which one or ones do you think are the most important and why?

6. The chapter mentions several factors that one has to consider in deciding how to describe a language usage/rule, such as learner age, learning purpose, and learning style. Can you think of any other factors that should also be considered and how you can take them into consideration in your pedagogical language description?

## Notes

1 Language description may also cover phonology (how speech sounds are formed to produce meaningful utterances), but it is beyond the scope and space of this book.

2 Capital initials are used for Cognitive Linguistics here to refer to the cognitive linguistic theory developed by Langacker (1987, 1991) among others so as to differentiate it from other cognitive linguistic theories such as Chomsky's generative linguistics.

3 The terms *theories* and *approaches* are combined as one with a slash because there has been a disagreement regarding whether corpus linguistics is a theory or merely an approach.

**PART I**

# Foundations: Key theories and approaches to language description

# 2
# PRESCRIPTIVE, STRUCTURAL, AND GENERATIVE LINGUISTICS

Prescriptivism, structuralism, and generativism are very different linguistic theories/ approaches, but they share two commonalities. First, they are all influential tradi- tional theories/approaches. Second, they all focus on the formal aspects of language, often overlooking semantics and pragmatics. Because of the commonalities they share, the three theories are discussed together in this chapter, but one at a time in the order of prescriptivism, structuralism, and generativism. The influence of each theory on language teaching is also addressed.

## 2.1 Prescriptivism

### 2.1.1 Overview

To begin with, it is necessary to note that prescriptivism (or prescriptive grammar/ linguistics) differs from structuralism and generativism in that it is not, in the strict sense, a linguistic theory, but merely an approach, because it does not offer any the- ory about how language works. The sole concern of prescriptivism as a linguistic approach is to tell speakers/writers how language *should* be used. Viewing language as a static system, prescriptive grammar tries to enforce what it considers to be cor- rect or standard grammatical rules and usages, i.e., it aims to establish language-usage rules that are often based on grammarians' views and preferences (instead of actual language usages). Specifically, it prescribes what usages are acceptable and what usages are incorrect. As such, prescriptive grammar is often contrasted with descrip- tive grammar, an approach that simply records or describes how language is actually used based on real language data.[1] One more point worth noting is that, unlike most key linguistic theories, prescriptivism was not developed by one linguist or by a small group of linguists. Yet a few linguists and writers have been recognized as important contributors to prescriptivism thanks to the specific prescriptive rules they helped create, including the famous seventeenth-century English poet John Dryden, for the rule that a sentence should not end with a preposition (*Merriam-Webster diction- ary of English usage*, 1994); and the eighteenth-century English grammarian Robert Lowth for setting up the rule that forbids double negative in his 1763 grammar book. While it is impossible to pinpoint specific individuals responsible for the origin and development of prescriptivism, the approach may be traced back to the Roman Latin grammar because quite a few of the famous prescriptive English grammar rules, such as the rule forbidding the use of split infinitives, are believed to be based on Latin. So modeling language rules on a dead language contributed to the development of prescriptivism.

Because prescriptive grammar is often based on personal views and preferences, many of the prescriptive rules are arbitrary, i.e., not backed by sound linguistic or logical reasons. A good example of the arbitrariness of prescriptivism can be found in the rule that prohibits the use of double negation. The fact is that the double negative form was once not only acceptable but quite prestigious in English (Old and Middle English) as can be seen in the following lines by Chaucer and Shakespeare: "Ther nas no man nowher so virtuous" (Chaucer's description of the Friar in *The Canterbury tales*); "Nor never none/Shall mistress of it be, save I alone" (lines of Viola in Shakespeare's *Twelfth night*). Furthermore, double negation is still the acceptable and prestigious form in some other languages such as French.

Due to the arbitrariness of many prescriptive rules, the usages considered unacceptable by prescriptive grammar are often widely used in everyday language. Here are some examples given in the "don't ..." prescriptive rule format:

Don't start a sentence with a coordinating conjunction (e.g., "<u>And/But</u> he showed up eventually").

Don't end a sentence with a preposition (e.g., "He's the one I'm looking <u>for</u>").

Don't use a non-count quantifier before a count noun (e.g., "20 items or <u>less</u>").

Don't use a plural pronoun to refer back to a singular noun (e.g., "<u>Everyone</u> should do <u>their</u> best").

Don't split infinitives (e.g., "We have decided to <u>seriously</u> investigate the issue").

Don't use who instead of whom as the object of a verb or preposition (e.g., "<u>Who</u> did you speak to?").

Don't use adverbs such as "hopefully" and "interestingly" initially as sentence modifiers (e.g., "<u>Hopefully</u>, we can reach our goals").

Don't say "It's <u>me</u>" when referring to oneself as the doer of something; say "It's I."

A check of any spoken and/or written English corpus of an adequate size will show that some of these prohibited usages are in fact quite common both in speaking and writing (such as sentence-ending prepositions and split infinitives). Many of the others are also fairly frequent, although occurring mostly in speech. A few of them such as "It's me" are in fact the dominant usages, for most speakers would not say "It's I" when knocking on someone's door and asked who it is. More importantly, even some of the usages branded as the worst offences by prescriptive grammarians are also not uncommon in informal speech context. Here are a few examples:

The use of an object pronoun for a subject pronoun in a conjoined subject (e.g., "John and <u>me</u>").

The use of adjectives as adverbs (e.g., "Drive <u>slow</u>/<u>real</u> good)".
Double negative (e.g., "He <u>doesn't</u> like <u>nobody</u>").
Ain't (e.g., "He <u>ain't</u> a good person").

More importantly, even individuals of important social positions sometimes also use these forbidden usages in formal context in order to help communicate their ideas more effectively. For example, Neville Chamberlain, Prime Minister of Britain from 1937 to 1940, reportedly said "We ain't going to have war" after he signed the Munich Agreement with Hitler. Also, former U.S. President Ronald Reagan said at the 1984 Republican National Convention, "You ain't seen nothing yet" as a promise to show both his supporters and opponents that he was going to bring about more positive changes to their lives if he was re-elected. Obviously, both political leaders used the "unacceptable" language (ain't and double negative) to draw their audience's attention to the messages they each wanted to convey.

It is also important to point out that although many of the prescriptive rules (such as those condemning split infinitives and sentence-ending prepositions) are not what the majority of the language speakers/writers abide by, many of the others, including those against the use of double negative and *ain't*, are indeed widely followed by the majority of the speakers/writers of the language in most contexts. The latter rules, if given descriptively, can become sound and helpful for language users. For example, the prescriptive rule on the use of double negative can be rewritten descriptively as follows: The use of double negative in English often carries the social stigma of being the language of the uneducated. However, while most English speakers/writers do not use it, especially in formal settings, some speakers do, especially in informal context, for emphasis purposes. Such a description gives a more complete representation of the double negative usage.

### 2.1.2 Influence of prescriptivism on language teaching

The influence of prescriptivism on language teaching has been direct and significant. Prescriptive grammar was taught in Latin as a classical language for centuries. This approach was later (especially in the nineteenth century) spread to the teaching of modern languages as foreign languages, including English, resulting in the rise and wide use of what we now call the grammar-translation teaching method (Rivers, 1981). As its name suggests, this teaching method focuses on grammar, using grammar study and translation exercises as the main teaching activities. A typical lesson begins with students studying target vocabulary and grammatical rules followed by translation exercises in which students use the learned vocabulary and grammatical structures to translate expressions and sentences from their L1 into the target language and sometime from the target language back into their L1 (Richards & Rodgers, 2001).

In fact, the influence of prescriptivism on language teaching continued until the 1970s. Many English-language textbooks and examinations (including TOEFL—Test of English as a Foreign Language) closely followed the prescriptive grammatical rules. Some textbooks, especially those examination preparation books, include lists of "incorrect" usages and explanations about why the usages were wrong, as well as many exercises designed to help learners become better able to identify and correct usage errors. The following is a sample question taken from Rudman's (1981) TOEFL test preparation book. In this type of question, a word is underlined and the test taker is asked to select, from five provided choices, the correct form for the underlined word or structure (Rudman, 1981, p. 3 of test 1, question 7):

> Leisure promotes health, efficiency and happiness, for there is time for each individual to live <u>their</u> own "more abundant life."
>
> 1. their 2. his 3. its 4. our 5. your

According to Rudman, the correct answer is "his," not "their," because the subject is "each individual," a third-person singular noun.

Obviously, the teaching of such prescriptive rules ignores the fact that the "incorrect" usages are actual language produced by a large number of English speakers/writers. However, it is also important to point out that while some of the errors that prescriptivism-based teaching focused on were not really errors, many indeed were, as can be seen in the following example taken also from Rudman's TOEFL book (1981, p. 3 of written expression test, question 17):

> I <u>am</u> <u>so tired</u> I <u>can't</u> <u>scarcely</u> stand. <u>No error</u>
>   A     B         C      D              E

The error is "scarcely" because the negative modal "can't" before it is already negative. This type of double negative is almost never produced by native English speakers. ESL/EFL learners should learn to avoid such errors because most native speakers consider them incorrect. It is clear again that while some prescriptive rules are not based on actual usage, many are what most speakers/writers abide by. The latter rules can and should be taught if they apply to the language that students are learning. In fact, even prescriptive rules that are not followed by all the speakers and writers (e.g., the rule forbidding the use of "different than") should be also be covered (descriptively, of course) in teaching in order to help learners attain a sound, complete understanding of what the actual usages are. Concerning *different from* vs. *different than*, learners should know that the actual usage pattern based on corpus data (specifically based on the 425 million-word Corpus of Contemporary American English) is that while *different than* is used by some speakers, it is far less common than *different from* (the ratio is 1:3.5). Even more importantly, *from* is used much more in academic writing than in speaking (with writing and speaking ratio of 2.4:1) whereas *than* is used far more frequently in speaking than in academic writing (with a speaking and writing ratio of 4.4:1). Learners need this information so they can make informed decisions concerning which of the two to use in a given context.

In short, if they are useful for learners, prescriptive rules that are generally true based on actual language data should be taught as long as they are presented descriptively with adequate contextual information provided. It can be done in the way shown in the usage-based description about double negative given at the end of the Section 2.1.1 and also in the above description of the use of *different from* vs. *different than*. Of course, in actual teaching, we often can ask and guide students to discover such descriptive information via corpus queries, a practice that will be discussed in Chapter 5 and many Part II chapters.

## 2.2 Structuralism

### 2.2.1 Overview

Structural linguistics also focuses on form. It originated with Swiss linguist Ferdinand de Saussure's work published posthumously in 1916 in an anthology titled *Course in General Linguistics*. His linguistic theory was later further developed by, among others, American linguist Leonard Bloomfield, whose 1933 seminal book *Language*, along with his other works that followed, helped establish structural linguistics as the most dominant linguistic theory in the 1930s and 1940s. Striving to analyze and describe language with a precision equal to that of science, structural linguistics focuses exclusively on the mechanistic or formal aspects of language, completely overlooking semantics and pragmatics (the aspects of language Bloomfield and his follows considered unsuitable for scientific inquiry). In other words, structural linguistics "attempts to explain grammatical relations solely in terms of the formal features observable with the language corpus" (Rivers, 1981, p. 70). Using such a formal approach, structural linguistic treats language largely as a static system of interconnected units in a hierarchical order starting with phonemes and morphemes, moving to words/ phrases, and then finally to clauses/sentences.

This formal approach to language is best shown in the **immediate constituent (IC) analysis**, a unique structural analysis technique used in structural grammar. Developed by Bloomfield as a scientific discovery procedure for identifying the basic units of language, IC analysis breaks down a sentence first into major immediate constituents/parts, i.e., the noun phrase that serves as the subject and the verb phrase that works as the predicate. Then it divides these two identified parts further into smaller parts until it reaches the smallest meaningful

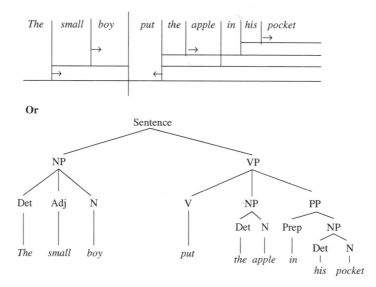

**FIGURE 2.1** Examples of sentence structure IC analysis.

constituents, as illustrated in Figure 2.1. In this figure, an IC analysis of a sentence is performed using two different common diagramming methods found in IC analysis: the IC cut method and the syntactic structure tree method. As can been seen in this example, IC analysis helps show that a sentence or phrase is not made up of a string words in a simple linear order. The words form a hierarchical relationship with the linguistic items (lexical and structural) at each level forming constituting pairs.

It is clear from these examples of IC analysis that, in structural linguistics, the focus is exclusively on **syntagmatics**, i.e., the structural relationship between the linguistic items or structures at various levels in an utterance. Very little attention is paid to the semantics. With a focus on structural patterns, structural grammarians also try to identify the basic sentence patterns. For example, Stageberg (1981, pp. 197–217) identified nine basic English sentence patterns (with some additional sub-patterns):

| Sentence Pattern | Example |
|---|---|
| 1. N *be* Adj (adjective) | "Mike is happy." |
| 2. N *be* Adv/Prep phrase | "The dog is downstairs/under the table." |
| 3. $N^{1*}$*be* $N^1$ | "Tom is a student." |
| 4. N LV (linking verb) Adj | "The man appeared tired." |
| 5. $N^1$ LV $N^1$ | "Jean became/remained the company manager." |
| 6. N InV (intransitive verb) | "The boy smiles a lot." |
| 7. $N^1$ TrV (transitive verb) $N^2$ | "The man cleans his car every day." |
| 8. $N^1$ TrV $N^2$ $N^3$ | "He gave Mary a rose" or "He gave a rose to Mary." |

| Sentence Pattern | Example |
|---|---|
| 9. $N^1$ TrV $N^2$ plus: $N^2$ (or: | "The members elected Mike *president*." |
| *Adj* | "They consider her *very competent*." |
| *Pronoun* | "I thought the visitor *you*." |
| *Adv (of place)* | "The couple assumed the *baby downstairs*." |
| *Present Participle* | "They witnessed her leaving." |
| *Past participle* | "We assumed him *defeated*." |
| *Prep phrase* | "They believed him *out of mind*." |
| *Infinitive phrase with to be* | "Everyone considers her to be a great singer." |

*Ns with the same superscript number have the same referent (e.g., Tom and student refer to the same person), while Ns with different numbers have different referents.

For this sentence pattern classification system to be truly accurate and complete, there should be a N LV Adv/Prep phrase between the two LV sentence patterns (4 and 5) to match the first three patterns that involve the be verb because English does have sentences like "Jack remained upstairs/in the room." However, for pedagogical purposes, all of the "be" verb and "linking verb" patterns can be combined as just one pattern described as $N + be/LV + adj/adv/N^1$ because the fewer patterns and rules for students to remember, the better it is for them. Clearly, having a list of basic sentence patterns can be helpful for language learners and teachers alike as it may enable learners to sort out the English sentence structures more quickly and easily. However, it is important to note that the usefulness of such a list of sentence patterns is limited because there are many various sub-sentence patterns (or subcategories) in English, including the many different structures that can be used as the object complement in sentence pattern 9 above. These sub-patterns often present serious difficulty for ESL/EFL learners, an issue that will be discussed in detail in Chapter 7.

## 2.2.2 Influence of structuralism on language teaching

Arguably, few other linguistic theories have had a more direct and significant influence on language teaching than structuralism. As the dominant linguistic theory in the 1940s, structuralism, together with behaviorism in psychology (a theory developed by Skinner, 1957), forms the theoretical underpinnings for the audiolingual method, the most popular language teaching method in the 1940s through the early 1960s. Structural linguists and language educators Charles Fries and Robert Lado, among others, were key figures in the development of this approach (Richards & Rogers, 2001). Based on the behaviorist theory that language is learned mainly through habit formation and motivated by the focus of structuralism on language structures (rather than meanings), the audiolingual method makes extensive use of sentence pattern drills. In this method, target grammatical features or structures are identified and isolated for students to practice using drills. The students are given only enough vocabulary to make such drills possible. The reason to focus on structure, rather than vocabulary, is motivated by the belief that learning by heart basic sentence patterns and structures is the starting point and key to successful language learning. In other words, it is assumed that repeated pattern drills will help learners develop new habits in the target language so they can use it fluently (Richards & Rogers, 2001).

In the audiolingual approach, the description of a language rule or usage pattern is form-focused, with little attention paid to meaning. In fact, very little description of language rules/usages is given by the teacher, for in this approach, "[t]here is little provision for grammatical explanation or talking about the language" (Richards & Rodgers, 2001, p. 64). The teacher simply provides students with sentence patterns by way of pattern drills. Students are supposed to induce the usage rules and patterns by themselves from the sentence pattern drills they are doing. While letting learners themselves discover grammar/vocabulary usage rules and patterns is a very good practice that should be encouraged, it cannot be successfully done without appropriate support and guidance from the teacher (an issue that will be discussed in detail in Chapter 4 in the section on how to help learners learn to use corpus data for discovery learning). Unfortunately, little is done in this regard in the audiolingual method. Students are often left to struggle on their own because most of their time is spent on pattern drills.

The drills used in the audiolingual approach include, among others, the following types: *repetition* in which students simply repeat what they hear; *replacement* or *substitution* in which students substitute one of the words or structures with a different one; *completion* in which students hear an utterance that is incomplete and restate it in a complete form, and *transformation* in which students change the form of a sentence, e.g., change a declarative sentence to question or change it from affirmative to negative; *integration* in which students combine two or more separate sentences into one (Richards & Rogers, 2001, pp. 59–62). The following are examples of a few of the drill types:

> **Substitution**
> Tom is a student. → I'm a student. → They're students.
> They all like their teacher, Mr. Smith. → They all like him.
> **Transformation**
> Tom is a student. → Is Tom a student? → Tom isn't a student.
> They repair TVs. → They don't repair TVs. → What do they repair?
> This young man is my brother. → Who is this young man? → Whose brother is this young man?
> **Integration**
> It was raining and hot. The children were all playing outside. → Although it was raining and hot, the children were all playing outside.

Such structure-based mechanic drillings lead mostly to rote learning and unproductive language knowledge. The aforementioned lack of meaningful and clear descriptions of grammar and vocabulary usages may also help contribute to the learners' mechanical grasp of language structures without a true understanding of them. However, it is important to note that the problem is not with the sentence structural patterns themselves. In fact, the patterns identified and focused on by structural grammar and the audiolingual approach are all sound. The problem is only with the mechanical way these patterns are learned.

## 2.3 Generativism

### 2.3.1 Overview

Generative linguistics (also known as generative-transformational linguistics), developed by Chomsky (1957) and his followers, also treats language as an autonomous system separate from semantics/pragmatics, but it differs from structural linguistics in that it focuses almost exclusively on syntax. It is important to note, however, that the generative linguistic theory has changed over the years with many additions and revisions, such as the addition of a semantic component to its syntactic system by Chomsky (1965) and the advancement of the Minimalist framework (Chomsky, 1995) in which the lexicon is given greater importance. Still, it is the main goal of generative linguistics to identify a set of grammatical rules that will generate all and only correct sentences. It is also the assumption of generativism that many of the rules arrive from a posited innate faculty known as **Universal Grammar** (**UG**, a concept Chomsky first referred to as "language acquisition device" or LAD). Consequently, in generativism, human language knowledge is largely innate, activated or acquired simply by exposure to language input. This theory of language knowledge is based on an assumed paucity of language input and an assumed ease with which children acquire a language, but both assumptions have been seriously challenged in recent research (see Tomsello, 2003). Chomsky also refers to this human knowledge to produce correct language as linguistic competence, which he contrasts with linguistic performance, the way speakers use language in communication. Yet, generative linguistics is interested only or mostly in linguistic competence, i.e., it is not interested in any external factors related to language use. Before we move on to the discussion of the typical procedures and methods of linguistic analysis used in generative linguistics, it is necessary to point out that, because of its focus on the mind as the locale of language, generative linguistics is also a type of cognitive linguistics. However, it differs significantly from Cognitive Linguistics in many key issues including where our linguistic knowledge comes from and how language is acquired.

As mentioned above, generative grammar focuses on syntax. As a result, all the linguistic analysis and description done in generative grammar relate to syntax. Generative grammar analyzes and describes syntax by using a phrasal-structural approach involving phrasal-structural rules. These rules determine what types of lexical items go in a given phrase and how they are ordered. The following are the key English phrasal-structural rules (the categories in parentheses are optional for the phrasal structure):

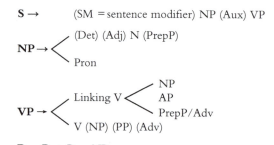

**S →** (SM = sentence modifier) NP (Aux) VP

**NP →** (Det) (Adj) N (PrepP)
Pron

**VP →** Linking V NP / AP / PrepP/Adv
V (NP) (PP) (Adv)

**PrepP →** Prep NP

**AP →** (intensifier) Adj (PrepP) (e.g., fond of, conducive to, dependent on)

**AdvP →** (intensifier) Adv

**AdvCl →** adv sub S

*Also, words and phrases of the same category can be joined by conjunctions as illustrated below :*

NP → NP Conj NP; VP → VP Conj VP; S → S Conj S.

In each phrasal structure, there is a head word, e.g., N in NP and V in VP, and the phrasal structure is named after the head. In other words, lexical categories (such as noun or verb) form the heads of phrasal structures or categories. Phrasal-structural rules are very important information for L2 teachers and students (of course, not in the form of the abstract notations shown above) because these rules often vary from language to language. For example, the NP structural rule in Thai is N (Adj) (Det), which is the opposite of the NP rule in English. Also, the VP rule in Japanese and Korean is (NP) V, which is the opposite of the VP rule in English.

Using phrasal-structural rules, generative grammar parses a sentence into constituent parts or syntactic categories in the form of a syntactic structure tree diagram. It uses the syntactic structure tree diagramming method because it can better show the underlying relations among the phrasal structures (especially when they're ambiguous) as well as the transformations that helped derive the surface sentence structure from its deep structure—the underlying primary grammatical structure of the sentence that shows the core meaning, a point that will be exemplified below. Let us first look at how structure tree diagramming may reveal the ambiguity in a sentence structure as exhibited in Figure 2.2. The sentence analyzed is "The young lady saw the soldier with a binocular."

In the first structure diagram, *with a binocular* is part of the verb phrase, i.e., it modifies the verb *saw* as an adverbial of manner/instrument. In contrast, in the second diagram, the prepositional phrase is part of the noun phrase, i.e., it modifies the noun *soldier*. This type of syntactic analysis/description clearly has

Meaning 1 = *The young lady saw the soldier by using a binocular.*

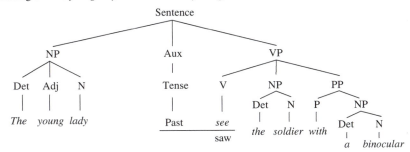

Meaning 2 = *The young lady saw the soldier who carried a binocular.*

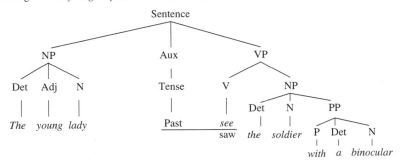

**FIGURE 2.2** Structure trees showing sentence ambiguity.

its roots in structural grammar where structural analysis/description, as already shown above in Section 2.2, also centers on breaking down an utterance into constituent parts. However, generative grammar differs from structural grammar in that its analysis does not stop here. As just mentioned, it also examines how a sentence arrives at its surface structure from its deep structure through the application of transformational rules such as *addition*, *deletion*, and *movement*. In other words, generative grammar also analyzes/describes utterances with reference to their underlying thoughts. Let us look at a very simple example to illustrate this transformation process. As we know, the following two utterances mean essentially the same although each has a different focus.

1. Carol helped Mike.
2. Mike was helped by Carol.

The second utterance differs from the first structurally in that it is in the passive voice. In other words, the surface structure of the second sentence is derived from the deep structure shown in the first utterance via a series of transformations, including movement (moving Mike to the subject position) and addition (adding *be* and *by*).

Using deep structure analysis, we can also account for the semantic difference between sentences that are identical on surface structure as shown in the two examples:

| Surface structure | Deep structure |
|---|---|
| 3a. Jean is easy to please. | 3b. (For others) to please Jean is easy. |
| 4a. Jean is eager to please. | 4b. Jean is eager to please others. |

The two sentences with the same surface structure (3a/4a) differ in meaning because they are derived from different deep structures (3b/4b). Such analysis does deal with meaning but it is limited to syntactic structure-based meaning only. It does not deal with meaning and use in context: when and why one surface structure is used instead of the other. For example, it does not address when and why would one use the passive "Mike was helped by Mary" rather than the active voice.

## 2.3.2 Influence of generativism on language teaching

Generativism has had some influence on language teaching, but its influence has not been as direct and as strong as that of structuralism. Specifically, there are three theoretical foci or assumptions of generative linguistics that have each influenced language teaching. The first is the strong focus of generative linguistics on the cognitive and rule-governed nature of language. This focus attracted special interest from those language educators who believed that explicit study of grammatical rules was crucial for successful language learning. These educators had been very concerned about the lack of systematic grammar study in the then popular audiolingual teaching approach. Energized by the cognitive and rule focus of generative linguistics, these language educators pushed for more grammar instruction in language teaching. They wanted to engage learners in more cognition-based learning and hence liberate them from the "'mindless' drilling" of the audiolingual approach (Rivers, 1981, p. 78). Their effort resulted in the development of a new language teaching method named "Cognitive-Code Learning." Yet, due to lack of a clear understanding of what cognition was and what cognitive-code learning would actually involve, the approach was not clearly defined and it "never gained the status of what one might call a method" (Rivers, 1981, p. 49). At the risk of overgeneralization/simplification, the method and its procedures could be summarized as follows: the teacher begins the class with a deductive explanation of the target grammatical rules; then the class continues with exercises that allow students to practice the grammatical forms in context; and it concludes with reading and listening activities in which students communicate their ideas using the new forms learned.

The second theoretical assumption of generative linguistics that has influenced language teaching is its UG hypothesis. This hypothesis led to some interesting studies on the role of UG in L2 acquisition and its implication for L2 teaching (e.g., Hilles, 1986; Schwartz & Sprouse, 1996; White, 1985, 1989). The questions examined in this line of research included, among others, the accessibility or the level of accessibility of UG in L2 learning and the effects of the **superset/subset** principles. Before discussing the main findings of this line of research, it is necessary to note that some scholars on L2 acquisition (e.g., Bley-Vroman, 1989; Schachter, 1988) do not believe UG has a role in adult L2 learning. They argue that adult L2 learning differs fundamentally from child L1 learning. In their argument, child L1 acquisition is domain-specific (UG-based) whereas adult L2 learning relies on general learning strategies. Their theory is based mainly on the fact that there is often a lack of complete success in adult L2 acquisition and that the language of adult L2 learners, including advanced ones, often contains some non-target language structures and usages. However, the findings of the studies on the accessibility of UG in L2 learning contradict such a theory, because they generally indicate that UG is still accessible (Schwartz & Sprouse, 1996; White, 1989).

For example, a study reported in White (1989) examined the accessibility of the UG principle of **structure dependence**. According to this principle, language is composed of structured segments, not just a string of unstructured words. This can be seen in the fact that when we move things around in a sentence to form questions, the movement is structure-dependent, not word-bound. For example, to form a "yes/no" question with a complex subject (one modified by a relative clause), we move the "be" verb of the main clause to the front (i.e., in front of the entire subject including the relative clause), not the "be" verb of the relative clause as illustrated below:

5.  <u>The boy who is crying</u> is her brother.
6.  Is <u>the boy who is crying</u> her brother?
7.  *Is the boy who crying is her brother?

In the study, a group of Japanese subjects were asked to form questions from declarative sentences with the type of a complex subject described above. In Japanese, questions are formed by simply adding a question marker at the end of a sentence, i.e., it does not involve any structural movement or word-order change as it does in English. The Japanese subjects had learned how to form "yes/no" questions with a simple subject in English, e.g., "Tom is a student" → "Is Tom a student?" However, they had not learned how to do so with sentences that contained the aforementioned type of complex subject, but almost all of the subjects completed the task successfully by moving the right "be" verb to the front of the sentence. White attributes the Japanese subjects' success to the availability of the structure dependence principle through UG, i.e., not through the subjects' L1 because, as noted above, Japanese does not have a principle of structure dependence related to question formation. In other words, the results of the study demonstrate the accessibility of UG in L2 learning.

Other research findings that have supported UG accessibility in L2 learning include the availability of the subset/superset principles. According to UG, a language that has the superset for a particular structure must also include the subset but not vice versa. For example, regarding adverb placement in a sentence, in French, adverbs can be positioned in many more different places than in English. Thus, French has the superset and English contains the subset in this case: the positions where an adverb can be placed in French include all of those in English but not the reverse. For learners with the superset (French in this case) learning a language with a subset (English), they would often assume that adverb placement in L2 is the same as in their L1, causing them to produce unacceptable sentences like "*Mike is reading <u>closely</u> the article." Therefore, learners with the superset in their L1 learning an L2 with the subset need negative evidence, i.e., correction so they would know where adverbs cannot be placed in English. In contrast, for learners with the subset learning a language with the superset, positive evidence suffices. This is because, as in the case of English speakers learning the placement of adverbs in French, they will first place adverbs the way they do in English, which is correct as the French superset includes the English subset. Then, when they see adverbs can also be placed in other places in French in the input they receive, they will gradually adopt the new practice. Such findings are useful for L2 teaching because they enable teachers to know when and where they need to provide negative evidence to learners and how to best present the L2 usage information in question.

The third theoretical assumption of generative linguistics that has influenced language teaching is the innateness hypothesis, which posits that human language knowledge is prewired and activated by language input and that children acquire language effortlessly without the need of formal instruction. Some L2 educators, for example Stephen Krashen (1977, 1981), applied this generativist theoretical assumption to L2 language acquisition. Krashen's (1981) Monitor Theory about language learning was a result of this effort. The Monitor Theory consists of five hypotheses. The first is the "acquisition vs. learning" hypothesis, which postulates that language acquisition is a subconscious process that takes place in natural language use, whereas language learning is a conscious process that often involves formal instruction. The second hypothesis is the "natural order" hypothesis, which posits that the acquisition of grammatical rules follows a predictable order. The third hypothesis is the "monitor" hypothesis, which assumes that only acquisition contributes to language proficiency; learned language knowledge does not because it serves only as a monitor for checking production but several conditions must be met before the monitor can function, including sufficient time for the speaker to access the monitor and the focus of the context being on form, such as when one is taking a language test. In other words, the monitor or learned knowledge is generally not accessible in actual communication. The fourth hypothesis is the "comprehensible input" hypothesis, which asserts that comprehensible language input (i.e., input that is a little beyond learners' existing language knowledge) is essential for language acquisition. The fifth and last hypothesis is the "affective filter" hypothesis, which states that high anxiety, low esteem, and low motivation pose as a filter that prevents language input from becoming language intake, severely hindering language acquisition. Based on these hypotheses, formal instruction is of very limited value in language acquisition. It is important to note, however, that Krashen's theory, especially his rigid separation between acquisition and learning, has drawn a lot of criticism ever since it was first proposed (Gregg, 1984; McLaughlin, 1978). Most L2 researchers and teachers today do not accept such a separation of acquisition and learning, and believe, instead, in a certain level of interface between learning and acquisition.

Despite its aforementioned influences, generativism has not yielded, however, the level of influence that structuralism has had on language teaching including pedagogical language description. There are several likely reasons for this. First, the innate hypothesis about human language knowledge makes formal instruction essentially unnecessary in language learning, hence reducing the relevance of the theory to L2 teaching. Second, generative linguistics is comparatively much more abstract and theoretical than structuralism, and its sentence analysis procedures are also more complex. Finally, its focus on form and its inadequate attention to language meaning and use may have made it less relevant and less appealing for language teachers. For example, the major goal of generative linguistics is to identify all the possible sentence structures in a given language and explore how these structures can be used to generate endless utterances speakers/writers use to communicate, i.e., the creative nature of language. Yet, the generalization is entirely structure-based and is completely about grammaticality, i.e., about how to generate grammatically correct sentences. It pays no attention how contextual factors may affect the actual choices of utterances learner make. In other words, it does not deal with why and how different grammatically-correct utterances are used for basically the same communicative purposes as shown in the following examples:

8. Turn on the light.
9. Would you mind turning on the light?

Both utterances are grammatically correct and the purpose of each is essentially the same: requesting the hearer to turn on the light. However, which one to use depends on context, an issue that generativism does not address but sociolinguistics and functional linguistics do, as will be shown in the next chapter.

Similarly, the narrow focus of generative linguistics on the sentence structures and their use for generating utterances entails an overlook of another important aspect of human language in use: the embodied conceptualization processes such as metaphor (analogy) and metonymy. As contemporary linguistics such as

Cognitive Linguistics has shown, language is usage-based and motivated by our embodied conceptualizations. We do not mechanically generate an utterance from an abstract sentence structure. Instead, based on the meaning we would like to communicate and motivated by our urge to communicate effectively, we produce an utterance often modeled on an established construction through use, as can be seen in the following utterance:

10. I don't think he can <u>talk his way out of it</u>.

Clearly, this utterance is modeled on what Goldberg (1995) and Taylor (2002) call the *way* construction. The construction consists of *v + one's way + preposition phrase*, as shown in the more prototypical ones of the construction: "He found/fought his way home/to safety." Except for the most prototypical form of the construction, *find one's way home*, the sentences modeled on this construction are only sensible metaphorically because *way* is not something one can *lie/sleep/spend/work* (as in "He lied his way out of it/He slept his way through college"). In fact, some of the verbs used in this construction such as *lie* and *sleep* are not even transitive verbs. In other words, they are not used grammatically if we follow the strict grammaticality principle of generative linguistics. This example further highlights the limitations of generativism in describing and explaining language.

## Questions for consideration and/or discussion

1.  Based on your reading and understanding, tell whether each following grammar descriptions is prescriptive or descriptive and why.
    a.  Do not use "that" as a nonrestrictive relative pronoun in a relative clause; use only "which" in such a case: "The house, which (not that) was built in 1902, is still in an excellent condition."
    b.  "Like" is often used in conversation as a conjunction as shown in the following utterances: "It's just <u>like</u> she said" and "It looks <u>like</u> it's going to rain." However, in formal writing, such use of "like" is not common and is usually replaced by "as" ("The situation is just <u>as</u> she described") or "as if" ("It appears <u>as if</u> the meeting is to take place after all").
    c.  "Hopefully" should not be used as a sentence modifier, e.g., *"Hopefully, we can get this done in time." The correct usage is "It is our hope that we can get this done in time" or "I/We hope that we can get this done in time."
2.  Think of a few prescriptive rules that are generally followed in actual language use. Rewrite them as pedagogical rules, taking into consideration the necessary contextual information required to make your descriptions accurate. In the process, also bear in mind the clarity and simplicity principles.
3.  What are the major weaknesses of structuralism and generativism-based grammar description (consider especially the scope of its coverage)? Also

think about and explain what you can do to reduce or eliminate the weaknesses. What are the strengths or potential strengths of structuralism/generativism-based language description?

4. In Chinese (also Korean/Japanese), the subject and the object of a sentence are often omitted although they can be used. In contrast, in English, such omission is very rare. If you apply the superset/subset concept discussed in Section 2.3.2, which of the two types of language has the superset and which has subset in this case? Also, for Chinese speakers learning English, do they need negative evidence in relation to the issue of subject/object omission? Why? What would be your answer in the case of English speakers learning Chinese?

5. Generativism has never had the kind of influence on language teaching and pedagogical language description that structuralism has had. The chapter lists three most likely reasons why this is the case. Do you agree and can you think of any other likely reasons?

6. Based on your language learning and/or teaching experience, which of the three linguistic approaches to language description is most helpful and which is least helpful? Support your answer with specific examples.

## Note

1 While it is true that descriptive grammar aims only to observe and describe language rules and usages as they are found in actual language data, it is also important to note that the observation and description of language rules and usages always involve interpretation on the part of the person who is doing the observation and description.

# 3

# SOCIOLINGUISTICS AND SYSTEMIC FUNCTIONAL LINGUISTICS

Unlike prescriptivism, structuralism, and generativism (which focus on the formal aspects of language), sociolinguistics and systemic functional linguistics center on language as a tool for communication or social interaction and strive to explain language mainly in terms of meaning and function. This chapter first overviews the two linguistic theories, one at a time, and then discusses the impacts that they have had on language teaching.

## 3.1 Sociolinguistics: an overview of communicative competence and speech act theory

First, it is important to note that, in the strict sense, sociolinguistics is only a branch of linguistics rather than a complete linguistic theory because it deals with only one aspect of language (the social). Furthermore, sociolinguistics is a broad field which covers all of the areas or issues related to how language and society interact, including, among others, the influence of social factors (such as ethnics and socioeconomic class) on language, especially on its variety (dialects) and change; language policies (including policies on language use and language learning); and the influence of social contexts on individuals' language use. The latter issue is an area where sociolinguistics and **pragmatics**—the study of the ways in which contexts affect language meaning and use—overlap. The discussion here will cover only this latter issue because understanding how social/ situational contexts affect language meaning and use is extremely important for language learners. Three specific topics will be examined: **communicative competence**, **speech act theory**, and pragmatics across languages. An overview of these topics will help us gain a sound understanding of what communicative or pragmatic competence involves, why this competence is important, and why it is so challenging for L2 learners to develop pragmatic competence in the target language.

### 3.1.1 Communicative competence

Dell Hymes, a renowned American sociolinguist, introduced the concept "communicative competence" (a term he coined) in a 1966 article, and he elaborated on it in his 1971 book titled *Communicative Competence*. The concept refers to the ability to produce language that is not only grammatically correct but also socially appropriate. The development of the concept was a direct response to Chomsky's generativist theory, which gives primacy to linguistic competence and overlooks linguistic performance. Hymes's theory was based on findings from his empirical research known as the study of *ethnography of speaking* or *ethnography of communication* (1962, 1964). His research systematically examined the interaction or communication patterns among members of a speech community. Hymes's research findings suggest that linguistic competence alone is not enough for human beings to communicate successfully. Speakers also need sociolinguistic competence to do so. For example, if a person tries to obtain driving directions from a stranger by saying "Hey, tell me how to get to the closest gas station," he/she will be considered impolite and will likely not be able to receive the information he/she requested. Based on this simple example, we can easily imagine how a person who has only linguistic competence (i.e., who has no sociolinguistic competence) may behave and be viewed as a social monster. Hymes's theory was further developed and/or elaborated on by many other sociolinguists as well as language educators. For example, in 1980, Canale and Swain, two language educators, identified three specific components or competencies that they believed constitute communicative competence: (1) grammatical competence (or linguistic competence), which is the ability to produce grammatically correct utterances; (2) sociolinguistic competence (also called pragmatic competence), which concerns the ability to produce socially appropriate language; and (3) strategic competence, which refers to the ability to appropriately use communication strategies to communicate effectively. Later, Canale (1983) added one more competence: discourse competence, which deals with the ability to use organizational and other communication devices to produce language that is both cohesive and coherent.

### 3.1.2 Speech act theory

The concept of communicative competence has also been tied to and enriched by Speech Act Theory. First introduced by British language philosopher John L. Austin in his 1962 posthumous book *How to do things with words* and later enhanced by John Searle (1969), Speech Act Theory deals with how speakers use language to convey their intended meanings or to perform, in the terminology of the theory, various speech acts, such as *greeting, inviting, ordering, promising,* and *requesting*. Of course, the theory is also equally concerned with how listeners/readers correctly interpret the intended meanings of their interlocutors' utterances. Speech acts are analyzed at three levels: (1) locutionary act, which refers to the actual utterance and its surface meaning; (2) illocationary act, which concerns the social force or the intended meaning of the utterance as a verbal action; and (3) perlocutionary act, which deals with the actual effect of certain locutionary acts, including the effect of convincing, persuading, and scaring. The importance of this theory, especially the importance of its differentiation of the three levels of speech acts, is that it enables us to understand how and when we need to vary a locutionary act in order to best accomplish our illocutionary act in a given context as well as how to correctly understand the illocutionary acts of our interlocutors.

For example, to ask someone to open the window in a stuffy room, we can say any of the following (and more), although which one to use will depend on the context and the relationship between the interlocutors:

1.   Open the window.
2.   Please open the window.
3.   Can you open the window?
4.   Could you please open the window?
5.   Would you mind opening the window?
6.   It's quite stuffy in this room.

Even though the utterances differ significantly in form (e.g., 1, 2, and 6 are declarative sentences whereas 3–5 are questions), they all share the same intended meaning or illocutionary act: requesting the addressee to open the window. However, the utterances do vary in degree of formality and directness/politeness with some differing significantly, i.e., #1 and #2 are much more direct and much less polite than #4 and #5. In fact, #6 is so indirect that its illocutionary act is very weak and may likely be ignored intentionally or unintentionally by the addressee. The important point is that a speaker with pragmatic competence in English will know which one of the utterances to use in nearly any given context (i.e., to whom in where). Such a speaker will know that #1 may be used perhaps only when one is addressing one's child or subordinate, whereas #6 may be used when one is in a room interviewing for a job or seeing one's supervisor. By the same token, a competent addressee (listener) in this case will know how to correctly interpret the intended meaning (the illocutional act) no matter how indirect the utterances is, i.e., he/she will know that "Could you open the door" is not a question but a request and that "It's stuffy in this room" is a request, too, not a comment about the air condition of the room. As another example, while the following three utterances (locutionary acts) differ in form, they all serve to accomplish the same illocutionary act of greeting:

7.   Hi.
8.   How are you?
9.   What's up?

Again, however, the three utterances have different degrees of formality and used for different contexts, with #8 being the most formal and #9 being the most casual, used mainly for greeting close acquaintances. The above discussion and examples clearly show that Speech Act Theory is closely related to Hymes's communicative competence and pragmatics, because the knowledge about how to perform speech acts constitutes an important part of a person's communicative or pragmatic competence.

### 3.1.3 Pragmatics across languages

A very important issue that sociolinguistic research has uncovered is that socio-linguistic or pragmatic rules and routines (i.e., conventional formulae, such as *How are you?* as a greeting in English) often vary from one speech community to another, and this variation can be very significant across languages. There have been many studies on such differences among various specific languages and the serious challenges that L2 speakers face in acquiring L2 pragmatic competence (e.g., Barnlund & Araki, 1985; Beebe, 1980; Gass & Neu, 1995; Liu, 1995; Wolfson, 1981, 1989). A common method used in these studies was the discourse completion test (DCT). In this test, the subjects are typically given a series of scenarios of social interaction and, at the end of each scenario, the subjects are asked to describe how they would respond, i.e., what they would say and how they would act in the situation. This method enables a researcher to obtain a large amount of data in a fairly short period of time. A weakness of the method is that it may not have high validity and reliability (Wolfson, 1989). Therefore, using spontaneous (natural) speech data is more preferable if they can be obtained by audio/video taping (sometimes they may be available in existing recordings or transcripts for other purposes, such as court hearing transcripts). Of course, sometimes it may be difficult to find the instances of the types of interaction one wants in natural conversations, so researchers sometimes use both elicited and natural data in their research (e.g., Liu 1995).

Many studies identified specific cross-language differences in the performance of various speech acts, such as apologies, compliments (and responses to compliments), greetings, invitations, refusals, and requests (Barnlund & Araki, 1985; Blum-Kulka, House, & Kasper, 1989; Wolfson, 1981, 1989). A major shared finding of many of the studies is that L2 speakers often unconsciously use their L1 pragmatic rules/routines in L2 communication, a practice known as **sociolinguistic transfer**. Such transfers often lead to communication breakdowns or even conflicts between L2 speakers and native language speakers. Communication breakdowns and conflicts of this nature are also called **pragmatic failures**.[1] Here are two examples. The first example comes from Liu's (1995) study involving Asian, especially Chinese, students studying in the U.S. According to Chinese custom, an invited guest at a dinner party should generally decline the food offered by the host a few times before accepting it during the second and subsequent rounds of food offerings, especially if the host is one's superior at work. The host, on the other hand, should insist that the guest take the food and, if necessary, should force the guest to accept the food. However, in America or most Western cultures, if a guest declines the offer, the host usually will honor it instead of trying to force the guest to eat more food. Several Chinese students in the study told stories about how they left dinner parties at their professors' homes with half-empty stomachs because they followed the Chinese custom by saying "no" when their professors asked them if they would like more food.

The second example relates to problems in greetings. Common Chinese greeting formulae among friends and acquaintances include "Where are you going?", "What are you doing?", and "Where have you been?" Using such greetings expressions in English obviously can cause confusion. Furthermore, in Chinese culture, these initial greeting formulae may be followed by questions that are considered very inappropriate in American culture. To illustrate this point, a conversation is provided below that is written based on actual stories that I have heard from quite a few American students and colleagues:

> Chinese: "Hey, where have you been?"
> American (somewhat confused and hesitant): "Shopping."
> Chinese: "What did you buy?"
> American (becoming somewhat unhappy): "Uh, a laptop."
> Chinese: "How much did you pay for it?"
> American (growing more unhappy): "Uh … $950."
> Chinese: "Oh, you paid too much. You could have got it online for $550."
> American (growing really unhappy and starting to walk away)…

The problems in this conversation are obvious. The Chinese speaker did not know that "Where have you been?" was not a greeting form in English. More importantly, he/she did not realize that asking how much a person paid for something and commenting that the person overpaid for something were very inappropriate in America, even though such questions and comments are common Chinese ways to show one's care and concern for the addressee. In short, the Chinese speaker unconsciously and unintentionally offended his/her American friend, who, not knowing the cause of problem, would likely blame the offence on the former's personal character. It is clear that pragmatic failures caused by sociolinguistic rule transfers usually have much more serious consequences than linguistic transfer errors. This is because linguistic transfer errors are easily recognizable, such as missing articles or missing plural -s (errors that often result from a lack of such inflectional morphemes in L2 speakers' native language). Furthermore, linguistic transfer errors usually do not cause comprehension or communication problems. In contrast, sociolinguistic transfers or pragmatic failures are difficult for native speakers to recognize because there are no grammatical or surface errors involved. Without recognizing the source of the problems caused by sociolinguistic transfers, native speakers tend to attribute the problems to L2 learners' personal traits by considering the L2 speakers rude, ignorant, and/or weird and by viewing their language offensive and/or insulting.

To help L2 learners to avoid pragmatic failures so they can communicate successfully, it is very important to include pragmatic rules/routines in L2 language description and teaching. By doing so, we can help them develop sociolinguistic competence and avoid *unintentionally* offending native speakers. The latter point is very important because, as Thomas (1983, p. 96; italics original) correctly points out:

> It is not the responsibility of the language teacher qua linguist to enforce Anglo-Saxon standards of behavior, linguistic or otherwise. Rather, it is the teacher's job to equip the student to express her/himself in exactly the way s/he chooses to do so—rudely, tactfully, or in an elaborately polite manner. What we want to prevent is her/his being *unintentionally* rude or subservient. It may, of course, behoove the teacher to point out the likely consequences of certain types of linguistic behavior.

As for how to help L2 learners grasp pragmatic rules/routines, the issue will be addressed below in Section 3.3.2.

## 3.2 Systemic functional linguistics: an overview

Systemic functional linguistics (SFL), developed by Michael Halliday (1973, 1978, 1985), is a major theory in a group of linguistic approaches and theories called functional linguistics. The group includes, among others, Simon Dik's functional discourse grammar (1980) and Talmy Givón's (1984) functional-typological grammar. Halliday's SFL is chosen for discussion here because it is arguably the most comprehensive and most representative work of what we usually understand as functional linguistics. It is important to note that SFL is a complex theory and it is therefore impossible to cover every aspect of it in this short overview. Only those aspects that are important to the topics of language description in this book are covered.

### 3.2.1 Language as a system of choice

As noted earlier, SFL treats language as an instrument or system for social interaction rather than as an isolated structural system of its own, for, in Halliday's own words (1994, p. xxvi), language is a system and "resource for making meaning." Therefore, in language analysis and description, SFL focuses on the functional roles rather than the formal roles of linguistic structures. In fact, it distinguishes three types of functions: semantic, syntactic, and pragmatic. In doing so, it employs three different sets of terms. Terms of semantic functions include *agent*, *process*, *patient*, etc. Terms for syntactic functions consist of *subject*, *verb*, *object*, etc. Terms for pragmatic functions contain ***theme, rheme***, *topic*, etc.[2] The following offers an example illustrating how the three categories of functions are applied in the analysis of the composing structures in the sentence "Tom gave Mary flowers."

| *Syntactic:* | subject | verb | indirect object | direct object |
|---|---|---|---|---|
| *Semantic:* | actor/agent | process | recipient | patient |
| *Pragmatic:* | theme | rheme ——————————————————→ | | |
| | *Tom* | *gave* | *Mary* | *Flowers* |

By looking at the example, we can see that the syntactic function analysis is what is performed in traditional linguistic analysis. Semantic and pragmatic function analyses are new. Particularly worth discussing is the pragmatic function category because analysis in this category is performed from a discourse perspective, a very important perspective that SFL brings into language analysis. *Theme* refers to given or old information (what the listener/reader already know) while *rheme* means the new information. Typically, the information at the beginning of an utterance (often the subject) is the theme and the following predicate is the rheme. For example, in the utterance "He's a college student," *He* is the theme, the information we already know from discourse context; otherwise, the use of this personal pronoun is inappropriate or confusing. The predicate—*is a college student*—is the rheme, new information regarding the subject.

It is clear from this example that, in language analysis, SFL goes beyond the sentence level. It does so because (1) the use or selection of a linguistic item or structure is often heavily influenced by discourse context, and (2) the selected item also influences the choice of the following linguistic items/structures. In other words, discourse information is extremely important for language as a meaning-making "system network" (Halliday, 1994, p. xxvi) because it enables speakers/writers to make sensible choices to effectively communicate their meanings. As Halliday puts it, "Each system in the network represents a choice, not a conscious decision made in real time but a set of possible alternatives ... These [choices] may be semantic, lexicogrammatical or phonological" (ibid., p. xxvi). In other words, in SFL, meaning, form, and function are described as a unified system network and each choice is affected by the previous one, which simultaneously affects the next choice. There is no description of a single linguistic feature in isolation, for "there is no difference between describing something and relating it to everything else, because the description of any feature *is* its relationship to all the others" (ibid., p. xxvii).

### 3.2.2 Semantic functions of language

In dealing with linguistic functions and meanings, SFL identifies three functional meanings or semantic functions, "ideational, interpersonal, and textual," and these functions "are realized throughout the grammar of language" (Halliday, 1994, p. 179). In other words, language elements or structures at every level are used to fulfill one or more of the three functions. Ideational function refers to the use of language to convey one's experience, thoughts, and views. The following are two examples of utterances that fall into this semantic function:

10.  Tom had a car accident yesterday.
11.  It rained this morning.

Interpersonal function concerns the use of language for social interaction with other individuals. Examples of utterances that belong to this function include:

12.  Could you please explain your questions again?
13.  Hey Mary, our class is cancelled, isn't it?

Textual function relates to the use of language to organize information, high-light a theme, and/or provide cohesion, as illustrated in the underlined structures in the following sentences:

14.  As a result of his hard work, Tom won first place in the contest.
15.  It is time that we start to undertake that.

As already mentioned above, not only full clauses but also linguistic structures at a lower level, such as phrases or words, may be used to perform these language functions, an issue that will be discussed in Chapter 14.

It is important to note that there are two sub-functions under the ideational function category: *informational* (language used simply to convey information about one's experience and thought) and *evaluative* (language used mainly to express one's view or opinion). The utterance "An earthquake occurred in that region last night" is informational while the statement "John chickened out at the last moment" is more evaluative than informational because it expresses largely the speaker's view about what John did. The interpersonal function category also contains two sub-functions: *interactional* (language used to interact with an interlocutor, e.g., *What's up?*) and *modality/qualification* (language used to express one's stance or to qualify/modify one's message for more effective inter-action and communication, e.g., *so to speak*). The *textual* category involves many subcategories such as *additive* (*in addition*), *causative* (*because of*), *resultative* (*as a result*), and *sequential* (*First of all*). [3]

### 3.2.3 Register

Viewing language as a system of choice, SFL also attaches great importance to the context, or what it refers to as **register**, in which language is used. Like pragmatics, register also deals with the influence of social/situational contexts on language use, but it differs from the former in that it is concerned with the influence of context on language style, not on the use and interpretation of language utterances. In other words, although the two interact to a certain degree, register and pragmatics are two different domains. Register is defined as a style of language used in a given social or situational context. While some social contexts require a much formal style (e.g., job interviews and court hearings), some call for an informal style (e.g., family gatherings and pool parties). Also, generally, the language style we use in speech differs significantly from that used in writing. Furthermore, many professions such as law, medicine, religion, and many academic fields have their own distinctive language styles or registers (known as professional or technical registers). Thus, in linguistic analysis, it is important to examine and identify the unique linguistic features and patterns used in each register. Such information is necessary for speakers/writers because it enables them to use language appropriately and effectively in the register(s) in which they function.

## 3.3 The impacts of sociolinguistics and SFL on language teaching

As explained above, sociolinguistic theories (such as Hymes's communicative competence) and the theories of SFL have brought us important new perspectives on language and language use and have drawn our attention to issues that were overlooked in previous linguistic theories and traditional language teaching practices. As a result, sociolinguistic and SFL theories have had very significant impacts on language teaching. Specifically, they have helped contribute to the following major changes in language teaching: (1) a shift of language instruction from form-focused to meaning/communication-oriented; (2) the inclusion of pragmatics as an important component of the second language curriculum; (3) a strong or special focus on discourse; and (4) an enhanced attention to register and semantic function in language description and teaching.

### 3.3.1 From form-focused to meaning/communication-oriented instruction

The shift of language teaching from form-focused to meaning/communication-oriented in the 1970s was best evidenced by the emergence and spreading of the communicative language teaching (CLT) approach (the most important and most widely promoted/used language teaching approach since the 1970s). CLT grew directly out of (1) language educators' dissatisfaction with the then dominant teaching method—the audiolingual method, and (2) the increasing need of individuals who could communicate with speakers of other languages in a more and more globalized world. Yet sociolinguistics and SFL provided the theoretical drive and foundation for this new approach. It is worth noting that, unlike many other teaching methods, such as the audiolingual and total physical response (TPR), CLT was not developed by one individual or one group of individuals working together. As such, it is a very broad and comprehensive approach. As Richards and Rodgers point out (2001, p. 155), "Its comprehensiveness thus makes it different in scope and status from any of the other approaches and methods ... There is no single text or authority on it, nor single model that is universally accepted as authoritative." Thus, CLT does not really have any hallmark teaching techniques of its own (nothing like pattern drills for the audiolingual method).

One of the early forms of CLT is the functional-notional communicative approach developed in the 1970s by the Council for Cultural Cooperation (CCC) of the Council of Europe (see Rivers, 1981, p. 232). As the key words in its title (functional and communicative) suggest, this approach was influenced by the theories of communicative competence and SFL. The approach aimed to identify and teach essential communicative functions and to help learners reach at least a threshold level in the performance of such functions. It also tried to identify and teach the specific notions or concepts speakers need to use in communication, such as "spatial and temporal properties and relationships; actions/ event relations; qualities of size, shape, texture; possessive relations; and logical relations" (Rivers, 1981, p. 233). The term *notion* also refers to a context of communication, and the term *function* concerns the specific purpose of communication in a given context. For example, the notion or context of attending school will involve many language functions such as following instructions, asking and answering questions, taking notes, and writing essays. Also, the notion of eating in a restaurant will call for certain language functions, such as asking for information about drinks and dishes that the restaurant serves, ordering drinks and food, and chatting with the servers. The approach also identified the vocabulary that learners needed to grasp in order to attain the established threshold level of the communicative competence. In discussing this early form of CLT, it is important to mention that this approach drew heavily from David Wilkins's (1976) influential work *Notional Syllabus*, a language teaching curriculum that focused on the teaching of meaning and communication instead of form. Even though Wilkins did not include the word *functional* in the title of the book, his syllabus does include language function as a very important component.

As a type of language teaching curriculum rather than a language method, the notional syllabus centers on how to select and organize teaching materials and content. According to Wilkins, the new type of syllabus differs markedly from traditional structural syllabi in that instruction in the notional-functional syllabus is not organized or sequenced by grammatical structure as was done in traditional methods such as the grammar-translation method. Instead, it is organized according to notions and functions. In short, with a new design in teaching contents and sequence, the Functional-Notional Communicative Approach, together with the notional syllabus, helped form the framework for the CLT approach we know of today, even though they did not provide many specific teaching activities and procedures.

In terms of the main procedures and activities used in the CLT approach, they often vary from classroom to classroom but they all seem to include simulated real-life situations that require meaningful communication. As Richards and Rogers (2001, p. 165) put it in summarizing the types and the nature of CLT teaching activities, they must "enable learners to attain the communicative objectives of the curriculum, engage learners in communication, require the use of such communicative processes as information sharing, negation of meaning, and interaction." In other words, the activities generally each contain an information gap for the participants to fill in. In such an activity, the two participating parties each have information that the other does not have, and they need to communicate in order to successfully complete the activity. In terms of procedure, the teacher first designs an activity that simulates a situation that students are likely to encounter in real life. The activity will require the participating students to use the language they have learned or are learning to obtain the information they need so as to solve whatever problem that is involved in the situation. The activity may be for a whole class, a small group, or a pair, although most activities in CLT are pair dyads. It is also important to note that, unlike the activities used in the audiolingual method (e.g., repetitions, sentence transformations, and scripted role plays), activities employed in CLT do not have prescribed or predetermined outcomes. Instead, the outcome of an information-gap activity may vary according to the reactions/responses of the participating parities. Also, the contents of the real-life simulation activities may vary from lesson to lesson but they must be meaningful and useful based on the students' learning purposes and objectives.

Finally, although CLT focuses on the meaning and use of language, it does not ignore the teaching of form or grammar. Grammar is—or should be—taught in CLT because, as noted above, grammatical competence is an important component of communicative competence. However, in the CLT approach, grammar is not taught in isolation as was done in traditional language approaches; instead, it is taught in a meaningful way, often involving the teaching of sociolinguistic rules. Also, often, grammar is taught implicitly and done without much use of metalinguistic terms. What the teacher typically does in CLT is draw "learners' attention to some specific grammatical form in such a way that it helps them … process it in comprehension and/or production so that they can internalize it" (Ellis, 2006, p. 84). The key point is that grammar in CLT is taught with the use of language in context. As Berns points out (1984, p. 5), language teaching in CLT focuses on "the use (function) of language in context, both its linguistic context (what is uttered before and after a given piece of discourse) and its social, or situational, context (who is speaking, what their social roles are, why they have come together to speak)." This context-focused grammar teaching practice certainly reflects the influence of both sociolinguistics and SFL, for, as already shown above, both linguistic theories attach great importance to the role of contexts in their descriptions of language rules and usages. What Berns refers to as "social/ situational context" is largely the domain of pragmatics and register: how to use language appropriately and effectively to communicate in various contexts. What Berns means by "linguistic context (what is uttered before and after a given piece of discourse)" falls into the domain of discourse, a key issue in language use according to SFL.

### 3.3.2 Teaching pragmatics

Arguably, the most noticeable change in language teaching that has resulted from the influence of sociolinguistic theories/research is the inclusion of the teaching of pragmatics as an essential part of the L2 curriculum. As already mentioned in Section 3.1.3 above, influenced by sociolinguists' work on communicative competence and speech acts in the 1960s and 1970s, many L2 educators and researchers have since studied the learning and use of L2 pragmatics (Barnlund & Araki, 1985; Beebe, 1980; Gass & Neu, 1995; Liu, 1995; Wolfson, 1981, 1989). Their research has focused on the following three issues: (1) L2 pragmatic rules for various speech acts; (2) differences between L1 and L2 pragmatic rules; and (3) L2 learners' understanding and use of L2 pragmatic rules, as well as the challenges they face in grasping L2 pragmatics. Research findings have repeatedly demonstrated that knowledge of pragmatics is imperative for L2 learners, because a lack of knowledge of L2 pragmatic rules/routines has frequently been shown to lead to serious communication breakdowns and conflicts or pragmatic failures. As a result of these research findings, many language educators have explored conscientiously how to help L2 students learn pragmatic rules/routines and develop pragmatic competence (e.g., Bardovi-Harlig, 2009; Bouton, 1994; Ishihara & Cohen, 2010; Koike & Pearson, 2005; Lyster, 1994; Soler, 2005). Their work has focused on two issues: whether instruction could help learners better grasp L2 pragmatics and how pragmatics could be taught effectively.

The findings of research on the first question have been overwhelmingly positive. Almost all of the studies on the topic have shown that students who received instruction on L2 pragmatics performed significantly better than students who did not receive instruction in tasks that tested their ability to use L2 pragmatic rules/routines (Bardvic-Harlig & Vellenga, 2012; Bouton, 1994; Lyster, 1994). As for research on the second question, it has been found that while both explicit and implicit instruction are helpful, explicit instruction is often more effective (Koike & Pearson, 2005; Soler, 2005). Explicit instruction always involves the provision of direct metapragmatic information by the teacher in various forms, such as (1) description/explanation of the pragmatic rules and teaching specific pragmatic routines/formulae for accomplishing a given specific speech task (e.g., "Thank you for having me" and "Thank you for inviting me" as formulae for expressing appreciation to a party host) and (2) explicit discussion of such information (Bardvic-Harlig & Vellenga, 2012, Rose, 2005; Soler, 2005). Implicit instruction does not offer metapramatic information but includes methods and/

or activities that assist students in figuring out such information by themselves, such as highlighting formulae for performing speech acts in reading materials (Soler, 2005) and having students compare differences in speech act performance patterns in transcripts or listen to/read transcripts that contain L2 speech act performance patterns (Takahashi, 2005). Teachers also often use role plays, video clips, and questionnaires (DCTs) to help learners better grasp L2 pragmatic rules and routines. It has been found that the teaching of pragmatic routines/formulae is effective for helping L2 learners develop pragmatic competence (Bardovi-Harlig, 2009; Bardovi-Harlig & Vellenga, 2012).

As for how best to describe and explain a pragmatic rule/routine, there are two things teachers can and should do. One is to draw students' attention to the unique feature or pattern in a given pragmatic routine. For example, it has been found that when expressing refusals, American speakers typically begin with a goodwill expression (e.g., "I'd love to help you, but ..."). Highlighting this routine can help students learn to give refusals more appropriately and effectively in American English. The other important practice is to explore the underlying sociocultural values and beliefs that have helped shape a given L2 pragmatic rule/routine. Such an exploration helps learners understand why the pragmatic rule/routine in the target language is the way it is, which should enable them to better remember and use it in communication. Take, for example, the conventional English response to a compliment: "Thank you." This routine is important for many ESL/EFL learners to learn because they have trouble using it due to the fact that in their L1, the usual response to a compliment is essentially the opposite: denying the truth of the complimented, as shown in the following made-up dialogue between an American and a Japanese student:

American: "Oh, you speak excellent English!"
Japanese: "Um, actually my English is still not very good."

To help these ESL/EFL learners better grasp this English routine, ESL/EFL teachers can ask students to explore the reasons for this difference. To guide the students, the teacher can encourage the students to think what cultural values and beliefs would motivate Asian speakers to not accept compliments about their accomplishments, talents, and abilities, and what cultural values and beliefs would drive Americans to quickly accept a compliment and thank the person who gave it. With appropriate prompting and help, students should be able to learn that a major reason why Asians do not readily accept a compliment is that Asian cultures place a very high value on humility and modesty. In contrast, Western cultures consider showing due appreciation to be an important and necessary act.

As another example, due to influence from their L1 pragmatic routines, some ESL/EFL students tend to express their requests and refusals in a very indirect and unclear manner, often leaving their native speaker interlocutor confused (Liu,

1995). To help these learners better adapt to the L2 pragmatic routines, teachers can have students explore the motivating cultural factors for the difference. The exploration, with the assistance of the teacher, should lead to the key reason: Japanese and many other Asian cultures are high-context cultures, whereas the U.S. and most Western cultures are low-context cultures (Hall, 1976). In high-context cultures, many things are not explicitly stated and need to be understood using contextual information and shared cultural understandings; in contrast, in low-context cultures things are often stated explicitly, and context does not play as important a role as it does in high-context cultures.

### 3.3.3 Discourse analysis and discourse grammar

The third key change in language teaching caused by the influence of SFL is the inclusion of discourse analysis in grammar description and teaching. In the past two decades, there have been many studies regarding the importance of doing discourse analysis in language teaching as well as textbooks about how to use discourse analysis to enhance language teaching (e.g., Celce-Murcia, 1991; Celce-Murcia & Olshtain, 2000; Hughes & McCarthy, 1998; McCarthy & Carter, 1994). Some language educators, e.g., Hughes & McCarthy (1998), consider discourse-based analysis of language so important and unique that they view it as a grammatical approach of its own and label it as **discourse grammar**. To them, discourse grammar differs from traditional grammar significantly: while traditional grammatical analysis is confined to structures at or below the sentence/clause, discourse grammar goes beyond the sentence level. As Hughes and McCarthy put it, discourse grammar analyzes "grammar as an aspect of discourse rather than as something that operates only within the boundaries of the clause or sentence" (Hughes & McCarthy, 1998, p. 264). In fact, many grammatical usage issues cannot be fully explained at or below sentence level. The use of pronouns is a case in point, for the choice of a given pronoun is always determined by the preceding discourse information. Furthermore, confined by its analysis at the sentence level or below, traditional grammar often uses grammatical categories or paradigms that are inadequate or even inaccurate. Hughes and McCarthy (1998) illustrate the point by examining the treatment of English pronouns in traditional grammar in which *this/that/these/those* form a demonstrative pronoun paradigm, whereas *I/we/you/it/they/...* constitute a personal pronoun paradigm. In the demonstrative set in this system, we contrast the singular *this/that* pair with the plural *these/those* pair and the *this/these* pair with the *that/those* pair. The pronoun *it* is treated as an item that has nothing to do with the demonstrative pronouns. However, based on McCarthy's (1994) corpus research findings, Hughes and McCarthy (1998, p. 265) demonstrate clearly that such a paradigmatic treatment of pronouns ignores the fact that "the relationship between the pronoun *it* and the singular demonstratives *this*" in real discourse often constitutes "a paradigm of three members (instead of the [traditional] four-member demonstrative set *this*, *that*, *these*, and *those*, with *it* as a member of the pronoun set)." (italics and parentheses original). McCarthy's corpus-based discourse analysis also reveals that while *it* may be a valid alternative for *this* in some cases, the three pronouns in the set each perform unique functions:

> (a) *it* signaled reference to continued, ongoing topics, (b) *this* signaled the raising of a new or significant topical focus, and (c) *that* had a variety of distancing or marginalising functions (e.g., the attribution of an idea to another person, emotional distance, the rejection of ideas or positions, the downgrading or defocusing of a topic, referral across different topics).
>
> *(Hughes & McCarthy, 1998, p. 267)*

This example clearly shows the value of discourse grammar. However, as Hughes and McCarthy acknowledge, while discourse grammar may provide more adequate and accurate grammatical description, it has its own weaknesses, such as rule complexity and the time and effort involved in the data analysis. These are important issues that must be considered in pedagogical description. Despite its weaknesses, discourse-based grammatical analysis is often invaluable in explaining some difficult language usage issues, an issue that will be discussed in Chapters 8, 9, and 11.

### 3.3.4 Register and semantic function analysis

One more result of the influence of sociolinguistics and SFL on language teaching is an enhanced awareness of register and semantic function in language description. As discussed above, sociolinguistics and SFL attach great importance to language registers and semantic functions. It has clearly shown how language use varies from register to register in various ways and how language is used to fulfill three major semantic functions: ideational, interpersonal, and textual. Equipped with such new understandings from SFL, many language educators and researchers have strived to produce teaching materials that can more effectively help learners develop register-awareness and grasp the semantic functions of the language structures they are learning. As a result, many corpus-based studies and reference/teaching materials have appeared in the past two decades (e.g., Biber, Conrad, & Cortes, 2004; Biber, Johnsson, Leech, Conrad, & Finegan, 1999; Cortes, 2004; Coxhead, 2000; Gardner & Davies, 2007; Liu, 2003, 2008c, 2011b, 2012a). These studies and reference/teaching materials have provided, among others, many register-specific lists of lexicogrammatical items, including the most frequently-used academic word families, spoken idioms, phrasal verbs, and other multi-word lexical units from various academic disciplines. These studies will be discussed again in Chapters 5 and 14.

## Questions for consideration and/or discussion

1. Of the four components of communicative competence proposed by Canale and Swain (1980) and Canale (1983), do you think they are of equal importance? If not, how would you rank them? Why?

2. The chapter mentions some examples of L2 pragmatic failures due to interference from learners' L1 pragmatic rules or routines. Can you also give one or two examples of L2 pragmatic failures based on your language learning and/or teaching experience? Also think about and explain what you can do to help students avoid such pragmatic failures.

3. Research has shown that there are pragmatic routines or formulae used for specific speech acts. Besides the examples mentioned in the chapter, e.g., "How are you?"/"What's up?" for greeting, think of and give a few more examples. You should not only mention the formulae but also explain the speech acts they typically each perform.

4. According SFL, language is used to fulfill mainly three semantic functions (ideational, interpersonal, and textual) as well as many sub-function categories. Determine the semantic function of each of the following sentences or the underlined part of a sentence.
   a. <u>What is more</u>, the gap between China and the U.S. will be greater than expected.
   b. President Obama dropped the ball on this issue [=failed to fulfill his responsibility].
   c. Hold on. Please let me finish.

5. It has been shown in this chapter that discourse (e.g., given/new information) may determine and explain our lexicogrammatical decisions. Keeping the role of discourse in mind, decide which of the two underlined sentences in the examples below you prefer and explain why.
   a. The copy of the book that I inherited belonged to my own grandmother … <u>The book was written by her mother—my great-grandmother.</u>
   b. The copy of the book that I inherited belonged to my own grandmother … <u>Her mother—my great-grandmother—wrote the book.</u>

6. While discourse-based language analysis can make language description more accurate and informative, it has some drawbacks such as rule complexity and the large amount of time it may involve. Considering both its values and weaknesses, when and where (i.e., for what types of learners and what types of classes) do you think discourse analysis can be used effectively? If you do not think it is appropriate for classroom teaching, think and explain with one example how you as a teacher can use it to help make your pedagogical description and explanation of grammar/vocabulary more engaging and effective.

## Notes

1 The reason for calling such problems failures rather than errors is that the term *error* would suggest that L2 pragmatic rules are correct and those in L1 are incorrect. That is not true.
2 There is some variation in the terms used by different functional linguists. For example, Halliday (1994) uses *actor* to refer to what most linguists call *agent*. For a thorough discussion on the classification of the different functions of linguistic structures by functional linguistics, the reader is referred to Dik (1980, 1989, 1997) and Halliday (1994).
3 For more information about the classification of the subcategories, see Biber, Conrad, and Cortes (2004) and Liu (2008c, 2012a).

# 4

# COGNITIVE LINGUISTICS

Arguably the most important contemporary linguistic theory over the past two decades, Cognitive Linguistics has had a profound impact on our understanding about language including its use and acquisition. In recent years, it has also begun to have a significant influence on language teaching. This chapter offers a discussion of the theoretical underpinnings of Cognitive Linguistics (including its key concepts) and an examination of the unique features of Cognitive Linguistics-inspired language descriptions as well as its value and potential for enhancing the effectiveness of language teaching.

## 4.1 Theoretical underpinnings and important basic concepts

Cognitive Linguistics has developed as a result of work done by a group of linguists who were devoted to the study of language and mind but were dissatisfied with or dissenting from generative linguistics. It is a linguistic theory consisting of a family of interrelated approaches to the study of language, including, among others, Cognitive Grammar (Langacker, 1987, 1991), Construction Grammar (Fillmore, 1985, 1988; Goldberg, 1995, 2006), metaphor theory (Lakoff, 1987; Lakoff & Johnson, 1980), and conceptual semantics (Talmy, 1988, 2000).[1] As a new theory, Cognitive Linguistics is best known for positing the following assumptions about language: (1) language (including grammar) is a symbolic system where human experience-based conceptualization plays a key role and, as such, language is motivated; (2) meaning is fundamental to language and should be the main focus of language study; (3) as a symbolic system, language is made up of symbolic units/constructions (i.e., pairings of form and meaning), rather than rigidly and hierarchically divided subsystems of lexis and syntax; and (4) language knowledge is usage-based, not innate. To understand Cognitive Linguistics, an elaboration of these important positions is in order.

### 4.1.1 Language is symbolic and conceptual in nature

According to Cognitive Linguistics, language (including grammar) is symbolic and conceptual in nature, and is motivated by our general cognitive processes and experiences, especially embodied experience. A particular point about this symbolic nature of language is that, in addition to lexical items, grammar (in the form of units or constructions) is also symbolic, for, as Langacker (1987) argues, "language as symbolic in nature extends beyond lexicon to grammar" because "morphological and syntactic structures themselves are inherently symbolic, above and beyond the symbolic relations embodied in the lexical items they employ" (p. 12). We will return to this point in the next section (4.1.2).

Evidence for the conceptual nature of language and language knowledge is ubiquitous in language usages and structures. For example, based on our embodied experience, we conceptualize *being balanced/bright/high/up* as being desirable/positive while *being unbalanced/dark/low/down* as being undesirable/negative. The way language symbolizes these conceptualizations can be seen in the following contrastive English examples: *a balanced argument/view* vs. *an unbalanced approach/growth*; *a bright future/student* vs. and *a dark side/period*; *high achievement/spirit* vs. *low grade/moment*; and *brighten/cheer up* vs. *bog/fall down*. Embodied conceptualizations are also shown in some grammatical and phonological structures. For example, the use of past tense in the present to make one's request or suggestion less direct or imposing (e.g., "Could you help me?"/"Here is an article I thought you would like") is based on the concept that time is spatial and a past time creates distance. Also the use of repetition (e.g., "She is very, very smart") as well as the addition of inflectional morphemes to lexical words for expressing grammatical meanings (e.g., the plural -*s*, the past-tense -*ed*, and the possessive -*s*) is based on the conceptualization that more form means more substance/force and hence more meaning (Kövecses, 2006). As an example of how our embodied conceptualization is shown in phonology, we use /i/, a short speech sound with a high harmonic content, to express diminutiveness and endearment (e.g., the Chinese word *qing*, meaning light in weight, and the English words *little bit/Johnny*) because this sound feels brisk and pleasant to the ear; in contrast, we use sounds or sound sequences with a lower harmonic content to express heaviness and unpleasantness (e.g., the Chinese word *zhong*, meaning heavy, and the English words, *bomb/bulk/junk*) because such sounds feel dull and unpleasant to the ear. Furthermore, the Chinese word *qing* is also pronounced with the first or the lightest tone whereas *zhong* is given the fourth or the heaviest tone.

In discussing language use as conceptual, it is also necessary to mention metaphor, especially conceptual metaphor. According to Cognitive Linguistics, language and its usages are to a great extent metaphorical in nature (Kövecses, 2002, 2006; Lakoff & Johnson, 1980; Liu, 2002). Metaphor is so pervasive in language that often it is not easy to differentiate between metaphorical and non-metaphorical use of language, e.g., not many English speakers would think of *budget one's time* as a metaphor. Other examples of everyday metaphors include "The couple has split" (based on the conceptual metaphor that "marriage is a union") and "The argument fell apart" (stemming from the conceptual metaphor that "arguments are buildings"). Even many grammatical terms and concepts are metaphorical in nature, e.g., *structural tree*, which is based on the conceptual metaphor that "syntactical structures are plants." The analysis of language use in terms of conceptual metaphor offers a very interesting and in-depth understanding of a key principle under which language operates. It also provides useful explanations of the motivations behind many language usages and structures.

All of the above examples demonstrate that language indeed symbolizes our conceptualizations. However, because language and cognition are both built on the experiences and environments of the speakers/writers of the language, and because human experience may vary from culture to culture, there are cross-language/culture differences in the symbolized conceptualizations (Kövecses, 2002, 2006; Liu, 2002, 2007). A well-known example is presented by Talmy (1991, 2000): Romance languages, which he classifies as **verb-frame** languages, tend to express the path (direction) of a motion in the verb but the manner of the motion in an adverbial or gerund, e.g., "He entered the room by walking"; in contrast, **satellite-framed** languages such as English tend to express the manner of a motion in the verb with the path shown in a satellite structure such as a prepositional phrase, e.g., "He walked into the room." A less well-known example is that in many languages such as English, time is conceptualized and expressed in linear, sequential terms, e.g., *last* and *next night/week/year/generation*. However, in Chinese, the language spoken by a people who have been historically well-known for respecting (even worshipping) ancestors and hierarchy, time is often conceptualized in vertical/hierarchical terms, e.g., *shang wu, shang xingqi/yue/nian*, and *shang yidai* (translated literally as *upper noon* [=morning], *upper week/month/year*, and *upper generation*) vs. *xia wu, xia xingqi/yue/year*, and *xia yidai* (translated as lower noon [=afternoon], lower week/month/year, and lower generation). Also, as Liu (2002) shows, due to historical and cultural reasons, while eating metaphors are much more extensively used in the Chinese language than in American English, sports metaphors figure much more prominently in American English than in Chinese.

This understanding of the cultural experience-based nature of language is extremely important for second-language learning. It helps L2 learners become aware that linguistic differences often result from differences in cultural experience, which in turn enables them to better understand the motivations behind the L2 structures and usages that may seem strange and difficult to understand otherwise. This is true not only of the use of idioms and metaphorical language, but also of some grammatical structures, as has just been shown. In short, because language is conceptual in nature and based on human experience, language usages and structures are generally motivated rather than arbitrary as traditional linguistic theories have assumed. Exploration of the motivations of language usages is a hallmark feature of Cognitive Linguistics.

### 4.1.2 Meaning is fundamental to language

Cognitive Linguistics considers meaning central to language and language study. Langacker (1987, p. 5) makes this point very explicitly in an overview of the theoretical foundations of Cognitive Linguistics: "The most fundamental issue in linguistic theory is the nature of meaning and how to deal with it." The theory of language as a symbolic system based on human conceptualization makes the issue of meaning especially important and interesting in Cognitive Linguistics. Since language is a symbolic system based on human conceptualization, the meaning of language is mediated by the human mind via conceptualization.[2] Hence, Cognitive Linguistics "equates meaning with conceptualization (explicated by cognitive processing)" (Langacker, 1987, p. 5). Also, the symbolic nature of language means that language is above all a system of representation of meaning. Therefore, meaning is inherent in every aspect of language. As Langacker (1987, p. 12) puts it, "From the symbolic nature of language follows the centrality of meaning to virtually all linguistic concerns." Furthermore, cognitive semantics differs from traditional semantic approaches such as the structural and the logic approaches in that, instead of defining meaning using semantic features and truth conditions based on models of the real world as traditional approaches do, it views meaning in terms of conceptualization, i.e., viewing it as a concept or mental image formed in the mind based on a person's experience. For example, the word *house* symbolizes a concept or a mental image conventionally associated with the word in a person's mind rather than a specific house in the real word. The meanings of linguistic symbols correspond, therefore, to "a mental representation of reality, as construed by the human mind, mediated by our unique perceptual and conceptual systems" (Evans & Green, 2006, p. 7). In this sense, conceptual representations may be heavily influenced by the experience of an individual or a speech community, context, etc. Such an approach to semantics more accurately and fully covers language meanings than traditional approaches.

Take, for example, the meanings of the English words *boy* and *girl*. Despite sharing the semantic feature *+young/-old*, the two words do not actually refer to the same age group of individuals of their respective gender: "for many people, the term girl is used for female humans at a significantly higher age than the term boy is used for male humans" (Fillmore, 1982, cited in Croft & Cruse, 2004, p. 9). Similarly, as Fillmore also points out, *bachelor* and *spinster*, while sharing the semantic property of being single, differ more than just in gender because *spinster* has a much more negative connotation. The type of semantic differences shown in the above examples, often overlooked or un-described in traditional linguistics, is well explained by **frame** or **construal** in Cognitive Linguistics. *Frame* refers to the background knowledge that shapes our understanding of an object, event, etc. This knowledge provides a special reference for understanding a concept. Due to cultural traditions, we use different frames in deciding the age range covered by *girl* and that covered by *boy*.

In fact, often the same event may be described using different expressions or structures, conveying different meanings resulting from a difference in construing and/or framing, as can be seen in the following examples from Lee (2001, p. 3):

1. John bought the car from Mary for a good price.
2. Mary sold the car to John for a good price.

Although referring to the same event, the two sentences differ in that 1a is framed from the perspective of the buyer whereas 1b is from the perspective of the seller; the meaning of "good price" is thus tied to the perspective taken in the utterance.

To adequately discuss the importance of human experience in the understanding of meaning in Cognitive Semantics, a discussion of encyclopedic (or background) and pragmatic knowledge, which is not covered in traditional semantic analysis, is also called for because such knowledge is essential in the understanding of language and concepts. In fact, the understanding of any concept requires some necessary background knowledge, including the concepts upon which it is built (Langacker, 1987, 1991; Croft & Cruse, 2004). More importantly, such knowledge is not always universal for all concepts. In some cases, it may be culture-specific. For example, the word *hospital* cannot be adequately defined and understood simply as a medical institution or facility. The term has several concepts associated with it, e.g., doctors, nurses, patients, labs, emergency room, and surgery rooms. These concepts are not related to hospital by structural semantic relations as defined in structural semantics, and they are not listed in dictionary definitions. These concepts are, however, tied closely to it based on our experience or encyclopedic knowledge. The concept of *hospital* differs noticeably between Americans and Chinese. First, in America, people go to hospital either for emergency purposes or for certain medical procedures including surgeries. They do not usually see their doctors at a hospital. In China, however, a hospital is the place where people see their doctors. They do not have what we call *family doctors*. When they need to see a doctor, they go to a hospital to first wait in line and obtain a number for the specific department (internal, dental, gynecology, etc.) that they would like to see a doctor in. Then they go to that department waiting for their turn. It is also at the hospital that patients have all of their necessary tests done and their prescriptions filled. Thus, for Chinese ESL learners to correctly and fully understand *hospital* in English and for American learners of Chinese to understand *hospital* in Chinese, they will need to have the necessary encyclopedic knowledge in the target language.

### 4.1.3 Language is composed of symbolic units/constructions

As a symbolic system, language is made up of symbolic units/constructions. A symbolic unit is a pairing of form and meaning consisting of a phonological pole (form) and a semantic pole (meaning, including pragmatics). The concept of symbolic units collapses the traditional rigid division between lexis and grammar. As Langacker (1987) puts it, a symbolic unit is "the construct deployed in Cognitive Grammar for the representation of <u>both lexical and grammatical structure</u>" (p. 58; underline added). A symbolic unit can be as small as a morpheme or a word and as large as a clause or sentence, e.g., the plural -*s*; *by and large*; *How are you/What's up?* Syntactical rules, key issues in traditional grammar (especially generative grammar), are not important topics in Cognitive Linguistics. Instead, symbolic units or constructions are, because, as already mentioned, language is built on constructions, or levels of construction. A large symbolic unit consists of smaller ones, e.g., the symbolic unit *tie up loose ends* is composed of two smaller constructions *tie up* and *loose ends*, and the latter are each in turn made up of smaller units (e.g., *tie* and *up* in the case of *tie up*).

Structurally, a symbolic unit/construction "may be defined, very generally, as any linguistic structure that is analysable into component parts" (Taylor, 2002, p. 561), although some cognitive linguists do not believe a construction is entirely analyzable, for "some aspect of its form or function is not strictly predictable from its component parts or from other constructions recognized to exist" (Goldberg, 2006, p. 5). In other words, in the view of linguists such as Goldberg, even when a construction may be analyzable in form, its meaning may not be strictly predictable, an issue that will be discussed below. Whether entirely analyzable or not, however, a symbolic unit/construction is entrenched (stored and accessed) as a whole structure (i.e., as one entity) in the minds of the language speakers or in their language system via repeated encounters. The fact that symbolic units are entrenched whole constructions allows speakers and writers to process and use them automatically without much effort, even in the cases where speakers need to employ them together with other structures to produce larger, novel expressions.

Fortunately, there is not a very high demand for speakers to construct completely novel expressions in actual language use due to the fact that language is largely made up of prefabricated or semi-prefabricated units, a fact that has been well supported by corpus research (Biber et al., 1999; Liu, 2003, 2011b, 2012; Sinclair, 1987, 1991). There appear to be two main reasons for the extensive use of prefabricated or semi-prefabricated expressions in language. One is that language is conventional, which is a well-established understanding about language, and conventionality tends to lead to prefabricated expressions. The other reason is practicality: "Without a substantial inventory of prefabricated expressions, fluent real-time speech would hardly be possible" (Langacker, 2008a, p. 19). Interestingly, some language educators (Nattinger & DeCarrico, 1992; Pawley & Syder, 1983) appear to have long recognized the existence of pre/semi-prefabricated units (what they call lexical phrases) in language and argued for focusing on these units in language teaching. A very important point to note here is that linguistic units are not always either completely prefabricated or entirely novel: there are semi-prefabricated expressions. More importantly, even many completely prefabricated expressions, such as idioms, are sometimes used creatively with novel forms, as has been evidenced by corpus research (Langlotz, 2006; Liu, 2003; Moon, 1998), an issue we will return to in Chapter 14. By the same token, linguistic expressions or structures are neither completely entrenched nor completely un-entrenched. As Langacker (1987, p. 59) elaborates:

> Linguistic structures are more realistically conceived as falling along a continuous scale of **entrenchment** in cognitive organization. Every use of a structure has a positive impact on its degree of entrenchment, whereas

extended periods of disuse have a negative impact. With repeated use, a novel structure becomes progressively entrenched, to the point of becoming a unit; moreover, units are variably entrenched depending on the frequency of their occurrence ...

As a result, there is no particular quantifiable level of entrenchment that can be used as a "cutoff point in defining [symbolic] units" (ibid.). To understand this point, it is necessary to understand the different types of symbolic units, especially the schematic ones, as well as the concept of **schematicity**.

Symbolic units/constructions fall roughly into three major categories: **filled**, **partially-filled**, and **unfilled** (Goldberg, 1995, 2006; Holme, 2009). Filled constructions are those whose individual components, and the order of the components, are all specified, such as morphemes and individual or compound words, e.g., *pre-* and *housesitter*, as well as idioms, e.g., *kick the bucket* (die) and *What's up?* Being specific and fixed in form, filled-constructions are low in schematicity and productivity, although they can be quite productive when used creatively as illustrated in the following example related to the use of the idiom *pull a rabbit out of one's hat*. In reporting and commenting on the news that a Congressman from Arkansas unexpectedly and magically secured Federal funds to build a new highway in Arkansas, a news reporter stated that the Congressman "pulled a highway out of the hat," an expression clearly adapted from "pull a rabbit out of the hat" (Liu, 2003). Partially-filled constructions refer to those where only some of the words or bound morphemes are filled, such as partially-filled idioms (e.g., *cut <someone> short* and *rake <someone> over the coals*), the N + s noun plural construction, and the *more ... the more ...* constructions (e.g., "The more you practice it, the more proficient you will be"). Being units with some items unspecified, partially-filled constructions are more schematic and hence more productive than filled-constructions.

Unfilled constructions refer to those that are highly abstract or schematic, such as the *determiner + N* construction (which may be instantiated as "a/the book") and the N + V + N + Adj *resultative* construction that signifies the meaning of "X causes Y to become $Z_{state}$" (which can be instantiated as "The police shot the suspect dead/He forced the door open"), a construction first identified by Goldberg (1995). Being highly schematic, unfilled constructions are therefore highly productive. Schematic constructions or constructional schemas play an extremely importance role in facilitating language comprehension and production. "They allow expressions which are constructed in conformity with the schemas to be rapidly and reliably categorized and interpreted" and they also enable "the rapid and effortless creation of an indefinite number of new expressions, in conformity with the specifications of the schema" (Taylor, 2002, p. 233). Of course, there are some constraints on the creative use or the generalizability of some schematic constructions, an issue that will be discussed below in section (4.2.4.)

It is also important to note that all grammatical constructions, being schematic in nature, are unfilled. As Langacker (1991) explains, "all grammatical elements—morphemes, classes, and rules—are properly described in terms of schematic symbolic units" because they are "simply schematizations of particular expressions" (p. 46). This view differentiates the function of grammar in Cognitive Linguistics from that in traditional theories of grammar where grammatical rules are fully responsible for constructing sentences or expressions. In Cognitive Linguistics, the role of a schema or schematic symbolic unit "is not to construct new expressions, any more than a set of blueprints is responsible for constructing a building. The schema does, however, provide a model that the speaker can employ for computing a novel expression ... or assessing its conventionality" (Langacker, 1991, p. 47). In other words, schematic symbolic units are models based on which utterances are produced. Here is a good example showing how this works. During a protest at a prison against the execution of an inmate, Jessie Jackson was being arrested for trespassing; during the arrest, he said to the policemen, "Please don't Rodney King me." His utterance was clearly modeled on the expression "Don't baby me," which, I would like to argue, has acquired the status of symbolic unit or construction due to its frequent use, i.e., it has evolved into what I will call the *don't + noun-converted-verb + me* or *don't x me* construction with the meaning of "don't treat me the way the person (now serving as the verb in the construction) is treated." Of course, to understand the intended meaning of Jackson's utterance also requires the encyclopedic knowledge about the Rodney King incident, which adds further support for the need to include encyclopedic knowledge in the study of semantics as called for and practiced in Cognitive Linguistics.

A final important point about grammatical constructions is that, as briefly mentioned above, they are mostly meaningful. This includes not only those small units such as grammatical morphemes that symbolize plurality, tense, possession, etc., but also those syntactic constructions at the clause level, such as the "Cause to Receive" ditransitive (V + N + N) construction and the resultative (V + N + Adj$_{state}$) constructions mentioned previously. That syntactic constructions are meaningful is another key point that distinguishes Cognitive Linguistics or Cognitive Grammar/Construction Grammar from traditional grammars, especially generative grammar, which treats syntax as an autonomous system apart from semantics and lexis. The point that syntactic constructions are meaningful and motivated has been well argued by Goldberg (1995, 2005, 2006), among other scholars.

According to Goldberg, the meaning of an **argument structure** construction lies largely in the construction itself rather than the verb in it. Argument structure constructions refer to syntactic constructions described in terms of the number and the roles of the arguments (nouns) in relation to the verb in a structure, e.g., the N + V+N + N and N + V + N + Adj constructions just mentioned. For example, the verb *cut* does not by itself convey the meaning of "causing something/someone to become X$_{state}$. However, when it is used in the resultative N + V + N + Adj construction, as in the utterance "The police officer cut the hostage free," we understand it to mean that the hostage was freed as a result of the officer cutting off the materials that bound him. In other words, the resultative meaning comes from the construction, not from the verb "cut." The same is true of the "Cause to Receive" V + N + N construction, an issue that will be discussed in Chapter 11.

### 4.1.4 Language knowledge is usage-based

It has been shown above that Cognitive Linguistics views language as a symbolic system built on human conceptualization and experience, a system made up of symbolic constructions that serve as models for speakers to use to produce language in communication. Given this view of language, language knowledge is usage-based, rather than being innate as hypothesized by generative linguistics. Specifically, Cognitive Linguistics denies the existence of an autonomous language faculty that is capable of generating all and only correct sentences of a language. In other words, it rejects the notion of an innate faculty as the source of human language knowledge. In place of the innateness hypothesis, Cognitive Linguistics posits that "linguistic knowledge is acquired 'bottom-up' on the basis of encounters with the language, from which schematic representations are abstracted" (Taylor, 2002, p. 592). Furthermore, it is also the theory of Cognitive Linguistics that a very large part of our linguistic knowledge comprises "knowledge of low-level generalizations" and even "knowledge of specific expressions" (ibid.), a theory that also contrasts sharply with the highly abstract generalizations that form the core of language knowledge in the generative linguistic theory. Langacker (1987) states the difference between the two theories by stating that grammatical knowledge "is simply an inventory of linguistic units," not "a device that carries out a series of operations and gives well-formed sentences as its output" (p. 63).

Empirical studies on L1 child language acquisition by cognitive linguists have provided substantial evidence for this usage-based language acquisition theory (Casenhiser & Goldberg, 2005; Goldberg 2006; Goldberg, Casenhiser, & Sethuraman, 2004; Tomasello, 2000, 2003, Tomasello & Brooks, 1998). According to these studies, what children do in acquiring a language is essentially acquiring linguistic units or constructions of varying lengths and growing schematicity; they do so by matching the forms of constructions with their meanings, by generalizing patterns (i.e., schematizing) through repeated encounters of the constructions, and by using the acquired linguistic units to construct language in communication. As Tomasello (2003, p. 307) puts it, in learning a language children are "constructing utterances out of various already mastered pieces of language of various shapes and sizes, and degrees of internal structure and abstraction – in ways appropriate to the exigencies of the current usage event." In other words, language acquisition is usage-based, relying on language input and use in meaningful context.

According to Cognitive Linguistics, the acquisition of a construction requires the language speaker/learner to have both a high **token frequency** exposure and a high **type frequency** exposure to the construction (Bybee, 1998). Token frequency refers to the frequency of all of the occurrences of the construction. For example, in the case of the ditransitive "Cause to Receive" construction, each occurrence of any of the forms of the construction (e.g., "someone *gave* someone something" "and someone *faxed* someone something") is a token of the construction. A high token frequency is essential for the acquisition of the construction, but it is not enough: if a learner is exposed frequently to only one form of the construction (e.g., only to the *give* verb form of the construction), s/he will have difficulty acquiring the construction. This is because the learner also needs to be exposed frequently to the different forms of the construction, i.e., the different verbs used in the construction (e.g., *cook*, *fax*, *knit*, and *mail*) in order to generalize the use of the construction. The frequency with which different forms of the construction occur is called type frequency.

In short, a construction needs to have both high token frequency and type frequency in order to be entrenched and acquired. Tomasello (2000, pp. 76–77) explains clearly the important roles that the two types of frequency each play respectively in child language acquisition when he writes:

> Fluency with a construction is a function of its token frequency in the child's experience (entrenchment); creativity with a construction emanates from the child's experience of type variation in one or more of the constituents (abstraction). In this way, children build up in their linguistic inventories a very diverse set of constructions—concrete, abstract, and mixed—to call upon as needed in particular usage events.

Tomasello's explanation highlights a crucial point that differentiates Cognitive Linguistics from structural/behavioral linguistics in their theories about language acquisition. On the surface, both theories emphasize the importance of practice and patterns. Yet they differ fundamentally. If we recall, in the structural/behavioral theory, practice in the form of mechanical pattern drills (habit formation) is the key to language acquisition. In contrast, Cognitive Linguistics calls for repeated exposure and use of language constructions in meaningful contexts: instead of mechanical drills of constructions, learners should schematize them through repeated, meaningful and situated use so they learn to understand, to use Tomasello's (2000, p. 77) words again, which constructions are "needed in particular usage events." In short, it is the theory of Cognitive Linguistics that "first-person experience of language (by children or adults) during situated, communicative language use" is essential for language acquisition because such experience "provides evidence of *patterns* in the input that carry *meaning*" and allows learners to grasp language patterns "while doing something with communicative intent …" (Robinson & Ellis, 2008, pp. 494–495).

An important related issue is the role that the **prototype** or the prototypical form of a symbolic construction plays in the acquisition of the construction. A prototype of a construction is the form with which the construction occurs most frequently and it serves as the basic model for the language learner. For example, concerning the ditransitive construction, "*give* someone something" is the proto-type of the construction based on corpus data (Goldberg et al., 2004). It is impor-tant to remember, though, that prototypicality is a matter of degree, not dichotomy. Therefore, concerning the forms of a construction, besides the prototype, some of the rest of the forms are more prototypical than the others. According to research, the prototype of the construction is also usually the first form of the construction to be acquired, and it plays a very important role in the ultimate acquisition of the construction (Campbell & Tomasello, 2001; Goldberg, et al., 2004). By the same token, those more prototypical forms of a construction are acquired earlier than those much less prototypical forms. As a result, in language teaching, the prototypi-cal forms should not only be taught early but also be repeatedly practiced.

As for evidence for the theory that human language is largely knowledge of low-level generalizations and abstractions, it appears to be ubiquitous and abundant. The aforementioned statement by Jessie Jackson to the police, "Don't Rodney King me," may serve as a good example because, although it was quite creative on the part of Jackson in making this utterance modeled on the *Don't baby me* expression and the generalization needed to produce the utterance does not appear to involve a high level of abstraction.

Clearly, all of the above findings and new understandings produced by Cognitive Linguistics have significant implications for language description, as will be shown below.

## 4.2 Cognitive Linguistics-inspired language description

This section deals with the distinctive features of and approaches to linguis-tic description associated with Cognitive Linguistics, specifically with Cognitive Grammar and Construction Grammar. Due to a lack of space and the high tech-nicality of some aspects of the linguistic descriptions in Cognitive Grammar and Construction Grammar, only selected features and approaches used in dealing with certain language structural issues will be covered here. They will help illus-trate how language usages and structures are generally motivated by human expe-rience and conceptualization. As mentioned before, presenting language usages and structures as motivated phenomena should help make language learning and teaching more interesting and effective.

### 4.2.1 Cognitive grammar and construction Grammar

Cognitive Grammar and Construction Grammar[3] are two important strands or approaches of Cognitive Linguistics and they share essentially the same tenets regarding language and grammar. They differ mainly in their foci and the terms used in linguistic description. Because the two grammars are essentially the same, the following discussion offers a combined coverage of the unique features, approaches, and notation methods they use in linguistic description. Furthermore, in the discussion of the unique features and approaches, mention will be made, where appropriate, about how they may be used and adapted for effective pedagogical description.

Before proceeding, it is important to note that although both Cognitive Grammar and Construction Grammar each make an extensive use of specialized terminology, many of the well-known traditional grammatical terms and concepts such as *noun*, *verb*, and *modifier* are still functional in the two new grammars. However, the role and importance of these traditional terms and concepts in the two new grammars are much smaller than in traditional grammars where they are not only essential but also preponderant. In Cognitive Grammar and Construction Grammar, the description of conceptualization, meaning, and function is more important than the discussion of traditional grammatical terms and concepts. More importantly, the traditional terms or concepts are often given new meanings based on the understandings of language from the perspectives of Cognitive Linguistics.

For instance, in the classification of parts of speech in Cognitive Grammar, a noun is defined as a word that profiles or designates a conceptually-reified *thing* (i.e., what is conceptually construed as a thing); a verb is described as a word that "designates a 'process'" that expresses a temporal processual relationship, i.e., a relationship viewed sequentially as it unfolds; the other word classes such as prepositions and articles "designate atemporal relations," e.g., prepositions profile space relations (Taylor, 2002, p. 179). In such a classification, the distinction between nouns and verbs is based largely on "the manner in which a situation is conceptualized," not on "any objective' properties of the situation" (Taylor, 2002, p. 179). For example, the two sentences "Mike fought heroically against brain cancer" and "Mike's fight against brain cancer was heroic" portray the same situation or event, but each construes the situation differently, and, more importantly, each will be used in a different discourse context for a different purpose. The former construes the event as a process, i.e., the process of "fighting against brain cancer," and it is used when one tries to inform others of what Mike did likely as new information. The latter (the nominalization) construes the said process as a thing, and it is mostly likely used as a summary statement of a narrative about what Mike did or as a comment made by a listener after hearing the narrative. In short, the process construal foregrounds (profiles) the temporal aspect of the situation, whereas the thing construal backgrounds (de-profiles) the temporal aspect by nominalizing the verb and by presenting the process as a nonprocessual relationship. In Cognitive Grammar, nonprocessual relations (expressed by nominalized verbal structures such as gerunds and infinitives) and things are grouped together as nouns because they "represent a natural grouping" in the sense that "both construe a situation in a summary fashion" instead of a sequential fashion (Langacker, 2008, p. 119).

### 4.2.2 Focusing on construal and conceptual motivation

Given the high importance of conceptualization in the theory of language espoused by Cognitive Linguistics, the most noticeable feature of Cognitive Linguistics-inspired linguistic description is obviously its focus on construal and conceptual motivation of linguistic structures. As already mentioned above, according to Cognitive Linguistics, the use of a particular linguistic form, be it concerned with tense/aspect or syntax, often reflects a particular construal on the part of the speaker/writer, as shown above regarding the noun and verb distinction.

Because many examples will be provided on how the use of a given grammatical form is the result of construal in Chapters 8, 10, and 11, just one example will be looked at here. At a White House news conference in 1995, a reporter asked the then President, Bill Clinton, whether he and his wife had made mistakes in their handling of the firing of some personnel at the White House travel office (an event known as Travelgate). The President answered, "Mistakes were made in the handling" instead of "We made mistakes." In the answer, Clinton changed the subject or the **figure/trajector** (terms of Cognitive Linguistics referring to the more prominent participant in a relationship or event) from the Clintons to *mistakes*, the object or **ground/landmark** (the less prominent participant) in the original question. This change was the result of President Clinton's re-construing of the event and the relationship of the participants for the purpose of shifting the audience's focus away from him and his wife as the mistake makers.

### 4.2.3 Focusing on embodied experience and conceptualization: use of visuals

Given its focus on embodied experience and conceptualization, Cognitive Grammar makes an extensive use of visuals, especially diagrams, to help illustrate the conceptual workings of language, particularly its semantic and syntactic patterns. Langacker (2008a, p. 10) justifies the extensive use of visuals as an expected practice in an age that is "witnessing the emergence of 'scientific visualization' and the growing recognition of its importance to theory and research." In fact, for language learners and teachers, the heavy use of visuals is perhaps not only justifiable but also desirable because research has long shown the usefulness of visuals in assisting language learning (Brown, 2007). To illustrate the use of visuals in Cognitive Linguistics, two examples are given below.

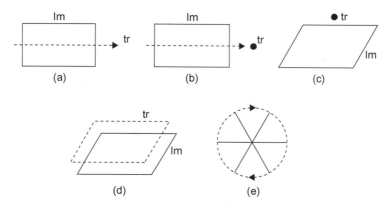

**FIGURE 4.1** Meanings of *over*. Note: *lm = landmark; tr = trajector. Source: Taylor (2002, 475) reprinted by permission of Oxford University Press.*

The first example, Figure 4.1, shows the visual schematic representations of five of the key meanings of *over* created by Taylor (2002, p. 475), who also provided sentences exemplifying the meanings. Only one sentence from his examples for each meaning is given below with the letters of the sentences matching the letters of the diagrams they each exemplify, e.g. sentence A illustrates diagram A.

3a.   She walked over the bridge.
3b.   They live over the hill.
3c.   The lamp hangs over the table.
3d.   The tablecloth is over the table.
3e.   We drove all over the city.

The second example, Figure 4.2, displays four of the ten cartoon sketches that Tyler (2008, pp. 473–475) created to help visualize the root and the metaphorically-extended meanings of model verbs based on the cognitive semantic theory of force dynamics develop by Talmy (1988).

Looking at the sketches, we can tell that while both *will* and *would* involves force from within the doer, the dotted lines of *would* suggests lessened commitment from the doer than *will*. Also, whereas *may* conveys the meaning of an external authority allowing action, *must* expresses the meaning of a strong external authority exerting irresistible force shown with a figure pushing the doer from behind.

It is important to point out that some of the visuals are meant to help explain complex grammatical issues and should not be used directly in the language classroom. Yet many of the diagrams used in Cognitive Linguistics-based discussion may be employed or adapted for language teaching. Of course, the technical terms need to be replaced with everyday language.

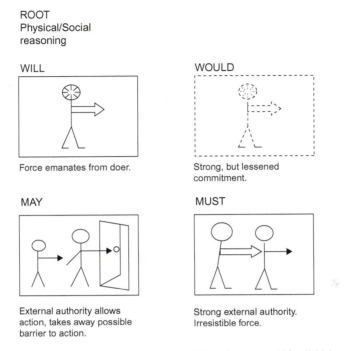

ROOT
Physical/Social
reasoning

WILL

Force emanates from doer.

WOULD

Strong, but lessened
commitment.

MAY

External authority allows
action, takes away possible
barrier to action.

MUST

Strong external authority.
Irresistible force.

**FIGURE 4.2** Root meanings of four English modal verbs. *Source: Tyler (2008, pp. 473–475), reprinted by permission of Routledge.*

### 4.2.4 Description of constraints on the generalizability of constructions

As mentioned before, schematic constructions are extremely important in language because they enable speakers to quickly process and also creatively construct expressions that conform to the schema of a construction. However, there are constraints on the generalizability of some of the schematic constructions, e.g., the unacceptability of *suggest/explain* in the "Cause to Receive" ditransitive construction mentioned before. Understanding such constraints is very important for language learners. It is well known that language learners tend to over-generalize or over-extend the use of a construction (Goldberg, 2006). Providing learners with a clear description of the constraints on the use of a construction should help them avoid making mistakes or make fewer mistakes in the acquisition of the construction. Cognitive and Construction grammars strive to provide good explanations of constraints on construction generalizability.

Take, for example, the resultative "X causes Y to become Z-state" construction in the form of $N + V + N + Adj_{state}$. In this construction, the agent X performs an action that causes or results in the patient becoming a certain state. Yet whereas many verbs of action may be used in this construction (e.g., sentences 7–10), some may not or they may sound unnatural, as can be seen in 11–14. Most of the examples are adapted or taken from Goldberg (1995, Chapter 8) and Taylor (2002, Chapter 27.4):

4   The policeman shot the murder suspect dead.
5   She slashed the parcel open.
6   He broke the door down.
7   They painted the fence white.
8   *The policeman shot the abductor wounded.
9   *They beat the suspect paralyzed.
10  *They fed the girl overweight.
11  *They beat the suspect dead.

According to Goldberg (1995), there are three constraints on the use of the construction that may help explain why sentences 8 through 11 are unacceptable. The first is that the result caused by the action must occur at the same time when the action designated by the verb ends. For example, in sentence 4, the murder suspect died the moment he was shot, not sometime after he was shot. This may explain why sentence 10 is not acceptable because it is impossible for the girl to become instantly overweight after being fed. The second constraint is that the resultative state the adjective designates must be at the "end-of-a-scale," i.e., the patient/object must go "over the edge" (Goldberg, 1995, p. 196). This constraint may be a cause preventing us from producing sentences 8 and 10 since *wounded* and *overweight* are not end-of-scale adjectives. The third constraint is that participle-derived adjectival, such as *paralyzed* and *wounded*, are not allowed in this construction.

One may wonder why sentence 11 is unacceptable since none of the three constraints apply to it. According to Taylor (2002), there does not appear to be any particular reason, and this fact provides evidence that there is some degree of idiomaticity in the use of constructions. While I agree with Taylor's latter point to a certain extent, it seems that our encyclopedic/pragmatic knowledge may actually help explain in part why sentence 11 is not used. As we know, beating usually does not result in death, whereas shooting often does. Also even when a beating results in death, it was not usually as instantaneous as it is in shooting. More examples will be given in Part II of the book to show how many of the usages that have been considered unexplainable in the past can actually be explained based on Cognitive Linguistic approaches.

Before we end the chapter, it is necessary to note, however, that some of the cognitive analyses called for in Cognitive Linguistics-inspired description may be challenging, especially for lower-level language learners. Language teachers should therefore always make sure of the appropriateness of the Cognitive Linguistics-based teaching materials they use and should always be ready to make any necessary adaptation and adjustment. With effort and care from teachers, Cognitive Linguistics-inspired linguistic descriptions can be beneficial to language learners of all proficiency levels. As Pütz, Niemeier, and Dirven (2001, p. xiv) argue, "Not only intermediate and advanced learners can be better catered for in CL-inspired learning materials; also absolute beginners and the group from beginners to intermediate learners can profit from CL findings about language" (p. xiv). For example, according to Holme (2012), for beginning and young learners, we can use enactment/embodied experience (the fundamental base for our conceptualization according to Cognitive Linguistics) to help learners better grasp language. An example from Holme (2012, p. 11) is that, when teaching verbs like *walk*, the teacher can actually walk and have students walk because doing so "reinvests the word in the physical activity from which its meaning was conceptualized and may therefore make it more memorable." Another note of concern is that while there have been some empirical studies about the effectiveness of Cognitive Linguistics-based descriptions (e.g., Boers, 2000; Kövecses & Szabó, 1996; Tyler, 2012), a lot more are needed in this regard.

## Questions for consideration and/or discussion

1.  Cognitive Linguistics posits that language is metaphorical in nature and that we cannot really divide language into metaphorical and non-metaphorical use. Do you agree or disagree? You need to support your position with language examples.
2.  In Cognitive Linguistics, the basic language units are symbolic units, which are pairings of form and meaning established through repeated use and which can vary greatly in length (e.g., the past tense -*ed* morpheme and the "*What's up?*" clause-length utterance). Consider the implications of such a theory on how language should be taught, especially how grammar and vocabulary should be taught (separately or jointly) and what types of language analysis to include.
3.  It is mentioned in the chapter that while there are many conceptual metaphors that appear across learners' L1 and L2, there are many language-specific metaphors as well. Based on your experience, can you think of some specific metaphorical expressions (including idioms) that appear only in learners' L2? Also think what you can do to help your students better grasp these expressions.
4.  A major focus of Cognitive Linguistics is to explain language usages based on our embodied experience and conceptual processes, such as metaphor and metonymy. Try to use this approach to explain some language-usage issues (either in English or another language) that have puzzled you in the past.
5.  Cognitive Linguistics places a great emphasis on the role of embodied experience in language use. Can you think of any things or activities teachers can do to capitalize on learners' embodied experience to help them more effectively grasp grammatical and vocabulary rules and usages?

6.   This chapter mentions various challenges involved in the development and use of Cognitive Linguistics-inspired language descriptions. Think of some specific likely challenges of using such descriptions based on your language learning and teaching experience. Then decide whether the challenges can be overcome. If your answer is yes, explain how.

## Notes

1   For lack of space and the purpose of the book, only some of the most important Cognitive Linguistic approaches and some of the best-known scholars working within each approach are mentioned. In fact, this chapter will focus primarily on Cognitive Grammar and Construction Grammar, two key approaches or strands of Cognitive Linguistics.

2   This notion that meaning is mediated by the human mind differentiates Cognitive Linguistics from systemic functional linguistics, a theory that, while also focusing on meaning, treats language as "an external entity" unmediated by the individual mind. In other words, systemic functional linguistics views language simply as "an unmediated response to social need" (Holme, 2009, p. 5), failing to recognize that the human mind has to create categories and interpret experiences in language use.

3   Construction Grammar actually consists of not just one model but several slightly different models. However, it is beyond the purview of this chapter to cover the different models.

# 5

# CORPUS LINGUISTICS

In the past two decades, corpus linguistics has gained increasing popularity among language researchers and teachers. It has had a tremendous impact on our understanding and description of language as well as on the way language is taught. Because of its growing popularity and importance in language teaching, this entire chapter is devoted to corpus linguistics. The chapter consists of an overview of corpus linguistics, a discussion of the contributions corpus linguistics makes in our understanding of language usage patterns/rules, and an examination of its use in language description/teaching.

## 5.1 Overview

### 5.1.1 What is corpus linguistics?

Corpus linguistics is the study of language through the examination of a collection of real language data or texts. As such, it is not a linguistic theory per se, but an approach. However, it is a principled approach shaped by several important linguistic theories and assumptions about language, including (1) language rules are usage-based, (2) language rules and usages may change over time, and (3) there is no rigid separation between vocabulary and grammar (Gries, 2008; Lindquist, 2009). The theory about language rules being usage-based differs drastically from the generativist theory that language is largely innate. Guided by this usage-based theory of language, corpus linguistics strives to uncover the rules and patterns of language by scrutinizing large amounts of natural language data using various query and analysis techniques and procedures. To understand how corpus research works, a quick definition/description of corpus is in order.

A corpus refers to a collection of spoken and/or written texts. Before the computer era, such collections were stored in paper form (e.g., cards, slips of paper) and the examination of the data was done manually. The first electronic corpus—the one million-word *Brown Corpus*—appeared in the U.S. in 1961. Since then, corpora have become generally electronic. Today's corpora are often equipped with powerful search engines that allow researchers to do language analysis quickly and often automatically. To assist and enhance their searchability, many corpora are tagged for a variety of information, such as parts of speech and demographic characteristics of the speakers/writers. Today's corpora are also well designed with systematically-selected representative language data. Careful designs and large sizes have greatly enhanced the reliability of corpus-based language research. Furthermore, the machine-search capability of contemporary corpora has significantly enhanced the value and effectiveness of corpus research. It makes it possible to easily and accurately analyze enormous language data in mega-sized corpora (which typically contain over 100 million words each). In addition, to accommodate various research purposes, different types of corpora have been developed, such as specialized spoken or written corpora, learner (L2) corpora, monitoring corpora that are used to observe language changes or variations, and large multi-purposed corpora that typically contain a variety of types of data in various registers. Examples of specialized corpora include the free two million-word online *Michigan Corpus of Academic Spoken English* (MICASE) and Barlow's two million-word *Corpus of spoken, professional American English* (CSPAE). Well-known examples of large multi-purposed corpora include the 100 million-word *British National Corpus* (BNC) and Mark Davies' free online 400+ million-word *Corpus of Contemporary American English* (COCA).

### 5.1.2 Types of information corpus queries may generate and the procedures used

The types of usage information that corpus queries can obtain or generate may vary depending on the search-engine capability and the way and extent that the data are tagged in a given corpus. In general, a corpus query can generate any of the following types of information:

1. frequency of words/phrases/structures;
2. common **collocations** of a word (including *V + N/V + preposition/adj + N* collocations, as well as the adjacent neighbors of a word);
3. typical **colligations** of a word (this refers to the typical grammatical words or structures a word co-occurs with, e.g., while *amazing, astounding,* and *surprising* are synonymous and can be used in the affirmative structure, usually only *surprising* is used in the negative structure, e.g., "It's not surprising that …", but not "*It's not amazing");
4. distribution of a word or structure across different registers;
5. comparison of any of the above information between two words or Structures.

One of the most basic and common corpus query and displaying methods is **concordancing**. A query of a word using this method will generate a list of all of the contexts in which the word appears, as shown in Figure 5.1 for the

**FIGURE 5.1**  Concordance lines for *pleased* in SCPAE using MonoConc Pro.

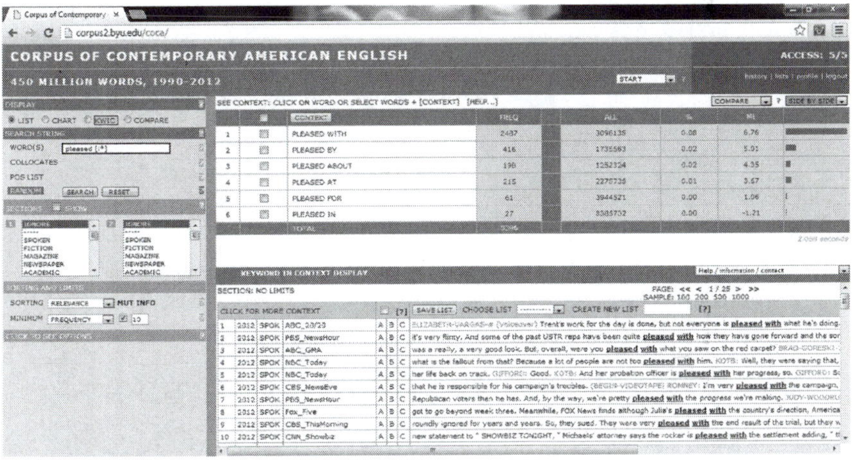

**FIGURE 5.2**  Prepositions used after *pleased* in COCA.

word *pleased* in the SCPAE corpus. Many concordance programs will highlight all of the *key words in context* (KWIC) by using different colors for different parts of speech. From the results above, one can see that *pleased* is used mainly as a predicate adjective (*be pleased*). The words that occur most frequently after *pleased* are the infinitive sign *to* and the preposition *with*. Furthermore, *pleased* is often modified by intensifiers, such as *very*, *quite*, and *really*.

In a corpus search, one can also query for a specific type of collocate of a word that appears either before or after the word. For example, one can query for the typical verbs used before a noun or the typical prepositions after an adjective or verb. Figure 5.2 shows the result of the query for the prepositions used after *pleased* in COCA. The query method is very simple: enter into the query space "pleased [i*]" where "i" is the searching code for prepositions and [i*] stands for any prepositions. For information about the methods for querying other types of information in COCA, visit the online corpus.

The results indicate that the prepositions used after *pleased* are, in order of frequency, *with/by/about/at* (the remaining two prepositions are not meaningful due to their low frequencies and low MI scores). The numbers in the first "All" column each refer to the total frequency of the given "pleased + preposition" phrase. The numbers in the second "All" column each mean the total frequency of *pleased* plus the total frequency of the preposition in COCA. The percentage numbers each indicate how many percentages the given *pleased + preposition* phrase accounts for the total frequencies of the two words in COCA. For example, the frequency of *pleased with* in COCA is 2,487 while the frequency of *pleased* plus the frequency of *with* is 3,096,135. So *pleased with* accounts for only 0.08 percent of the combined total frequency of *pleased* and *with* in COCA. The MI score is a measurement of how likely it is that the two words will co-occur given their total separate frequencies and their chances to co-occur with other words. The higher an MI, the more likely the two words will co-occur. A phrase that has a higher raw frequency than another phrase may not have a higher MI score. For example, *pleased at* has a higher frequency than *pleased about* (their frequency ratio being 215:190), but *pleased about* actually has a higher MI score than *pleased at* (4:35:3.67). In other words, the tendency for *please* and *about* to co-occur is higher than *please* and *at* considering the overall frequencies of the words involved.

As an example of how corpus search can generate register information of a lexical item, Figure 5.3 shows the results of the query for the frequencies of

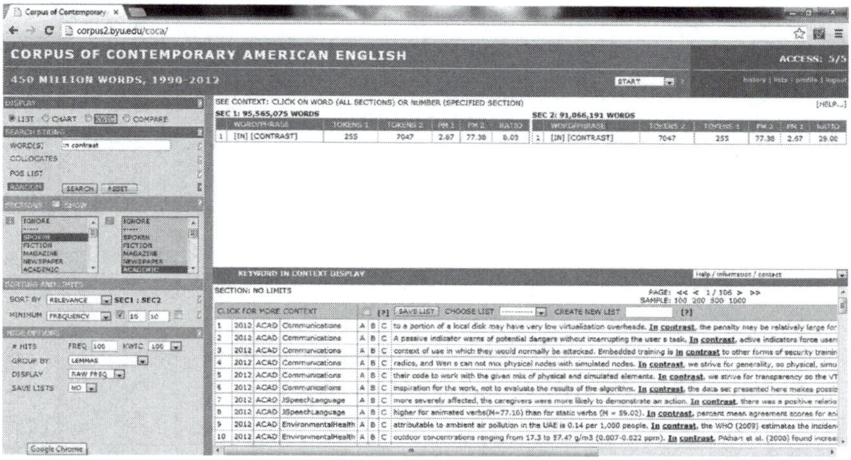

**FIGURE 5.3** Frequency of *in contrast* in speaking and academic writing in COCA.

*in contrast* in the spoken register (shown in the column "Tokens 1") and the academic writing register (shown in the column "Tokens 2") of COCA. The results indicate clearly that the phrase is used mostly in academic writing, with its frequency ratio between spoken and academic writing registers being 3:100. Such corpus query results can also be displayed in the form of a chart. Figure 5.4 illustrates the distribution of *in contrast* across all of the five registers (Spoken, Fiction, Magazine, Newspaper, and Academic writing) and all of the five time periods in COCA. The results reveal again that *in contrast* is used mainly in academic writing.

Finally, Figure 5.5 shows an example of a comparative query in COCA regarding the typical nouns that the adjectives *high* and *tall* each modify. The

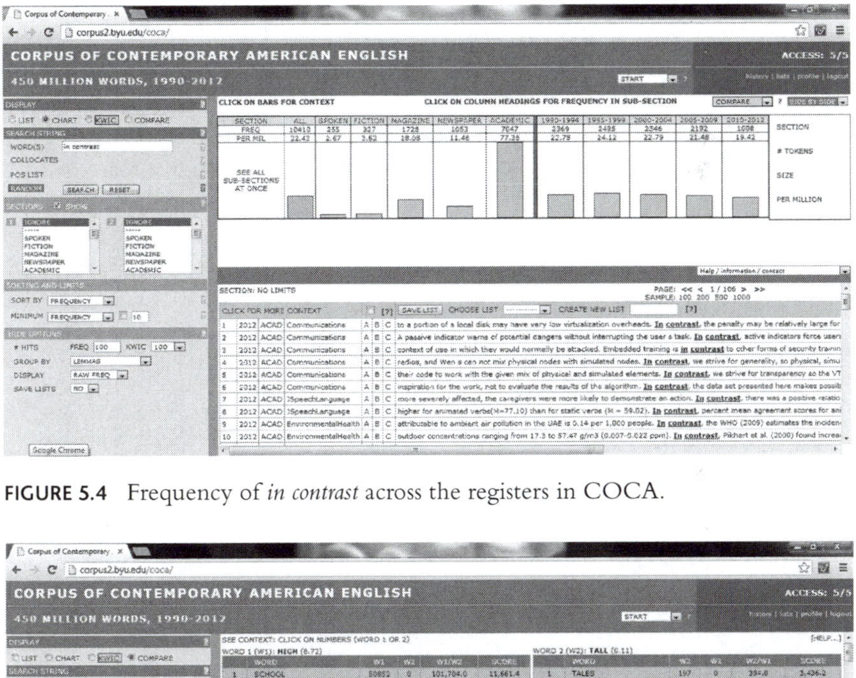

**FIGURE 5.4**   Frequency of *in contrast* across the registers in COCA.

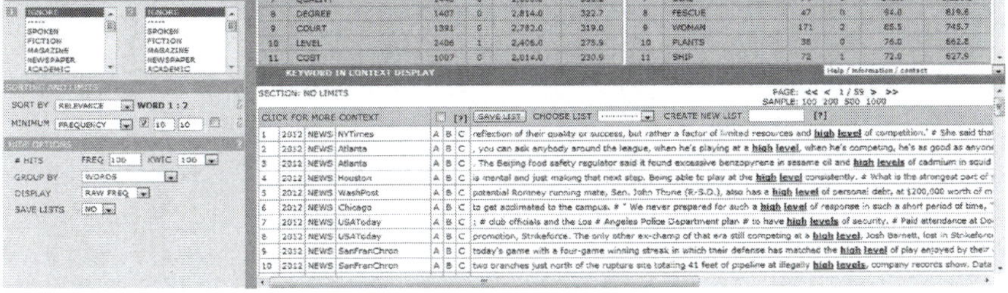

**FIGURE 5.5**   Comparison of nouns typically modified by *high* and *tall* in COCA.

query was intended to identify the differences between the two synonyms. As shown in the results, *high* is used much more frequently than *tall* (evidenced by the fact the frequencies of nouns modified by *high* are all in the thousands whereas the frequencies of the nouns modified by *tall* are all in the hundreds). Also and more importantly, *high* typically modifies abstract nouns (e.g., *school/ level/risk*) whereas *tall* usually modifies concrete nouns (e.g., *guy/man/woman*; note: *tall tale(s)* is an exception because it is a fixed idiomatic term). These results support the findings of Tsui's (2004) study that used a different corpus, which helps show the reliability of corpus research.

Based on these examples, one can conclude that the distributional patterns of a lexiogrammatical item/structure (i.e., in which context it occurs) and the frequency with which it occurs are two key issues that corpus linguistics looks at in uncovering general usage patterns and rules. This is completely understandable for a usage-based approach to language study. Frequency is important because it offers us the most basic information about how a linguistic item or structure is used. Yet this does not mean that corpus linguistics ignores or overlooks usages that are infrequent. Corpus linguists also scrutinize low-frequency items to understand why and how they are used (Liu, 2010b, 2013). Any usage, no matter how infrequent it is, must occur for a reason in communication. Context is another extremely important issue that corpus linguistics focuses on. This is again driven by the usage-based theory of language. By examining the typical contexts that a linguistic item is used in, we gain a good understanding of its meaning and usage patterns.

## 5.2 Significant contributions of corpus linguistics to the study of language

Corpus linguistics has significantly enhanced our understanding of the nature of language and the way language works and is used. Specifically, corpus linguistic research has produced several very important new understandings about language and has also uncovered many inaccuracies and/or inadequacies in the existing language descriptions. Each of the main contributions of corpus linguistics is discussed below.

First, numerous corpus studies have demonstrated that language is composed of a very large number of prefabricated/semi-prefabricated expressions, also labeled variously as *fixed/semi-fixed expressions, formulae, lexical bundles, multi-word expressions/units, phraseology,* and *word clusters* (Biber & Conrad, 1999; Biber, Conrad, & Cortes, 2004; Hoey, 1991, 2005; Hunston & Francis, 1998, 2000; Sinclair, 1987, 1991, 2004; Stubbs, 1995, 2001; Wray, 2002, 2008).[1] These expressions play a crucial role in communication and are largely responsible for a speaker's/writer's fluency in various contexts and functions.

Second, many corpus studies have provided ample evidence about the close correlation between linguistic items' formal distributional patterns and their semantic functions (e.g., Gries, 2001; Gries & Otani, 2010; Gries & Stefanowitsch, 2004; Hanks, 1996; Liu, 2010a; Liu & Espino, 2012; Sinclair, 1991, 2004; Stefanowitsch & Gries, 2003). In other words, the meanings and functions of a linguistic item are shaped by the contexts in which it is typically used, including with which words it frequently co-occurs and in which grammatical structure(s) and register(s) it usually appears. In fact, corpus-based behavioral-profile studies have repeatedly shown that a most effective way to understand the difference(s) among synonyms or near-synonyms is to examine their distributional patterns (an issue that will be discussed in detail in Chapters 12 and 13). The corpus research findings in this regard offer solid empirical support for the Firth's (1957, pp. 7, 11) theory that "the complete meaning of a word is always contextual" as we "know a word by the company it keeps".

Third, corpus linguistic research has revealed that the typical distributional patterns of a linguistic item often help create a **semantic prosody**—a unique connotative meaning for the item (Gries & Stefanowitsch, 2004; Louw, 1993; Sinclair 1991; Stefanowitsch & Gries, 2003; Stewart, 2009). For example, the emphatic adverb *utterly* is typically used with a negative word and hence has a negative semantic prosody, e.g., *utterly useless/ridiculous/incapable*. Also, as Sinclair (1991) shows, the phrase verb *set in* has a negative semantic prosody as it is typically used with a negative subject: *Panic/depression/fatigue sets in*. Similarly, as Stefanowitsch and Gries (2003) demonstrate, the N+*(be)+waiting to happen* construction (or **collostruction** in their terminology) also has a negative semantic prosody because the nouns in this collostruction are exclusively negative, as shown in examples of *accident/disaster/tragedy … waiting to happen*.

The fourth contribution of corpus linguistics is that it has identified the usage patterns and semantic functions of many lexical items across various registers—very useful information that we would not be able to learn otherwise (Biber, et al. 1999, Biber & Conrad, 1999, Biber, Conrad, & Cortes, 2004; Carter & McCarthy, 2006; Francis, Hunston, & Manning, 1996, 1998; Hoey, 1991, 2005; Hunston & Francis, 1998, 2000; Liu, 2003, 2008c, 2011b, 2012a; Moon, 1998; Sinclair, 1991, 2004; Stubbs, 1995, 2001). For example, based on a close analysis of corpus data, Francis, Hunston, and Manning (1996, 1998) compiled two books on the grammar patterns of words (one book on verbs and one on nouns) in which they describe the typical structural patterns that the main English verbs and nouns typically appear in. Also, Biber and associates (1999, 2004) and many other scholars (e.g., Carter & McCarthy, 2006; Hyland, 2008; Liu, 2003, 2012a; Moon, 1998) have identified thousands of frequently used three- to six-word-long lexical bundles or multi-word constructions used in various registers and academic disciplines. Furthermore, Coxhead (2000) identified and compiled a list of the most frequently used academic words or word families (words that are related, e.g., "analysis/analytical/analyze"). Finally, corpus work in this area has led to the publication of new type of dictionaries, including *Collins COBUILD* (1987, 1996) dictionaries and Davies and Gardner's

(2010) frequency dictionary in which word entries are listed by order of raw frequency and each entry also lists the most frequent collocates of the word.

The fifth important contribution of corpus linguistics is that corpus linguistic research, especially the work on **pattern grammar** (to be explained below) and the aforementioned collostructions (Gries & Stefanowitsch, 2004; Stefanowitsch & Gries, 2003), has seriously and successfully challenged the rigid separation between lexis and grammar held in traditional linguistic theories and approaches. Sinclair (1987, 1991), a founder of contemporary corpus linguistics, was the pioneer and leader in the research in this area. He explicitly questioned the "wisdom of postulating separate domains of lexis and syntax" (1991, p. 104) and laid the foundation for the development of the pattern grammars by Francis, Hunston, and Manning (1996, 1998) and Hunston and Francis (2000). A pattern grammar is a lexicogrammar; it describes the typical structural patterns in which given nouns or verbs are used. In pattern grammars as well as in the collostrations identified by Stefanowitsch and Gries, one can clearly see how the use of a word is tied to specific grammatical structures and how a grammatical structure is often connected with certain lexical items. Corpus research findings on this issue are of great importance because they have significantly changed the way we approach language: we now view vocabulary and grammar as an interconnected system rather than as two separate domains.

One more unique contribution of corpus linguistics is that it has made it much easier to accurately identify and trace languages changes over time and the differences between language varieties (e.g., American English vs. British English). For example, via a synchronic comparison of the BNC and COCA and a diachronic comparison of COCA, Lindquist (2009) found that the use of *likely* as an adverb (e.g., "Tom will likely do that") was far more common in American English than in British English and that its use in American English was also on the rise. Also, Liu's (2011b, 2012a) comparative studies of the American and British use of phrasal verbs and multi-word constructions in BNC and COCA identified some specific usage differences between the two English varieties (e.g., *fill in* a form in British English but *fill out* a form in American English) and the increased use of some structures (e.g., the significant increase in the use of the phrasal verb *check out* in American English in the past decade).

Last but not least, corpus linguistic research has uncovered many inadequacies and inaccuracies in the existing language descriptions. For example, corpus studies have found that many of the language usages (such as idioms and unique constructions) that have been marginalized or ignored by structural and generative linguistics are common language features that perform important and often indispensable functions in communication. Idioms (e.g., *by and large* and *raining dogs and cats*) and unique multi-word constructions (e.g., "One more absence and you fail this class") do not conform to established grammatical and semantic rules. This "one more x and y" or "do x and y" construction (e.g., "Do this one more time and you're fired") is unique in several important ways (Taylor, 2002, pp. 571–572). The usual coordinating conjunction *and* is used in this construction to conjoin two unparalleled parts: a noun phrase and a declarative clause or an imperative clause and a declarative clause. More importantly, the noun or the imperative clause before *and* actually serves as a conditional structure meaning "if you do x." Such unusual uses of language clearly violate established grammatical rules, but they are left unexplored in structural and generative grammar. Corpus linguistics has substantially raised our awareness of these overlooked language usages and the important roles they play.

Another inadequacy in the existing language descriptions uncovered by corpus linguistic research is that grammatical usage patterns/rules used in spoken language often differ from those in written language and this finding has led to the development of spoken English grammar (Carter & McCarthy, 1997; Leech, 2000). One more finding of inadequacies in the existing language descriptions is that some of the well-known prescriptive grammatical rules are not supported by actual language data. These rules include the prohibition of the use of *and/but* as linking adverbials to begin a sentence, the ban on the use of *hopefully* as a sentence initial modifier, and the stipulation that the *none of a plural noun* subject (e.g., "none of the students") should be treated as singular, not plural. Corpus data have shown that these rules are often not followed in actual language use. In fact, some of the banned usages (*and/but* as linking adverbial and *hopefully* as sentence modifier) have even found their way into academic writing and their use is on the rise (Liu, 2011a). Furthermore, corpus research has also found that, contrary to what has been traditionally believed, many so-called fixed idioms often vary in form in actual language use (Liu, 2003; Moon, 1998), an issue that will be discussed in Chapter 14. Some scholars have also specifically examined language descriptions in student textbooks against corpus finding and found noticeable inadequacies (e.g., Conrad, 2004, Alejo, Piquer, & Reveriego, 2010). Conrad (2004) compared four textbooks' descriptions of the contrastive linking adverbials with their actual use patterns in corpus data. Her comparison reveals several discrepancies. For example, while *though* was used mainly as a linking adverbial in the corpus data, the textbooks presented it only as a conjunction, entirely overlooking its adverbial function. Also, whereas corpus data indicated that *however* and *on the contrary* were used most often in academic writing, one of the textbooks recommended the two contrastive adverbials for use in conversation.

In short, based on the above discussion, corpus linguistics has greatly enhanced our understanding of language and enabled us to make language description more accurate and informative.

## 5.3 Impact of corpus linguistics on language teaching

Corpus linguistics has had an enormous impact on language teaching in the past two decades. It has provided language learners, teachers, and material writers with an invaluable new tool and resource, making language learning/teaching more engaging and teaching materials more authentic, accurate, and informative. The use of corpus in the classroom will be discussed first and then the use of corpus in teaching curriculum and material development will be explored.

## 5.3.1 Corpus use in the classroom

Thanks to the rapid advancements in both computer/internet technology and corpus linguistics, the use of corpora in the language classroom has increased tremendously in the past two decades. This significant increase of corpus use is driven by the fact that corpora can provide learners with not only enormous amounts of authentic language input but also various valuable deductive and inductive language learning opportunities that come with corpus queries and analysis (Aston, 2001; Burnard and McEnery, 2000; Francis, 1993; Hunston & Francis, 1998, 2000; Liu, 2010c; Liu & Jiang, 2009, O'keeffe, McCarthy, and Carter, 2007; Reppen, 2010; Sinclair, 2004). With regard to deductive learning opportunities, language learners can use corpus data to test the rules or patterns they have learned or are learning. For example, after learning that *get rid of* is an informal expression used mainly in speech, learners do a corpus study of its frequencies in both speaking and academic writing registers to ascertain whether this description of the phrase is truly correct. Concerning inductive (or discovery, data-driven) learning opportunities that corpora offer, learners can observe in the concordance data the actual uses of grammatical and/or vocabulary items and then discover/generalize the usage patterns or rules regarding these language items. For instance, in order to find out the semantic and usage differences between *high* and *tall*, learners can query for and examine the typical nouns each of the two adjectives modify and the results will enable them to reach the conclusions already mentioned above in Section 5.1.1.

It is necessary to mention that deductive learning with the use of corpus is also known as corpus-based learning whereas inductive learning via corpus data analysis is also called corpus/data-driven learning. For simplicity purposes, hereafter the term "corpus-based" learning will be used to refer to both types of corpus-involved learning. Research has shown that in general the majority of L2 students like corpus-based learning activities and find them more engaging and more beneficial than learning without corpus use (Chan & Liou, 2005; Liu & Jiang, 2009; Sun & Wang, 2003; Yoon & Hirvela, 2004). Furthermore, corpus-based inductive learning activities are "particularly effective for the acquisition of grammar and vocabulary" because they help learners to notice and retain lexicogrammatical usage patterns better by engaging them in "deep [language] processing" (Aston, 2001, p. 19). The types of lexicogrammatical knowledge that corpus-based learning can help students learn more engagingly and effectively include, among others, a lexical item's typical collocations/colligations, its register information, and its semantic functions (covering both its denotative and connotative meanings) generated from its usage patterns in the corpus data. Specifically, corpus searches can help learners find the necessary information to deal with some of the most challenging learning issues they face, such as the use of prepositions and verb–noun/adjective–noun collocations as well as whether a word is appropriate for a particular context or register.

For example, if a learner wants to use the word *disillusioned* in expressing his/her lost faith and trust in someone/something but does not know which preposition to use after *disillusioned*, s/he can do a quick corpus query and find out that *with* is the typical preposition to use in this case. As another example, if a learner is not sure whether it is correct to say *make a step*, s/he can quickly find out that in English we use *take* rather than *make* in this case by querying which verb(s) are typically used before the noun phrase *a step*. It is necessary to point out that direct corpus queries are not suitable for students with beginner or low-level English proficiency due to the level of difficulty of the language in most corpora. However, even for low-level students, corpora can be useful. Teachers can use corpus data to find appropriate authentic examples and then screen and simplify them for use with these students. In other words, corpora can be a very valuable indirect source for low-level learners.

It is important to note, however, that corpus-based learning can be very challenging due to a variety of reasons. First, such learning requires students to possess a good command of corpus query and analysis skills as well as a decent English proficiency. Frequently, students do not know which query method/procedure to use to obtain the usage information they need. This is especially true of students without much corpus research experience. Second, corpus data analysis and pattern/rule-finding can take a lot of effort and a large amount of time. Some students may find it too labor-intensive or time-consuming. There are also various other factors that may affect the success of corpus-based learning. Besides students' language proficiency and motivation, their learning styles, the class time available, and level of accessibility to corpora are just some of the factors teachers should consider when involving students in corpus-based learning. It is imperative that teachers provide students with adequate training and support in corpus-based learning before as well as during its implementation in the classroom. The following are some useful procedures, principles, and strategies for corpus-based language teaching taken from Liu (2010c, 2011a) and Liu and Jiang (2009):

- Show students how to conduct various corpus searches by modeling them step by step and doing them together with your students in class using specific query examples. Also give students a simple manual that describes in detail how to do each type of the queries students are supposed to learn.
- Concerning actual corpus-based learning activities, begin with guided and controlled learning activities. For example, we can first select some easy concordance examples, screen out irrelevant examples and examples that contain

difficult words or structures, and print out the selected examples on a piece of paper for students to work on. By screening out the difficult and irrelevant examples, we make the data analysis much simpler for the students.

- Have students conduct deductive learning activities before doing inductive ones because deductive learning is easier. In a typical deductive learning activity, give students a rule or pattern and ask them to test it by finding examples in a corpus. For example, after teaching your students that *bring up* can mean to raise an issue/question or mention something as well as to raise a child, ask students to find examples of the use of the phrasal verb in each meaning in a corpus. Such activities are simpler than those inductive ones where they have to examine many examples to identify the meaning or a rule by themselves.

- Have students work in pairs or groups. Research shows that pair or group work is an effective corpus learning practice (Liu, 2011a; Liu & Jiang, 2009). Corpus data analysis is time-consuming and labor-intensive. When students work together, the work can be divided. More importantly, it is much easier for several people to figure out a language rule or pattern than for one individual. Of course, it is of paramount importance that the groups are made up of individuals who can work well together.

- Make the corpus-learning assignment as specific and as clear as possible. For example, if you want your students to understand that phrasal verbs are generally used in spoken and informal written language while one-word verbs are preferred in formal writing, you can have your students do a comparative corpus study of the use of, say, *get rid of* vs. *eliminate* in the BNC's or COCA's "spoken" and "academic" corpora. You may even want to give them instructions about the search techniques they can use. Also allow students to use dictionaries (either online or hardcopy) in their data analysis because the latter can help them tremendously in the process.

- Select the most appropriate learning and teaching activities. Deciding which activities to use and when and how to use them in a given class is a complex and challenging issue. This is because the effectiveness of corpus-driven language learning depends on many factors including those mentioned above. For example, for students who are new to corpus study, deductive learning activities will be more appropriate than inductive ones. For students who enjoy working with others, group projects will be more appropriate but for students who prefer working individually and who have developed good corpus analysis skills, individual projects may work better.

Finally, there have been quite a few books devoted exclusively to the use of corpora in language teaching, such as Aijmer (2009), Aston (2001), Burnard and McEnery (2000), Kettemann and Marko (2002), O'keeffe & McCarthy (2007), Reppen (2010), and Sinclair (2004). Teachers can find various types of useful information on the topic, including even the basics about corpora and their use as well as sample corpus-based teaching activities.

### *5.3.2 Using corpora for curriculum design and material development*

Corpora are especially helpful for curriculum or syllabus design, material development, and lesson preparation. In curriculum design, the most important issues are what language features (including vocabulary and grammatical structures) to teach and in what sequence to teach them. In the past, these questions were very challenging because it was often difficult to accurately identify the language needs for the students in a given language program. Corpora have now made such decisions much easier by providing curriculum designers with the needed authentic language data to identify the specific language needs of the learners that their curriculum targets for. By the same token, corpora also offer material writers the authentic language data they need in developing language reference books and textbooks. In fact, many publishers have built mega-sized corpora for the purpose of curriculum and reference/teaching material development, e.g., Cambridge University Press's *Cambridge International Corpus*, Collins *Birmingham University International Language Database* (COBUILD), Longman's *Longman Corpus Network*, and the Oxford University Press's *Oxford English Corpus*. As a result, many, if not most, of the reference books and textbooks published today are corpus-based. The use of corpus data have significantly enhanced the quality and usefulness of such reference and teaching materials. It has made the language description more accurate, the presentation sequence more sensible, the language features covered in them more appropriate and useful, and the examples included in them more authentic. Besides corpus-based reference books and textbooks, there have been many research journal articles that offer corpus-based lists of the most frequently-used lexical items in various registers and academic disciples, such as Coxhead's (2000) most frequent academic word list, Gardener and Davies's (2007) and Liu's (2011b) lists of most frequent English phrasal verbs across different registers, Liu's (2003) list of the most common spoken American English idioms, and Liu's (2012a) list of the most common multi-word constructions in academic writing. These lists are useful reference and learning materials for language learners and teachers.

Corpora are also a valuable resource for teachers in lesson preparations. For example, teachers can readily find, from corpora, authentic language examples for illustrating the language points they are teaching. Let us assume that a teacher needs to help her/his students understand the differences between the closely related verbs *hope* and *wish*. The teacher can do a quick corpus search regarding the typical usage patterns of the two verbs (i.e., the typical linguistic contexts and structures they each appear in) and select the examples that can best illustrate and highlight the semantic and usage differences between the two verbs. Another benefit of seeking examples from corpora is that they are authentic rather than made up, the dominant type of language examples many teachers used before corpora became easily accessible. Finding authentic language examples is especially important for nonnative speaker teachers teaching in a foreign-language context because these teachers have very limited access to authentic target language and because they are not always sure about the accuracy and appropriateness of the examples they create (Liu, 2010c; Liu & Jiang, 2009). In fact, corpora (especially free online corpora) are excellent comprehensive tools for teachers to use to look for answers to almost any language usage issues they are not sure of. They are in some aspects better than dictionaries and grammar books because the latter often do not provide specific examples and also because the latter do not always have information regarding every small aspect of usage questions. Furthermore, teachers can use corpus data for developing exercises or language-test items. Overall, as research has shown, teachers find corpora to be a helpful resource in this regard (Aijmer, 2009; Liu & Jiang, 2009; Sinclair, 2004).

Finally, it is necessary to mention that there have been some nonnative or L2 speaker/writer corpora, such as the *Longman learner corpus* (a part of the *Longman Corpus Network*) and Granger, Dagneaux, and Meunier's (2002) *International corpus of learner English*. These corpora are designed to help L2 educators and researchers understand the unique features and/or problems of **interlanguage**, the language produced by L2 learner. Language teachers can use such corpora to identify the typical errors or issues L2 learners have so they can tailor their instruction to help learners more effectively deal with these challenging problems.

## Questions for consideration and/or discussion

1. In addition to the listed types of language usage information that corpus queries can generate, describe and explain any other types that you believe corpus searches can provide based on your experience of using corpora for language learning and/or teaching purposes.
2. Visit the COCA web page at http://corpus2.byu.edu/coca/ and take its brief tour if you have not done so to learn the basic query techniques and procedures. Then if you are a first-time corpus user, query for the following simple information concerning the verb *make*:
    a. its overall frequency and its frequencies or distributions across the five registers; the most common nouns that function as its objects (i.e., the nouns used after the verb);
    b. whether its most common objects are predominantly concrete nouns (e.g., cars/dinner) or abstract nouns (e.g., decisions/plans).

If you are an experienced corpus user, query for the following information regarding the phrasal verb *make up*:

    a. its overall frequency and its frequencies across the five registers;
    b. its different meanings (e.g., *to compensate* as in "make up for your lost time"; *to compose* as in "Five members make up the committee");
    c. which of the identified meanings is used most frequently;

    d.   whether the most frequent meaning varies from register to register (i.e., whether the most frequently used meaning of *make up* remains the same or changes from register to register).

Then think and describe how the findings from the queries may be used in language teaching to help learners better grasp the verb "make" or the phrasal verb "make up."

3.   The chapter mentions the following types of lexicogrammatical knowledge that corpus-based learning is especially suited to teach: a lexical item's typical collocations and colligations, its distributions across various registers (i.e., its register information), and its semantic usage patterns. Think whether there are other types of knowledge that corpus-based learning can also be effective in helping students learn. Then decide which type(s) of knowledge you believe are most conducive to corpus-based learning/teaching based on your learning/teaching experience. Explain and support your decision.

4.   The chapter also mentions some challenges involved in using corpus-based language learning and teaching. Based on your experience in using corpora (but if you have not used corpora, simply base your answer on your learning and teaching experience in general), are there any other challenges? If there are, how can teachers best deal with them?

5.   Find two old language reference and/or textbooks and two recently published ones that are corpus-informed. Compare the two different types of materials. In your comparison, pay particular attention to (1) the way grammar and vocabulary items are described and presented and (2) the quality and origin of the language examples used. Then describe any differences you found.

6.   Think about and explain how you may use corpora to enhance your understanding of the various aspects of the language you are teaching. Be specific and give concrete examples. You need to describe how you use corpora in your lesson preparations and how you use them in actual teaching activities in the classroom.

## Note

1 It is important to note that while these terms are near-synonymous, they are not entirely identical in meaning, an issue that will be discussed in Chapter 14.

**PART II**

# Putting theory to practice: striving for enhanced language description and explanation

# 6

# VOCABULARY DESCRIPTION

## Basics, parts of speech, and other challenging issues

This chapter discusses what pedagogical vocabulary description/teaching should cover. While it will touch on all of the key vocabulary description/teaching issues, it focuses on a few basic but challenging issues, such as parts of speech and count/non-count nouns. The remaining key issues related to vocabulary explanation/teaching (such as word meaning/pragmatics, register, collocation, and multi-word units) will be explored in Chapters 12, 13, and 14, respectively.

## 6.1 What information should be covered in teaching a word?

What should teachers cover when teaching a vocabulary item? The answer to this question is inherently connected with the question of what it means to know a word, because teachers should help learners eventually grasp every aspect of the knowledge of a word. Of course, vocabulary knowledge can be divided into receptive knowledge, which includes the ability to recognize the word and understand its meaning, and productive knowledge, which consists of the ability to say/write a word correctly and use it appropriately (for a complete list of the different abilities included in the two types of knowledge, see Nation, 2001, pp. 26–30). Furthermore, the knowledge of a word (even for a native speaker) is never a binary issue of knowing it or not knowing it (Nation, 2001; Schmitt, 1998). For the purpose of this book and language teaching in general, knowing a word means having an adequate receptive as well as productive knowledge of the word. With this definition in mind and based on a survey of scholarly discussions on this topic (Celce-Murcia & Larsen-Freeman, 1999, pp. 30–31; Laufer, 1997; Nation, 2001, pp. 23–59; Zimmerman, 2009), a full knowledge of a word includes knowing the types of information about it listed in Figure 6.1. The information is divided into two major categories: (1) form; and (2) meaning/use. While some linguistic theories make a distinction between meaning and use, which includes a distinction between semantics and pragmatics, the two are combined here for two reasons. First, meaning and use are often closely intertwined, for the meaning of a word may vary according to the context in which it is used. Second, contemporary linguistic approaches

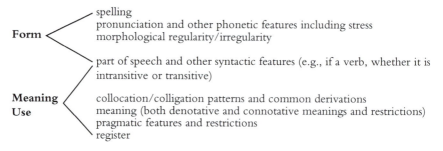

Form
- spelling
- pronunciation and other phonetic features including stress
- morphological regularity/irregularity
- part of speech and other syntactic features (e.g., if a verb, whether it is intransitive or transitive)

Meaning
Use
- collocation/colligation patterns and common derivations
- meaning (both denotative and connotative meanings and restrictions)
- pragmatic features and restrictions
- register

**FIGURE 6.1** What is involved in knowing a word.

such as Cognitive Linguistics include pragmatics in semantics, i.e., they do not distinguish the two, a practice that this book adopts. It is necessary to note that I have included "part of speech and other syntactic features" in both the form and meaning/use categories because, as will be shown in the discussion below, the part of speech of a word may also vary according to where and how it is used.

Let us take the word *do* as an example to illustrate how the different types of information are needed to know a word. To know the word *do*, a speaker would need to know it is spelled as *d-o* and pronounced as /dʊ/. The speaker also has to understand that *do* is an irregular verb with a past tense form of *did* and a past participle form of *done*, as well as the fact that, besides being used as a transitive verb, it can also function as an auxiliary. As a transitive verb, the common noun collocations of *do* include *do things*, *do business*, *do research*, and *do homework*. Words that are derived from *do* are quite limited, including only *doer*, *doable*, and *doability*. Concerning its meaning, the speaker needs to understand that, as a transitive verb, it expresses mainly the meaning of *perform/complete* while, as an auxiliary, it helps form negations and questions. Finally, for its pragmatic features and register information, the speaker should know that *do* is generally an informal word used much more in speech than in formal writing. Each aspect of the aforementioned knowledge is important and challenging and hence deserves attention from both language learners and teachers alike.

## 6.2 Describing/teaching spelling, pronunciation, and morphological rules

Word spelling and pronunciation in English are challenging because, unlike most other languages, English is developed from four different languages: German (Anglo-Frisian-Saxon German dialects in particular), French, Latin, and Ancient Greek; as a result, English spellings and pronunciations are not as consistent or systematic as they are in many other languages. Often, there are not only cases in which the same spelling (found in different words) may have different pronunciations, but also cases in which different spellings may have the same pronunciation. As an example of the former, the spelling *ea* may be pronounced either as/i/as in *beat/meat* or/eɪ/ as in *break/great*. As an example of the latter, the spellings *ea* (*meat*), *ee* (*meet*), *ei* (*deceit*), and *eo* (*people*) can all be pronounced as /i/. Of course, this does not mean there are no rules or patterns in English spelling and phonology. There actually are. For instance, the letter *a* when used in words composed of one onset (one consonant before the vowel) and one coda (one consonant after it) is almost always pronounced as /æ/, e.g., *cat*, *bag*, *map*. As another example, the letter *i* when used in words in which *i* is followed by a consonant plus a silent *e* is pronounced as /aɪ/, e.g., *bite* and *guide*. So when teaching spellings and pronunciations of words, we need, on the one hand, to teach students all the existing patterns/rules because these patterns/rules may enable them to learn new words better and faster. This is especially true with the morphological rules for forming words using derivational affixes (prefixes/ suffixes), such as *-dis/il/ir* for forming words with negative meaning and *en* for turning words into verbs meaning *cause to become* as in *enable/enlarge*. Another reason for teaching such compositional/decompositonal skills with vocabulary is that recent research (Sanchez-Stockhammer, 2010) has shown it helps learners to understand the motivations of word form and meaning and in turn to learn and retain words more effectively. However, on the other hand, we should also constantly remind students of the problems of irregularities, especially in spelling and pronunciation. One piece of advice we should give students is that they check a reference book or ask their teacher whenever they are not one hundred percent sure about the spelling and/or pronunciation of a word.

English morphology also includes many irregularities (i.e., irregular inflections for noun plurality and verb tense/aspect). The source of the problem is the same as the one for spelling and pronunciation inconsistencies: English words have different sources of origin. Different languages use different inflectional forms. Thus, English words of different origins have different inflectional paradigms. The good thing is that the original different inflectional forms in most of the contemporary English words have been regularized, e.g., *housen* (the plural form for *houses* in Old English) has become *houses*. However, some English words (mostly common words) have kept their original inflectional forms of their language of origin. For example, *be/do/have* still use their Old English inflectional paradigms. Many nouns of Latin origin (e.g., *syllabus/datum*) still use the Latin plural endings such as *i* (as in *syllabi/stimuli*) and *a* (as in *curricula/data*). To help learners more effectively grasp these irregular words, teachers can draw students' attention to the irregular inflections by highlighting them and also by explaining the origin of these words and their inflection rules. It is also helpful to provide learners a list of the irregular words organized by inflectional patterns, e.g., a list of those with Latin origin that have a common irregular plural inflection such as the plural *i* or *a* as just mentioned.

## 6.3 Defining/teaching parts of speech

Part of speech (also known as **word class** and **lexical/syntactic category**) is a major issue related to the syntactic features and restrictions of a word. The issue is important for language learners and teachers alike. For learners to use a word correctly and meaningfully, they will need to know its part of speech. Similarly, for teachers to discuss with students the meaning and use of a word either in isolation or in a sentence structure, we often need to talk about its part of speech. Yet how to define and classify parts of speech is a complex topic, and various definition and classification methods have been used. What parts of speech deal with, the major different methods of definition and classification, and the pedagogical implications of the defining and classifying methods will be discussed first.

### 6.3.1 The concept of parts of speech and categories involved

Parts of speech refer to lexical categories or classes, such as *noun, verb, adjective, adverb, conjunction, determiner, preposition, pronoun,* and *interjection.* They are also called syntactic categories. However, in phrasal structure grammars (i.e., those that use phrasal structural analysis such as generative grammar), syntactic categories involve not only lexical categories but also phrasal categories (e.g., noun phrase and verb phrase symbolized as NP and VP). In other words, under the umbrella of syntactic categories, phrasal structural grammars differentiate between lexical categories and phrasal categories. Lexical categories form the heads of phrasal categories, e.g., in a noun phrase, there must a noun serving as its head. However, a phrasal category may consist of other possible structures in addition to the head. For example, an NP may contain some other possible lexical constituents such as a determiner and/or adjective, as shown in "a young boy."

The number of parts of speech in English ranges from eight to twelve depending on which system of categorization one is using. While some traditional grammars do not include determiners as a category, most modern and contemporary grammars do (Celce-Murcia & Larsen-Freeman, 1999). Another reason for the number variation is that some of the categories each consist of a few subcategories that may be listed as separate categories. For instance, conjunctions include both coordinate and subordinate conjunctions. Furthermore, sometimes different terms have been used for the same part of speech. For example, some grammarians call intensifying adverbs like *rather* and *very* "qualifiers" (Stageberg, 1981, p. 167) while others label them as *intensifiers* (Celce-Murcia & Larsen-Freeman, 1999, p. 84). Of the English parts of speech, *noun, verb, adjective,* and *adverb* are the major classes and they are also called "open" word classes because they accept new members. The remaining classes are much smaller and are considered "closed" classes because they seldom, if ever, accept new members. In addition to the above differentiations, some grammarians (e.g., Culicover 1997) also distinguish between lexical and functional classes. Lexical categories refer to nouns, verbs, adjectives, adverbs, and prepositions. Functional classes refer to determiners, conjunctions, modal verbs, degree words (e.g., *more, too*, and *very*), and they are so called because words in the functional classes serve only grammatical functions. One may wonder why prepositions are classified as a lexical category, not a functional category. The reason is that while prepositions do have the characteristics of the functional categories, they are often associated with semantic roles such as *agent* (who does what to whom), *patient* (who is the recipient of the action) and *location* (Gass & Selinker, 2008, p. 166), as can be seen in in the sentence "The book was given *to* Mary *by* the author *in* Boston" where *to* indicates the recipient/goal, *by* the agent, and *in* location.

## 6.3.2 Meaning- and form-based definition methods

Historically, parts of speech have been defined mainly by meaning and word form, i.e., by semantic and morphological criteria. In meaning-based definition, a noun is a word that names a thing, place, or idea; a verb refers to a word that expresses an action or state of being. In form-based definition, a noun is a word that can inflect with the plural *s*, whereas an adjective is word that may take the *er/est* comparative/superlative forms. However, neither classification method is adequate. As far as the meaning-based method is concerned, there are some words whose part of speech will be difficult to define if we strictly follow the criteria set forth by the method. *Earthquake*, *completion*, and *walk* (used as a noun such like in *a long walk*) are just a few examples because, although these words are classified as nouns, they do not really name a thing or an idea. Instead, they essentially refer to an activity. As for the form-based method, its inadequacy is even more obvious. First, not all words in the same part of speech may take its typical category form(s) or marker(s). For example, some adjectives (e.g., *common* and *valuable*) do not take the *er/est* markers. Similarly, some adverbs (e.g., *often* and *very*) do not end with the typical adverb marker *ly*. To further complicate the matter, there are words that end with *ly* but are not adverbs (e.g., *friendly* and *holy*). Second, the form-based method does not work at all for some of the parts of speech, such as conjunctions, prepositions, and articles/determiners, due to their lack of a common category form marker. So the method has to lump all of these words together as *uninflected words* and then divide them into subclasses by function such as *conjunctions*, *determiners*, etc. (Stageberg, 1981, p. p. 164). Another major problem with both the meaning- and the form-based methods is that neither can really account for the parts of speech of words that are used outside their typical category domain, e.g., *rich* in "The *rich* are getting richer" and *baby* in "Don't *baby* me."

## 6.3.3 Structure (sentence position)-based definition method

In response to the inadequacies of the two aforementioned traditional methods, modern linguistic approaches, especially structural linguistics, have used a structure or syntactical position-based identification method for defining parts of speech. Some structural grammarians even went so far as to completely reject the meaning-based definition method. For example, Palmer (1971, p. 39) condemns the meaning-based definition of noun (i.e., noun = a word that names things) as "completely vacuous." Using two closely related utterances ("He suffered terribly" and "His suffering was terrible") as examples, he argues that the two sentences are identical in meaning and hence the word "suffering" does not refer to a thing. In other words, "suffering" cannot be really classified as a noun based on the meaning-based criterion.

In the structure-based method, the part of speech of a word is defined by the position that the word takes in the sentence structure. For example, a noun typically occupies the position of one of the following: the subject, the object of a verb or the object of a preposition. Also, a noun is often preceded by a determiner or an adjective. Using this method, we can easily classify the word *suffering* in Palmer's example as a noun or nominal because it is preceded by the determiner *his* and it occupies the position of the subject in the sentence followed by the predicate verb. By the same token, we can define the word *young* in "The *young* are needy" as a noun/nominal and *baby* in "Don't *baby* me" as a verb or verbal. Structural linguistics uses the terms *adjectival, adverbial, nominal*, and *verbal* for the parts of speech so defined in order to differentiate them from the parts of speech defined by using the traditional meaning/form-based methods.

### 6.3.4 Conceptualization/construal-based definition method

Finally, there is also the conceptualization/construal-based method advanced by Cognitive Linguistics (an issue already mentioned in Chapter 4). If we recall, according to Cognitive Linguistics, our understanding of anything in the world is always mediated by the human mind via conceptualization and categorization. Categories are thus what the human mind creates for understanding the world rather than preexisting entities. Therefore, the definition of parts of speech is also conceptual in nature and affected by construal. A noun refers to anything that is conceptualized/construed as a reified thing that is static and holistic, while a verb designates what is construed as a process, which is relational and sequential in nature, for, when a verb is used, the process it expresses always involves one more entities that participate in it, e.g., the verb *make* expresses a process that involves an agent who is doing the making and an object (a *patient*) that is being made. An adjective, on the other hand, is conceptualized as something between a verb and a noun: it is relational like a verb (as it depicts something) but it is not a process or sequential; instead it is static like a noun. Langacker (1999) illustrates how this construal-based method works by using the word *yellow*, which can function as a noun (e.g., "*Yellow* is my favorite color"), an adjective (e.g., "*yellow* shirts"), and even a verb (e.g., "The shirt *yellowed* with age"). Yellow as a noun refers a particular *thing* in the realm of color. As an adjective, it suggests a particular kind of color associated with whichever noun it modifies (e.g., the *shirt* in "*yellow* shirt"). As a verb, yellow expresses a process in which the color of a given thing gradually changes into the color yellow. Such a parts of speech definition system is rather abstract and generally not useful for language teaching. However, as will be shown in the next section, it is very helpful in defining those nouns that are either nominalized from verbs such as *completion* (from *complete*) or derived from adjectives such as *sadness* (from *sad*).

### 6.3.5 Using an eclectic method suited to learners' proficiency level and needs

From the above discussion of the different methods for defining parts of speech, it seems that the structure-based definition method is especially useful for classifying words used outside of their typical parts of speech category (e.g., *young* as a noun and *baby* as a verb). Also, as just mentioned, the conceptualization/ construal-based definition is particularly helpful for explaining the definition of the nouns derived from adjectives and verbs. As we know, it is difficult to use the traditional definition method to explain why nouns nominalized from verbs are nouns when they in fact refer to activities. For instance, "He completed the work" and "his completion of the work" essentially have the same meaning or refer to the same event. The same can be said of "He is genuinely sad" and "His sadness is genuine." Using the construal-based method, we can easily explain that in a nominalized expression, the action or event described by the verb has been construed as a reified thing. In other words, it is much easier for the conceptualization/construal-based method than the traditional meaning-based method to explain the definition of the nouns resulting from nominalization. Being able to better explain the definition of such nouns is important given that there are a large number of them in English. Basically, almost all of the verbs of process and states of being can be nominalized in English, e.g., *explanation* (from *explain*), *production* (from *produce*), *happiness* (from *being happy*), and *freedom* (from *being free*).

By now, one can see that, like grammar in general, parts of speech are not pre-existing language categories, but rather a system we use to classify the functions of lexical items. However, the most important question for language teachers and material writers is which classification method(s) to use in teaching ESL/EFL learners. In general, the meaning- and form-based methods seem easier to understand than the other two methods, especially for beginning and low-level students. This is because the meaning/form-based methods require less grammatical knowledge on the part of the learner than the structure-based method and less knowledge about cognition than the conceptualization/ construal-based method. Therefore, it may be best to start with the traditional meaning/form-based definitions. However, as the proficiency of the learners increases (along with their meta-language knowledge), it would be a good idea to introduce the structure-based method as it would allow them to have a more complete understanding of the concept of parts of speech and, in turn, enable them to use words more effectively and creatively. For instance, knowing that even words which are prototypical nouns in nature (e.g., *mother* and *room*) can be used as verbs, learners will be better able to understand and use sentences like "Don't <u>mother</u> me" and "He <u>roomed</u> with Tom for two years." For advanced learners, the conceptualization/construal-based method may also be helpful in cases described above.

Therefore, a sound coverage of the issue of parts of speech may be based on an eclectic method. For students of lower intermediate level and up, sometimes it may be beneficial to use both meaning/form- and structure-based method simultaneously, for it will allow them to more adequately and sensibly define the parts of speech of the words in question, which in turn may give them a better understanding of not only the issue of parts of speech but also the dynamic nature of language. Take, for example, the underlined words in the following sentence.

1.  The <u>college</u> student always wears a <u>smiling</u> face.

Using the structure method, students will find that both underlined words are adjectival because they each appear before a noun (*student* and *face* respectively) as its modifier. Then using the meaning/form-based method, they will decide *college* is a noun and *smiling* is a verb. In doing so, students can see clearly how words may function as various parts of speech. Equally importantly, being familiar with the different methods for defining parts of speech will also enable learners to develop the key grammatical knowledge needed for understanding basic sentence structural analysis. This is because the analysis of sentence structures often presupposes an understanding of syntactic categories—the basic constituents of a sentence, an issue that will be dealt with in the next chapter. Finally, it is important to point out that there are some cases where the part of speech of a word is very difficult to determine even by its position in a sentence, an issue that we will examine in section 6.5.1 with the example of the word "home" used in "go home."

## 6.4 Collocation/semantics/register: other key issues to be addressed

Knowing the typical collocations of a word is a crucial part of word knowledge (Celce-Murica & Larsen-Freeman, 1999; Laufer, 1997; Nation, 2001). This knowledge is especially important and challenging for L2 learners because the typical collocations of a word may vary significantly across languages. For example, one *makes a picture* in German, but *takes a picture* in English. As a result, L2 learners often make errors in lexical collocations. Due to its vital importance, collocation deserves special attention and will be explored in greater depth in Chapter 13.

Semantics, including pragmatics, is also a very important and challenging issue in L2 vocabulary learning. This is because when we discuss the meaning of a word, we often have to deal with several different types of meaning: (1) denotative vs. connotative meanings; (2) core vs. peripheral meanings; and (3) literal vs. figurative meanings (Laufer, 1997; Nation, 2001). Knowing the different types of meanings is very important for language learners because often a word that has the same denotative meaning in both the learner's L1 and L2 may have very different connotative meanings across the two languages. Also, while the core meaning of a word is the same in both L1 and L2, its peripheral meanings may vary significantly across the two languages. Like word semantics/pragmatics, word register (or register-appropriate use of words) is also crucial but difficult knowledge for L2 learners, who often have trouble knowing the right social and situational contexts for using a given word. Therefore, word meaning and use also call for special attention in L2 learning/teaching and will be examined thoroughly in Chapter 12.

## 6.5 Explaining/teaching challenging issues with new insights

Given that many challenging issues related to vocabulary learning, such as the learning of the various types of meanings, collocations, and multi-word units, will be addressed in Chapters 12, 13, and 14, here only two issues related to parts of speech will be covered.

### 6.5.1 Adverb or noun: the case of home in go home and more

Many grammars and dictionaries classify the word *home* used in *come/go home* as an adverb in order to explain the absence of the preposition *to* between the word *home* and the intransitive verb in the structure. However, this explanation becomes questionable when we consider the fact that either *stay home* or *stay at home* is commonly acceptable and also the fact that if we specify whose home, we need add *to: go to his/their home*. It would then seem rather strange to classify *home* in *stay home* (without the preposition *at*) as an adverb and the same word in *stay at home* as a noun. A better or more consistent explanation would be that the part of speech of *home* is noun in either case but the preposition *at* is optional. Based on this theory, *home* in *come/go home* should also be considered a noun and the use of *come/go home* can be viewed as a case in which the preposition *to* is always omitted—a case of *obligatory deletion* (Celce-Murcia & Larsen-Freeman, 1999, p. 404). The motivation for the deletion appears to be that *home* in such use refers to the home of the subject. This is why no determiner is used before *home* ("He's going home"/"I went home"), and this also explains why when the home is specified, *to* is needed ("He's going to her home"). This explanation about the absence of *to* in *come/go home* is more sensible, for it can also help explain similar issues in the use of words/phrase of time (i.e., words of days, dates, etc.) as adverbials. Some of these words and phrases (such as words of month and year) have to be used with a preposition, e.g., "born/published <u>in</u> January/<u>in</u> 1999." Some others (such as words of day and date) may be used either with or without a preposition, e.g., "born/published <u>on</u> Monday/on January 10" or simply "born/published Monday/January 10, 1999." In these cases, the preposition is optional. Still others must be used without a preposition (i.e., cases of obligatory preposition deletion), e.g., "born/published yesterday/last Tuesday/last week" and "will be published tomorrow/this Tuesday/next week."

Of course, as in the case of *home* in *go home* mentioned above, traditional grammar defines *tomorrow* and *yesterday* as *adverbs* when used as time adverbials, rather than nouns in a prepositional phrase with the preposition omitted. Yet, again, such an explanation does not work well for those phrases that can be used either with or without a preposition. It seems to be more consistent to describe every one of such words or phrases as a noun or noun phrase used in a prepositional phrase, treating the use or nonuse of the preposition as an issue of whether the preposition is (1) obligatory (must be used), 2) optional, or 3) omission-obligatory (must be omitted).

It is very important to point out that although such a description theory is sound from a pure linguistic perspective, it may not always be the case from a pedagogical language description perspective due to learner and teacher variables. The teacher may elect to classify the aforementioned words like *home*, *tomorrow*, and *yesterday* either as adverbs or nouns used with the preposition omitted. If time allows and students show interest, the teacher may offer both explanations. The advantage of doing the latter is that a discussion of two different explanations for a difficult grammar or usage issue may help highlight and reinforce the unique usage pattern of the language structure in question, and may in turn enable students to grasp the structure better. For instance, discussing the two different explanations for why we say *come/go home*, not *come/go to home*, should help learners remember the structure better.

### 6.5.2 Count vs. non-count nouns

The part of speech of a word is not the only thing a speaker needs to know in order to use it in a syntactically correct way. This is because there are subtypes in some of the parts of speech, such as *count* (also called *countable*) vs. *non-count* (also known as *uncountable* or *mass*) nouns in the noun category. Knowing that *book* is a count noun but *air* is a non-count noun enables a speaker to inflect *book* with the plural *-s* when referring to two or more *books* but not do so with *air* when referring to a large amount of *air*. Traditionally, *count* nouns are defined as those referring to things that we can count and *non-count* nouns are those designating things that we cannot count. In fact, based on my survey of eight ESL student grammar textbooks/series, this has remained the way count and non-count nouns are defined. The grammar textbooks/series surveyed include Azar and Hagen (2009, 2011), Byrd and Benson (1992), Celce-Murcia and Sokolik (2007, 2008, 2009), Conrad and Biber (2009), Elbaum (1996), Fuches and Bonner (1995), Keith (2010), Larsen-Freeman (1993), and Maurer (1995).[1]

The following are three examples of such definitions taken from the textbooks:

1. "A count noun: (1) can be counted with numbers ... (2) can be preceded by a/an in the singular ... (3) has plural form in -*s* or -*es*. A noncount noun: (1) cannot be counted with numbers ..." (Azar & Hagen, 2011, p. 292).
2. "Count nouns are nouns that can be counted ... Noncount nouns are not usually Counted" (Celce-Murcia & Sokolik's *book 1*, 2007, p. 156).
3. "Count nouns name things that can be counted ... Non-count nouns (or mass nouns) generally name things that cannot be counted because they exist in a 'mass'" (Maurer's *advanced course*, 1995, p. 52).

Also, a couple of textbooks give a circular definition by stating that count nouns take the plural -*s* and non-count nouns do not. Such simple definitions may work for beginning learners initially. Yet they would soon become inadequate when learners discover that the rules or criteria do not seem to work well with many nouns. For example, why is *rice* considered an uncountable noun when we in fact can see and count individual grains of rice? Why, on the other hand, do we sometimes say two (or more) *beers* when we cannot really count *beer*? While some of the series mention special/exceptional cases/uses (e.g., Celce-Murcia & Sokolik's book 3, 2008, p. 129 mentions that *two coffees* may be used to mean two cups of coffee), there is no real explanation of why such uses are possible. In other words, none of the series seems to have added any additional definition/explanation information in its advanced levels. Actually, the third example of definition above is for advanced students as indicated by the phrase "advanced course" in the title of the book.

Thanks to Cognitive Linguistics, we are now better able to define and differentiate the two types of nouns. In Cognitive Grammar, "The fundamental distinction between count and mass nouns depends on whether the profiled region [i.e., the thing or concept in question] is construed as being **bounded**" (Langacker, 1991, p. 18; emphasis original). Therefore, *lake* is a count noun because "it designates a limited body of water" whereas *water* is considered a mass noun due to its lack of boundaries as a substance. However, water can be used as count nouns when it is construed as being a bounded substance, e.g., *international waters*, *coastal waters*, and *two waters* (uttered in food/drink ordering). In these examples, water is used to refer to the specific water contained or bounded in a specific space, e.g., *international waters* refer to the areas of water owned by no individual country and two waters to the water in two glasses or cups. Of course, such use of mass nouns as count nouns can also be explained as a result of **metonymy** (the linguistic/metaphorical process of referring to X by mentioning something closely related to it), another important concept in Cognitive Linguistics, for when we say *international waters* or *two waters*, we are actually referring to the containers of the water in question (e.g., the geographical areas considered international that contain the water and the two glasses that contain the water in question). While we can construe unbounded things as bounded (as shown in *two waters*), we can also conceptualize and construe a usually unbounded thing as bounded, as shown in the case of using the indefinite article a/an and an adjective before a non-count noun such as *education* and *knowledge* to signify a particular type of it: *a good education* and *a strong knowledge*.

One other important issue related to bounded/unbounded-ness is whether the thing the noun designates is, as Taylor (2002, p. 367) notes, "an individual 'object'" or an "unindividuated 'substance'":

> An individual object has its own internal structure and composition—split it up and it loses its identity. Dismantle a car and you have car parts, not a car any more. But if you divide up a quantity of meat you still have meat, and if you put two quantities of meat together, you have again, meat.

In other words, *car* is a bounded, individual *object*, whose internal composition is made up of different things with no internal homogeneity. Meat, on the other hand, is an unbounded or unindividuated *substance* whose internal composition is homogeneous, i.e., any part of it "counts as a valid instance of it and a multiplication of instances also counts as an instance" (Taylor, 2002, p. 367). The same is basically true of rice and other substances like it such as sand. If we break a grain of rice, the broken pieces are still called rice. So, essentially the difference between count and mass nouns is the difference between *object* and *substance*.

However, as Taylor points out, although the concept of *object* and the concept of *substance* appear to be universal, how *object* and *substance* are conceptualized and how clearly the distinction is made between the two may vary from one language/culture to another. For example, Imai and Gentner's (1997) study shows that whereas speakers of Japanese (a language with no count/mass noun inflectional marking) are also sensitive to the object/substance distinction, adult Japanese appear less sensitive than Japanese children and native English speakers due likely to the influence of the Japanese conventional conceptualizations on the matter. In other words, the distinction between count (object) and mass (substance) nouns may not be made in exactly the same way by speakers of different languages. In addition, the fact that plurality is not encoded at all in some languages has made the learning of the English plural inflection very difficult for ESL learners with such an L1 background. The difficulty is exacerbated by the fact that the plural inflection is really a redundant feature, for the plurality of a noun is usually clearly expressed in the discourse. For instance, when we say *three chairs* or *two books*, the quantifier has already made clear the noun is plural (this is in fact how speakers of languages without noun plural inflection communicate and understand the concept of plurality: from contextual information).

Given the challenges that language learners often face in learning to distinguish count and non-count nouns and to use plural inflections correctly, it is important to find and use effective ways to help students in dealing with the challenges. The Cognitive Linguistics-inspired distinction between count and non-count nouns can be an effective approach, for we can give the following as a rule of thumb: count nouns are those things that when you break them apart, the broken pieces are not what the whole thing was, e.g., book, computer, house, plane, and train; mass or non-count nouns, on the other hand, are things that when you break them apart, each piece is still the same thing as the unbroken entity is, e.g., water, oil, steel, rice, and flour. Of course, in making such a distinction, we also have to deal with a special group of nouns called "plural mass nouns," such as *groceries*, *belongings*, *valuables*, *leftovers*, *clothes*, and *goods* (Taylor, 2002, pp. 373–374). According to Taylor these nouns possess some features of both count and non-count nouns. They resemble count nouns in that they each consist of different types of individual things (e.g., *groceries* may include various vegetables and other food items; *clothes* may include various apparel items). Yet they are similar to mass nouns in that the individual parts cannot each alone represent the whole concept of the noun they are a part of; e.g., a cell phone alone cannot be used to mean the concept of belongings. This is likely why we cannot really count the number of plural mass nouns: *two belongings*, *three groceries*, or *four clothes*.

## Suggested teaching activities

1. *Building up words with affixes and understanding of meaning.* First, give students a set of words that involve the same affix (can be a prefix or a suffix), e.g., *enable, encourage, enlarge*, and *ensure*; *cheerful, handful, meaningful*, and *roomful*. First, ask students to tell what the words have in common. After they identify the prefix or suffix, ask them to figure out the meaning. Then have them find additional words with the same prefix and meaning. Ask students to watch out for false friends (e.g., the *en* in *entire* does not mean *making tire*). As an alternative, the teacher can ask students to come up with other words with a different affix.

2. *Watching out for false friends.* The purpose of this activity is the opposite of the first one. It serves to make students aware of exceptions in the use of affixes in word formation. Give students words that may be easily misunderstood due to misinterpretation of the prefix, e.g., *ingenious, impassioned, invaluable*, and *priceless* (all positive words that may be misinterpreted as negative ones). The words may be given in context or isolation, depending on the teaching objective. Ask students to tell/guess the meaning of each. In the process, if students give the wrong meaning due to the false-friend affix,

first praise them for guessing the meaning of the word using affix, but then explain that there are sometimes exceptions. Tell them that they should not jump to conclusions about the meaning of a word using just one type of information. They will need to use contextual information and consult dictionaries if necessary.

3. *Noun to verb: Miming parts of speech.* This is an activity for low-level students, especially for young learners, to learn how words can be used as different parts of speech. This activity also capitalizes on learners' embodied experience and aims to help learners to use words more creatively and productively. It may involve two sub-activities: (a) turning names of natural or man-made things into verbs; and (b) turning names of body parts into verbs.

   *Activity A*: Place a series of things or pictures of these things in the front of the class, such as a container of water, ice, an iron, a phone, crayons (for teaching the verb use of the word "color"), a mop, plants (for the verb use "planting") … The teacher tells the class, "Many nouns can also be used as verbs. We'll show that in this activity." Then the teacher models the activity by holding up a container of water and saying "I have water" and then pouring the water onto some plants and saying, "I'm watering plants" or "I watered the plants." Then have one student repeat the action or do something else such as ironing clothes but have the class say, "X has an iron" and "He/she is ironing clothes." The activity can also be done in pairs.

   *Activity B*: Body parts that can be used in this activity include: elbow (elbowing one way through), eye (eyeing something), hand (handing in/off something), head (heading an organization/heading or headed to), shoulder … The teacher models the activity by holding up one of his/her elbows and say "These are my elbows" and then start to act as if trying to push through a crowd of people by using the elbows and say "I'm elbowing my way through" or "I elbowed my way through the crowd." Then have one student either repeat the action or do something else with a different body part and have the other students say what body part he/she showing and what he is doing or did, using the name of the body part as a verb.

4. *Green, grey …: Coloring parts of speech.* This activity has the same purpose as the third one but it may be more appropriate for students of lower-intermediate level and above. Most color words can be used in this activity. The teacher begins by saying, "Many words can be used as different parts of speech. In this activity, we will see how color words may be used as nouns, adjectives, and verbs." Then the teacher models the activity by saying and writing on the board, "I like the color green. I like green vegetables. Every March, my lawns begin to green." Then ask students to use at least three color words and make sentences that will use them as nouns, adjectives, and verbs.

5. *Oh, these nouns can be both count and non-count.* This activity is for lower-intermediate (and higher) level students to learn to understand and/

or to enhance their understanding that some nouns can be either count or non-count depending on whether the referent is being construed as bounded or unbounded. Give students a list of such words in sentences (as shown in the following examples) and ask the students to explain the reasons for the two different uses of the nouns involved and then to make sentences with the nouns used in both senses:

1a. We need more space.
1b. He cleared <u>a</u> space for her to sit down.
2a. There is room for improvement.
2b. There's still <u>a</u> room available at the hotel.
3a. Any comment made must have substance.
3b. The water contains <u>a</u> substance harmful to fish.

## Note

1 It is important to note that some of the series have newer editions, but I have no access to them. So the information gathered from these series is not the most recent. On a different note, Larsen-Freeman is listed as *director* (not *editor*) of her series. Also, Fuches and Bonner (1995) and Maurer (1995) are of the same series (*Focus on grammar*), but they are listed separately because the series has no series editor.

# 7
# SENTENCE STRUCTURE DESCRIPTION
## Basics, verb structure/subcategorization, and other challenging structural issues

Although an adequate description of grammar often must go beyond the sentence level (a point that has been discussed in Chapters 1 and 3 and will be explored again in Chapters 8, 9, and 11), sentence structural analysis is an indispensable basic issue in language description and teaching. To help learners understand and produce language, we usually have to explain how words and phrases are put together to form meaningful utterances or sentences. To address this important issue, this chapter will explore (1) sentence structural analysis and the typical procedures involved, (2) pedagogical structural analysis and the effective strategies recommended, (3) some challenging issues related to structural analysis as well as suggestions for how to deal with them. It is necessary to point out that some of the information presented in this chapter is meant for teachers only, i.e., not meant for use in actual language teaching. However, though not directly useful in the classroom, such information is needed to enable teachers to better deal with issues related to sentence structure analysis in teaching.

## 7.1 Sentence structural analysis: tasks and processes

### 7.1.1 Sentence structure types: a quick overview

In discussing sentence structural analysis, we should first know what a sentence is. A sentence is usually defined as a group of words that expresses a complete thought and can stand structurally alone. There are three types of sentences structurally: *simple, compound,* and *complex.* A simple sentence involves only one **finite clause**—a structure that is composed minimally of a subject and a predicate (a complete verb phrase), e.g., "*The young man completed the work in twenty minutes.*" A simple sentence may include one or more adverbials of *sentence modifiers,* as in "Perhaps Tom is coming." A compound sentence consists of two (or more) independent clauses joined by a coordinating conjunction, such as *for/and/nor/but/or/yet/so* (often called *fanboys* to help learners remember them), e.g., "I tried to get them out, *but* I couldn't." A complex sentence is made up of one independent (or main) clause and one or more dependent (subordinate) clauses conjoined by subordinate conjunctions such as *although, because,* and *if,* e.g., "Although he has a large house nearby, he spends most days and nights in this windowless shack." A subordinate clause cannot stand alone and must always be attached to a main clause. Sentences can also be classified by purposes into *declarative (statement)*, *interrogative (question)*, *imperative (command)*, and *exclamatory (statement expressing a strong feeling)*. For lack of space, the structural analysis in this chapter will focus on simple sentences, although some issues related to compound and complex sentences will also be briefly discussed, especially those with one or more **nonfinite clauses**. A nonfinite clause is a dependent clause structure that has the internal structure of a clause but it does not have a full (tensed) verb; instead, it typically contains only a gerund, infinitive or a participle, as shown in the underlined parts of the following sentences:

1. Drinking alcohol is harmful to your health.
2. They asked John to clean the dishes.
3. Although tired of the rules, she didn't dare break them.

Such nonfinite clauses are very common in written English for the purpose of packing more information into a sentence as well as for sentence variety.

## 7.1.2 Tasks and processes involved in sentence structural analysis

A complete structural analysis of a sentence in linguistic study (not in pedagogical grammar description) typically involves the following three tasks: 1) parsing the sentence into smaller units in terms of syntactic and lexical categories (such as *noun phrase* and *verb phrase*) until the smallest meaningful units (individual lexical items) are reached; 2) identifying the grammatical roles or functions (such as *subject* and *object*) of the parsed structures; and 3) specifying the semantic roles or functions (such as *agent* and *instrument*) of the parsed structures. It is very important to point out that whether and how much of any of the three sentence structural analysis tasks should be included in pedagogical analysis will need to be determined by various learner factors, an issue that will be returned to below. It is also worth noting that the three tasks of the structural analyses are not isolated but closely interconnected and are usually performed simultaneously. An even more important point is that an understanding of the meaning of the sentence is needed in order to accurately analyze its structure. In fact, according to Cognitive Linguistics, meaning and form are inseparable because, if we recall, language structures are symbolic units composed of pairings of form and meaning.

Let us now look at how each task of the sentence structure analysis is performed by analyzing the simple sentence, "The young man opened the door with a knife." Before we proceed, it is necessary to note that in sentence structure analysis, diagramming is sometimes used to help visualize the relations between the structural elements in a sentence. Three of the five English grammar books for language teachers (Celce-Murcia & Larsen-Freeman, 1999; Lester, 1990; Williams, 2005) include diagramming in their sentence structural analysis, but two (Parrott,

2000; Yule, 1998) do not. However, sentence diagramming does not appear to be used much in ESL/EFL teaching. Of the eight student grammar textbook series I examined, only a few (e.g., Byrd & Benson, 1992; Celce-Murcia & Sokolik, 2009) include a minuscule amount of very simple sentence diagramming. The use and discussion of diagramming here is meant for teachers only because knowing how to diagram sentence structures may enable teachers not only to better understand sentence structures but also to use it in teaching if needed.

There are several different diagramming methods. Besides the IC cut and the syntactic structure tree methods introduced in Chapter 2, there is also the well-known traditional Reed–Kellogg method, first developed by Alonzo Reed and Brainerd Kellogg in 1877. The method has been widely used in textbooks and grammar books for mainstream English, but not so much for ESL. Of all of the methods, the structure tree method appears to be the most widely known, so we will use this method as well. As we begin the three-part sentence structural analysis, it is necessary to note again that, in the actual analysis of a sentence, the three tasks are performed simultaneously. They are described one by one in sequence here simply for the purpose of showing more clearly what is involved in each task.

We begin with the syntactic category-based analysis. In parsing an English sentence, except for imperative and fragmented sentences, we first identify the NP (called the subject by grammatical function) and the VP (the predicate by grammatical function) of the sentence and diagram them as the two main branches of the sentence structure. We then continue the process by identifying and diagramming the smaller phrasal categories until we reach the individual lexical items, as is shown in Figure 7.1 (where the identified syntactic categories are written in normal font while grammatical roles are italicized and the semantic roles are underlined). Specifically, after identifying the main NP and VP, we need to identify the components of the NP and VP respectively. Thus, in parsing a sentence by syntactic category, a basic understanding of the phrasal structural rules will be very helpful. To recall the discussion in Chapter 2 (section 2.3), phrasal structural rules specify what each phrasal category in a language is composed of and in what sequential order its components are placed. Such information is very important for L2 learners because phrasal structural rules often vary from language to language. ESL/EFL learners will need to know, for example, that the sequential order of the components in the English NP structure is Det Adj N (not N Adj Det as in Thai) and the sequential order of the components in the English VP structure is V NP (not NP V as in Japanese).

Next we identify the grammatical roles of the elements of the parsed sentence. We begin by identifying the *subject* and the *predicate*, with the latter including the verb plus any of its constituents, such as the object(s) and adverbial phrases. After identifying the *subject*, the *predicative verb*, the *objects*, and the other main grammatical roles, we can then continue to identify the grammatical roles of the lower-level phrases and lexical items, e.g., *young* as the modifier of the noun *man*, etc., as can be seen in Figure 7.1. It is worth noting that, in phrasal structural grammars like structural and generative grammars, the object

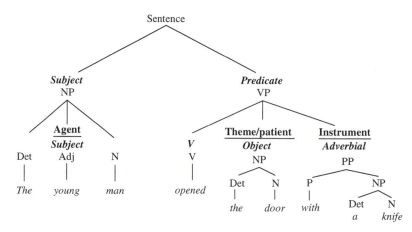

**FIGURE 7.1** Example of sentence analysis by syntactic category and grammatical/thematic roles.

(direct or indirect) of a verb is often called a verb complement. Given that the term *object* is used much more widely, it is more preferable than *complement* in pedagogical language description. Furthermore, using the term *object* this way also helps distinguish noun phrases that complement a verb from prepositional phrases that are needed to complement some verbs, such as *on friends* in "relied on friends during the crisis" and *on the table* in "put the books on the table." Verbs like *rely* and *put* require a prepositional phrase to be complete.

Finally, we determine the semantic roles of the parsed structures. In this task, we basically specify the semantic roles of the main noun phrases related to the predicate verb, e.g., *the young man*, *the door*, and *a knife*. In this sentence, the *young man* is the agent, the *door* is the theme or patient, and the *knife* in "with a knife" is the instrument or the adverbial of instrument. For reference purposes, the semantic roles so defined are called *thematic or theta/θ-roles* in generative linguistics but are labeled *cases* in case grammar, as developed by Fillmore (1968). There are other differences in the terms used for the semantic roles between the two grammars. For instance, in the sentence "John gave an iPhone to Mary." In generative grammar, *to Mary* serves the theta role of *goal*, whereas in case grammar, it is called a *beneficiary*. It is very important to point out that analyzing semantic roles in such a manner is generally difficult and hence not very helpful for language learners, especially in cases where the subject NP is not an agent. For example, in the sentence "The young man saw a bird," the subject (the young man) is an *experiencer*, not an *agent*, because in seeing the bird, the young man did not do anything to the bird but merely experienced the sight of it. In most cases, it will not be beneficial for language learners to make such subtle technical semantic distinctions.

Generally, semantic role analysis of this type should not be used in teaching, but they may be used with advanced learners to help them better understand some verbs or sentence structures that appear especially confusing to L2 learners, such as those of what Burt (1975) and Ellis (1995) call psychological verbs. These verbs express some affective state that people experience, such as love and fear. They are difficult because the experiencer may either be the subject or the object of the sentence as shown in the following examples:

4a. Tom adores his father.          4b. Tom concerns his father.
5a. Everyone loves Mary.           5b. Everything scares Mary these days.

Although the a and b sentences in each pair look similar in structure, they differ in meaning. In each of the a sentences, the subject (*Tom* in 4a and *everyone* in 5a) is the experiencer but in each of the b sentences, it is the object (*Tom's father* in 4b and *Mary* in 5b) that is the experiencer. The subjects in the b sentences are the stimuli, not the experiencers. Marking the semantic role of each of the nouns in such a sentence structure can help learners more accurately understand the meaning. Another potential benefit of this semantic role assignment activity is to help learners better understand how sentences that differ in structure may have essentially the same meaning but with different foci based on what the speaker wants to the listener to pay attention to.

6. Tom opened the door with his key.
7. The key opened the door.
8. The door was opened by Tom with a key.

Despite their structural differences, the semantic roles of the nouns in these sentences remain the same: Tom=*agent*, key=*instrument*, and door=*patient/theme*. Whichever noun is placed in the subject position is either what the speaker would like to focus on or the old/known information in the discourse context.

## 7.2 Established practices for describing/analyzing sentence structures

Perhaps no teacher would or should engage students in the type of structural analysis of a whole sentence showed above. However, to help learners better understand how to produce meaningful and grammatically correct sentences, teachers sometimes do need to let students know the structure types and functions of words and phrases in a sentence, such as the use of an *ing*-form as a gerund functioning as the subject/object or the use of an *ing*-form as a present participle modifying a noun. In other words, teachers sometimes have to engage students in some structural analysis. However, explicit structural analysis is not suitable or beneficial for young learners and beginning/low-level learners, especially those with no formal education, nor is it useful for learners whose goal in learning the target language is merely to gain some basic oral communication skills. For other learners, some sentence structural analysis may be helpful, especially for those learners who possess a strong literacy in their L1 and who are learning an L2 for academic purposes (Hudson, 2001). In fact, in most intensive academic L2 learning programs, there are classes devoted to language structure or to writing and structure combined. These classes often involve some explicit or implicit structural analysis. How to best carry out such analysis is an important question for language teachers.

### 7.2.1 How pedagogical structural analysis is generally done

The discussion in this section is based on the survey of the eight student grammar textbooks mentioned in Chapter 6 and observations of many ESL/EFL classes. The general practice in pedagogical sentence structural analysis seems to include using specific examples of sentences to describe and explain the types and functions of structures and the ways particular sentence structures are formed and used. Metalanguage or technical grammatical terms are often used, but, as noted above, diagramming is rarely used, although some simple forms of marking are sometimes used to help learners visualize and better understand the relationship between the structures in question. The following examples from Celce-Murcia and Sokilik's textbook series may help illustrate the general practices just mentioned. Example 1 is from Book 2 of the series (p. 129) and; example 2 from Book 3 (p. 167).

**EXAMPLE 1** How to form *wh/how* questions in the simple past tense

| *Wh- Word*<br>*How Phrase* | *did* | *Subject* | *Verb* | |
|---|---|---|---|---|
| When<br>Where<br>How long ago | did | Hippocrates | teach | medicine? |

**EXAMPLE 2** How gerunds and gerund phases are used

| *Gerunds and Gerund phrases* | *Examples* |
|---|---|
| A gerund is the base form of a verb + ***ing*** that is used as a noun. | **Teaching** can be an interesting career. |
| A gerund or gerund phrase can be the *subject* or *complement* of a sentence.<br>Use the third-person singular form of the verb after a gerund subject. | Subject<br>**Deciding on a career** is not simple.<br><br>Complement<br>My dream job is **teaching children**. |
| A gerund or gerund phrase can be the direct *object* of a verb. | Direct object<br>You'll imagine **working at certain jobs**. |

**Note**: This example shows some simple marking/diagramming used to indicate the gerund phrases and their grammatical functions.

The meta-language terms used by teachers and textbooks are mostly traditional grammatical ones, such as *subject, object, noun/noun phrase*, and *modifier*, and they are often mixed terms taken from the two sets of terms used in the first two of the three aforementioned tasks of sentence structural analysis: syntactic category (e.g., *noun/noun phrase, gerund, verb/verb phrase*) and grammatical function/role category (e.g., *subject, complement, object*). No teachers or textbooks use terms from the semantic category/role analysis (e.g., *agent*, and *theme*) because, as mentioned above, this type of analysis is not usually beneficial for language learners. The following is a list of the terms that teachers and textbooks often use, based on the results of the classroom observations and the textbook survey. Even though teachers and textbooks often use them in a mixed fashion (as noted above), the terms are organized according to whether they belong to syntactic or grammatical function categories:

A. *Terms used to describe syntactic or clause structures*: article (definite/indefinite), quantifier, (count/non-count/mass) noun, clause (main/independent clause and subordinate/dependent clause), (be/linking/intransitive/transitive) verb, infinitive, (present/past) participle phrase, gerund, (coordinate/subordinate) conjunction adverb, prepositional phrase,(personal/possessive) pronoun, phrasal verbs.

B. *Terms used to describe grammatical roles/functions*: subject, (direct/indirect) object, subject complement, object complement, adverbial of (frequency, goal, location/place, purpose, time …), noun clause as complement, noun clause as object, particle (e.g., adverbs used in phrasal verbs), relative/adjectival clause, adverbial clause.

## 7.2.2 The use of technical terms

Given that technical grammatical terms are needed in structural analysis, what terms to use and to what extent they should be used are important questions. There are three principles teachers should follow concerning these questions. First, the terms used should be those that are common and easy to understand. For example, in discussing parts of speech, we should simply use *noun/verb/adjective/adverb*, instead of *nominal/verbal/adjectival*; in discussing the part of speech of the word *college* in the phrase "college students," we should say it is used as *an adjective* rather than *adjectival*. One point worth noting is that, unlike *nominal/adjectival/verbal*, the term *adverbial* is actually used extensively in teaching. It has been used in a fashion in which *adjectival, nominal*, and *verbal* have not: whereas we usually say a *noun* clause (not a nominal clause), we say an *adverbial* (not an adverb) clause. In short, *adverbial* has been used as a conventional term for referring to any structures that function like an adverb. Other terms that teachers should avoid include those rare specialized terms, such as *theme/rheme* (we can simply use "given/new information"), *argument structure*, and *adjuncts/conjuncts/disjuncts*—terms some grammarians use to classify the functions of adverbials (an issue that will be returned to below). The second principle regarding the use of technical terms is that teachers should use as few of them as possible, so as not to burden learners with unnecessary terminology. They should also try to explain, whenever possible, any technical concepts by using plain language as illustrated in the aforementioned case of *given/new information* for *theme/rheme*.

The third principle is that teachers should use a consistent set of terms so as not to confuse students. This is important because in some cases different grammarians use different terms to refer to the same structural elements. For example, a *main clause* is also called an *independent* clause and a *subordinate clause* is also labeled as a *dependent clause*. Also, the *object* of a verb is called a *verb complement* in structural and generative grammars. As one more example, what is defined as an *appositive clause* in traditional grammar (e.g., the underline in the sentence "The news that he won the prize surprised us") is called a *noun complement clause* in structural grammar (i.e., the "that clause" completes the noun "news" by telling us what the news is). Therefore, in cases where some students have learned to use a term that is not the one used by the current teacher, it is necessary for the teacher to explain the fact that the two terms mean exactly the same thing.

It is necessary to note, however, that there are some cases where the related different terms are not entirely identical, for they reflect the different perspectives of different grammatical approaches. For example, traditional grammar classifies adverbs and adverbial structures into semantic/functional categories such as *adverbial of degree* (e.g., *very* and *extremely*), *of frequency* (*often* and *rarely*), *of manner* (*slowly*, and *strangely*). However, some contemporary grammars (e.g., Carter & McCarthy, 2006; Quirk, Greenbaum, Leech, & Svartvik, 1989) have introduced a new functional classification system that involves the following three (sometimes four) categories: (1) *adjunct* (an adverb/adverbial that is integrated into the sentence structure as a modifier of an adjective, adverb or verb, e.g., *He answered the question strangely*); (2) *conjunct* (an adverb/adverbial that is typically placed sentence initially to provide a discourse link between what has been stated and what is to be said in the ensuing sentence, e.g., *Consequently, he failed the test*); and (3) *disjunct* (an adverb/adverbial that is a sentence modifier, separated from the clause it modifies by a comma, e.g., *Surprisingly, he answered the question*). As a result of the different systems for classifying the functions of adverbs, an adverb, e.g., *strangely*, can be simultaneously classified as an *adverbial of manner* and an *adjunct*, with each term reflecting a different classification scheme. Of course, we may not want to use the new system because it does not appear to be helpful for language learners. Another example in this category relates to a type of clause or infinitive used after an adjective as shown in the following to example:

9. I'm very sad that our team lost.
10. I'm very happy to see you.

In traditional grammar, such a clause or infinitive is called an adverbial of reason, i.e., why "we're very sad" or "very happy." However, in structural grammar, such a clause or infinitive is labeled as an adjective complement, i.e., it complements the adjective. Obviously, the two grammars approach the issue from two different perspectives, with traditional grammar focusing on logic and meaning and structural grammar concentrating on structure. For upper intermediate and advanced learners, the teacher may use such examples to illustrate how grammatical analysis and description may vary according to grammarians' perspectives and foci.

### 7.2.3 The use of diagrams and other visual markings

As mentioned above, structural diagramming should be avoided in general. However, some simple form of marking and diagramming can be used to help learners better understand the relations among the elements in a given sentence structure, as shown in the aforementioned example 2 from Celce-Murcia and Sokolik's grammar textbook series. As another example, Byrd and Benson (1992, p. 32) introduced the following marking system for students to use when doing sentence analysis: underline the subject phrase, double-underline the verb, enclose the complete object or complement phrase, and mark modifiers using a slash, as shown below:

*In the United States/, you can hear many different languages.*

Another easy way for marking structural or functional elements is coloring. For example, red for subject, blue for verb, yellow for object. This is especially useful when doing structural analysis and marking on the board because it enables students to easily see them. For grammar classes of intermediate level and up, the teacher may use diagrams that are a little more complex and more informative, such as the IC cut diagramming as shown in Figure 2.1 in Chapter 2 and Figure 7.1 in this chapter.

## 7.3 Explaining/teaching challenging issues with new insights

### 7.3.1 Describing and explaining different verb structures

An essential part of sentence structure analysis and understanding is the analysis and understanding of verb structures. One aspect of verb structures that is especially difficult for ESL/EFL learners is verb **subcategorization**—the issue of how many noun phrases a given verb requires or allows in order to become a complete verb phrase. At a general level, there are the three major categories of verbs: (1) intransitive (which requires only one NP: a subject); (2) transitive (which needs two NPs: a subject and an object); and (3) ditransitive (which calls for three NPs: a subject, a direct object, and an indirect object). Then there are many subcategories. For example, in the transitive verb category, there are those that require, in addition to two NPs (subject and object), a prepositional phrase/ adverb as an object complement, such as *put/place/leave/hide* as can be seen in "put the book on the table." In the intransitive category, there are some that require or take a prepositional phrase, such as *depend/lurk* as shown in "depend on his availability/lurk behind a tree." Furthermore, there are also variations at even lower levels. A case in point is the variation in what types of syntactic structures a transitive verb can take as its object. For example, while *love/ hate* can take either an infinitive or a gerund (e.g., "Mary loves/hates reading/ Mary loves/hates to read"), *enjoy/dislike* can take only a gerund (e.g., "Mary enjoys/dislikes reading," but not *"Mary enjoys/dislikes to read"). Similarly, whereas *request* can have as its object/complement either a noun + infinitive structure ("Tom requested his boss to grant him a leave") or a that clause ("Tom requested that his boss grant him a leave"), "demand" can take only the clause structure ("Tom demanded that his boss grant him a leave") i.e., we do not usually say *"Tom demanded his boss to give him a leave"). Then there are also some verbs that can take only the infinitive, not the gerund, such as *hope/want* ("I hope/want to finish it", not *"I hope/want finishing it").

It is generally very difficult for ESL/EFL learners to grasp such verb variations. Often, learners tend to overlook the differences between them, resulting in errors such as *"enjoyed to read"/"demand you to do it." It is thus important to draw students' attention to the usage differences among those related verbs, i.e., verbs that look fairly similar in usage patterns and/or meaning. Many teachers and textbooks use various effective strategies to help learners notice and grasp the differences among the subcategories of verbs. These strategies include (1) offering explicit comparisons and contrasts among the various subcategories of verbs, (2) having students do exercises that reinforce the comparisons and contrast, and (3) providing lists of the verbs by subcategory as references (e.g., Azar & Hagen, 2009, 2011; Celce-Murcia & Sokolik, 2007–2009, Elbaum, 1996). However, one area in which not enough appears to have been done is explaining the reason(s) of the variations among the verb subcategories. The motivation for explaining the reason(s) is that knowing them can help learners better understand and retain the usage patterns of the verbs because it gives them additional useful information to organize and remember the usage patterns of the sub-groups.

Here are the main reasons for the usage differences among the aforementioned verb types. Regarding the difference between the *love* type and the *enjoy* type of verbs, the behavioral pattern of *love* is that of verbs of English (or Old German) origin. These verbs are generally short with only one syllable, such as *hate/like/love/try*. On the other hand, the usage pattern exhibited by *enjoy* is that of verbs of Latin origin. These verbs are usually long with multi-syllables, such as *abhor/despise/dislike/enjoy*. Concerning the *hope/want* type of verbs, although they are short and of German origin, they are all intending verbs (i.e., they express an intention to perform an action), e.g., *aim/hope/intend/want/wish to buy a house*. In other words, the intended action expressed by such a verb has not occurred yet. This meaning of the verbs fits well with the inherent function of the infinitive: to express a future action. This also explains why all of the other verbs that either express a commitment to a future action or cause others to be committed to a future action also take the infinitive, not the gerund, e.g., *agree/ promise to go* and *force/persuaded someone to go*. In contrast, the gerund is used typically to refer to either a timeless action (e.g., *enjoying reading*) or a finished action (e.g., *finished eating*). Therefore, gerunds are not a good fit for the intending and future commitment verbs. These examples show clearly that whether a verb takes a gerund or an infinitive is often motivated. It is important that the teacher helps students understand the motivations.

### 7.3.2 Participles/participle phrases and clause structure: form/ function

Participles/participle phrases are common structures that often pose great difficulty to ESL/EFL learners. For example, some learners use the present participle form when they should use the past participle (e.g., *"I'm interesting in it/I'm boring to death"); also, many learners seldom use participle phrases in writing—a register where such phrases are often preferred or required for reasons to be discussed below. Here you may wonder why participle phrases are being discussed together with the topic of clause structure. The reason is simple: participles and participle phrases are closely tied to clause structures. In fact, all participle phrases are nonfinite clauses (i.e., they are derived from finite, subordinate clauses), as shown below:

11.   The boy (~~who is~~) crying over there has just had a flu shot.
12.   (~~Because he was~~) critically injured, Tom was transported to the hospital by helicopter.

Understanding this fact and also why participle phrases are used can help learners better grasp the use of these structures.

Thus, in explaining/teaching the structures, the teacher should focus on how participle phrases are derived and where they are used. To help learners understand the difference between present and past participles, the teacher can illustrate the derivational process by using examples like the following:

13.   Politics bores me. → I'm bored (by politics), not I'm boring. Politics is boring.
14.   The rule pleases us. → We're pleased by the rule, not We're pleasing. The rule is pleasing.

Drawing/diagramming can be used to help explain the difference.

Concerning where and why participle phrases are used, the teacher can show with corpus examples that they are used mainly in writing, especially formal writing. The reason for their use is that writing requires not only a higher level of conciseness but also more variety of sentence structures (i.e., a more appealing style). The use of participle phrases, which are shorter than finite clauses, enables the writer to simultaneously pack more information and vary the sentence structures used. It is therefore a good practice in a writing class to have students transform some subordinate clauses into appropriate participle phrases. In a conversation class, the teacher can ask students do the opposite: expand participle phrases in a writing passage or article back into finite clauses so as to make the language more colloquial. An example of this type of activity is provided in the Suggested Teaching Activities section below. The teacher can give students parallel forms of passages with the A form containing marked finite clauses and the B form containing participle phrases in the place of the finite clauses in the A form; and then ask students to compare the forms and decide in which context each form will be more appropriate. These practices can help learners more clearly understand the form, meaning, and function related to participle phrases. The activities can simultaneously help reinforce learners' understanding of the clause structures.

### 7.3.3 Describing/explaining the dummy it and related sentence structures

A unique and common feature of the English syntactic structure that is difficult for ESL/EFL learners in structural analysis is the use of the so-called dummy pronoun *it*. As a dummy, it does not have a clear, specific referent. It fulfills two main functions.[1] First, it is used as the subject in an utterance about distance ("It's two hours from here"), time ("It's two o'clock"), weather ("It's raining") and environment ("It's stuffy here"). Second, it functions as a dummy subject or object (i.e., it is an expletive or redundant subject) as shown in the following examples (where the expletive *it* is italicized and the real subject is underlined):

15. *It* is strange <u>that the supervisor would ask anyone to go out to the treadmill at that hour</u> (taken from COCA).
16. They found *it* difficult <u>to develop new crops and markets</u>.
17. *It* is Mike
18. *It* seems that <u>John</u> has secured the job (this sentence involves a *raising to subject verb* "seem" and it is transformed from "John seems to have secured the job.").

The dummy *it* is difficult for many ESL/EFL learners because it is absent in many languages, particularly pro-drop languages (those that frequently permit the omission of the subject and/or object or both, such as all Romance languages and many Asian languages). In some of these languages, such as Chinese, subject-less utterances like "Is raining" are the norm for talking about weather. ESL/EFL learners of such an L1 background often do not understand why this *it* is necessary. Teachers and textbooks often do a good job explaining the function of the expletive "it" but not the reasons why it is used. It would be helpful to learners to know the reasons. Here are a few explanations teachers can provide to their students. The dummy *it* is needed in the discussion of distance, time, weather, and environment for the following reasons. English is not a pro-drop language but a subject-prominent language where a subject is required for every sentence except for imperative sentences and for some limited face-to-face interaction utterances (an issue that will be discussed in Chapter 11). Also, while we could use the topic words as the subject in some cases, such as "The distance/time is …," it is much simpler to use *it* instead.

As for the use of *it* as a dummy subject or object, the main reason is that it enables us to produce sentences with a more balanced structure by extraposing or moving a long subject or object to the end of the sentence. English favors a sentence with a clear, short subject or, metaphorically speaking, a clear small head but a strong predicative body so the sentence can stand firmly. A sentence containing a long subject and a short predicate would appear to have a very unbalanced structure, as can be seen in the follow sentence, which is reworded from sentence 15 above, resulting in an awfully long (fifteen-word) subject and a minuscule (two-word) predicate:

19. <u>That the supervisor would ask anyone to go out to the treadmill at that hour</u> is strange.

Knowing the reason for using the expletive *it* should enable learners to understand when and where to use it.

## Suggested teaching activities

1. *Sentence parsing and meaning.* This activity is intended to help students learn the importance of sentence parsing in understanding sentence meaning. Give students some ambiguous sentences (like the following) and tell them that the sentences each have more than one meaning depending on how they are parsed. Have them parse the sentences and tell the different meanings involved.
   a. Visiting relatives can be fun. (*Visiting* is either the subject or a participle modifier.)
   b. She hit the man with a laptop. (*With a laptop* modifies either *the man* or the verb *hit*.)
   c. They fed her dog food. (*Her* serves either as the indirect object or the modifier of *dog*.)

d. Tom likes Mary more than Jean. (*Jean* is either the object of *like* or the subject in the comparative clause.)

If students have difficulty, the teacher can work with the class to disambiguate this first sentence on the board as an example. Simple diagrams like the following may be helpful:

$$\text{Visiting } | \text{relatives} = \text{the act of visiting relatives}$$
$$\longleftarrow | \textit{object of the gerund}$$

$$\text{Visiting } | \text{relatives} = \text{relatives who are visiting}$$
$$\textit{modifier} | \longrightarrow$$

2. *Which verbs can take which structure(s) as their object?* Give students a list of verbs and have them query a corpus to see whether the verbs each can take both infinitives and gerunds as their objects. Have students organize the verbs into groups based on their query results, and then explore the motivations for their usage patterns (those mentioned in the chapter).

3. *Different structural use and different meanings.* This activity is designed to help learners understand two different verb structural patterns by examining two different uses of the verb *make* (the ditransitive vs. the object + complement). The activity should also help learners understand how different meanings arise from different underlying structures that appear identical on the surface. Give students two sentences like the following:
   1. Ms. Long's students <u>made her a birthday cake</u>.
   2. Ms. Long's students <u>made her a better teacher</u>.

Ask students to tell the meanings and also the structures of the two sentences. While students should have no difficulty differentiating the two sentences semantically, they may have trouble with their syntactic structures. Some may say that structurally the two sentences look identical: *make + her(NP)+NP*. Tell the students that they are right in that the verbs in both sentences are indeed followed by two noun phrases, but ask students to think and discuss whether the two noun phrases in both sentences perform the same grammatical functions. This discussion should lead to the conclusion that the functions differ completely: in sentence 1, *her* is the indirect object and *a birthday cake* is the direct object (i.e., it is the Cause-to-Receive construction), but in sentence 2, *her* is the direct object and *a better teacher* is the complement of the object (the Cause-to-Be resultative construction). Also remind them that the difference is shown, too, in the fact that in the Cause-to-Receive (sentence 1), the two nouns have different referents (*her* and *cake*), but in the resultative (sentence 2), the two nouns have the same reference (*her* and *teacher* = *her*). Then have students do a corpus query looking for more examples of both structures and/or make sentences that include both structures.

4.  *From participle phrases to clauses: Form and function.* As mentioned in the chapter, a common practice to help learners grasp the use of participle phrases is to have students shorten adverbial and relative clauses into participle phrases. This activity reverses the process by having students expand participle phrases back into finite clauses. It helps students understand the origins of participle phrases and their functions. It is best to include phrases that have come from both adverbial and relative clauses, as shown below, because it will allow them to see that participle phrases can come from different types of classes, which serve different functions:
    1a.  The boy rushed out of the room, <u>crying loudly</u>.
    1b.  The boy <u>crying loudly over there</u> is her brother.
    2a.  <u>Shot in the leg</u>, the man fell to the ground.
    2b.  The man <u>shot in the chest and head yesterday</u> has died.

    After students have expanded the underlined phrases, have them compare the meaning/function/form of the a and b sentences in each pair.

5.  *Making sentences more balanced with* <u>it</u> *as the expletive subject.* Tell students that each of the following sentences is unbalanced with either a long subject or object. Ask them to make the sentences more balanced by moving the long underlined subjects or objects to the end of the sentence and adding the dummy (expletive) subject *it*. For students who have difficulty identifying the subjects/objects, the teacher can have the subjects/objects underlined.
    1.  That over 10,000 people have been killed in this war is reported.
    2.  To keep the house tidy with so many children living in it is not easy.
    3.  We consider to protect the natural resources our duty.
    4.  That he completed two books and ten articles in three years is unbelievable.
    5.  Few people believe that he embezzled money from the charity to be true.

## Note

1  Besides the two functions explained here, *it* is also used in some idiomatic expressions where it does not have a clear referent either, such as *Just do it, beat it,* and *made it.*

# 8

# TENSE AND ASPECT

Tense and aspect play a very important role in the English language, but they are also among the most difficult grammatical issues for English teachers to explain and for L2 learners to grasp. Thus, this chapter is devoted to this challenging topic. The chapter begins with a brief overview of the English tense and aspect system, followed by a description of some of the most common practices for teaching tense and aspect. It concludes with a discussion of how contemporary linguistic theories of construal and discourse may enable us to offer more accurate and effective description and teaching of a few challenging English tense/aspect usage issues.

## 8.1 English tense and aspect system: an overview

Because there is often confusion about what tense and aspect mean, a clarification of the two terms is first in order. While both terms deal with time, they do so in very different ways. Tense refers to the location of an event in time relevant to a reference point (often the speaker/writer's) and the sequential ordering of the two points in time (Comrie, 1976). In other words, it concerns whether the event is in the *past*, *present*, or *future* according the speaker/writer's perspective. Aspect, on the other hand, refers to "ways of viewing the temporal constituency of a situation" (Comrie, 1976, p. 3), i.e., it deals with whether the speaker/writer views the event as being ongoing (progressive), completed (perfect), etc. The common confusion about tense and aspect is best evidenced by the widely-held belief or assumption that English has twelve tenses (a belief that has clearly resulted from a conflation of tense and aspect). Instead of having twelve tenses, English may be said to have twelve tense/aspect combinations. Technically speaking, English has only two tenses (*past/present*) and two aspects (*progressive/perfect*). There is no future tense in English because future is not marked by verb inflection as the present and the past tenses are. Instead, future in English is expressed by a number of words and phrases (e.g., the modal *will* and the phrasal modal *be going to*). Similarly, there is no marking of the simple aspect except for the simple present singular. Also, the perfect progressing aspect is indicated by the combination of the perfect aspect and the progressive aspect markings, i.e., it does not have its own marking.

**TABLE 8.1** English tense and aspect system

|  | Past | Present | Future |
|---|---|---|---|
| **Simple** | worked. | work/works. | will work. |
| **Progressive** | were/was working. | are/is working. | will be working. |
| **Perfect** | had worked. | have/has worked. | will have worked. |
| **Perfect-Progressive**[*] | had been working. | have/has been working. | will have been working. |

[*]The *progressive* aspect is also called *continuous*.

| Past | → | Present | → | Future |
|---|---|---|---|---|

**FIGURE 8.1** Common diagram of time sequence.

However, even though technically English has only two tenses and two aspects, an adequate description of the English tense and aspect system should give a full account of all of the tenses and aspects that it distinguishes and expresses, no matter what methods it uses to do so. In other words, the description should include all of the three tenses (*past/present/future*) and four aspects (*simple/progressive/perfect/perfect-progressive*), which together form twelve tense and aspect combinations as shown in Table 8.1 illustrated with the verb *work*.

Such a complete description of the English tense and aspect system is especially important for language learning purposes because it provides learners with the information they need in order to communicate accurately and effectively regarding time and aspect. It is important to note that the sequential order of the tenses listed in the table is *past/present/future* rather than *present/past/future*, the frequently-used order in the textbooks. While it is sensible to begin with the present tense in teaching English tenses due to its extensive use and its simplicity in form (no inflections except for the third-person singular), it is not so for listing the sequential order of the English tenses because it violates our typical conceptualization and visual representation of the sequence of time, which is usually a linear-line image that starts with the past on the left end and moves rightward/forward to the present and then the future as shown in Figure 8.1.

It is also important to note that the grammatical aspect (*simple/progressive/perfect/perfect progressive*) of verbs should not be confused with their lexical aspect. The latter is defined by the inherent semantic nature of a verb, such as *durative*, *punctual*, and *stative*. According to Vendler (1957), English verbs fall into four categories of lexical aspect: *activity*, *accomplishment*, *achievement*, and *state*. Later, Comrie (1976) added another aspect, **semelfactive**, which refers to verbs that express momentary actions. All of the five groups are listed in Table 8.2 with illustrative examples. The term *momentary action* is used to label the *semelfactive* group because it is easier to understand.

**TABLE 8.2** Verb groups by Lexical aspect

| Activity (durative with no clear starting/finishing point) | Accomplishment (durative with clear finishing point) | achievement (punctual) | Momentary action (punctual; may often be repetitive) | State (durative but involving no action/change) |
|---|---|---|---|---|
| dance | build | discover | blink | desire |
| jump | draw | notice | knock | have |
| play | knit | realize | punch | love |
| study | make | win | sneeze | understand |

Activity verbs each portray a durative action that does not have a clear-cut starting and finishing point. As such, activity verbs are particularly compatible with the progressive aspect. Accomplishment verbs, like activity verbs, are also durative, but they differ in having a clear finishing point. Achievement verbs resembles accomplishment verbs in having a clear ending point, but they are punctual, i.e., not durative. With a clear finishing point, accomplishment and achievement verbs are especially suitable for the perfect aspect. Momentary verbs are punctual like achievement verbs, but they are not achievement in nature. Instead, they are punctual actions that can be repeated multiple times in a short span of time, hence suited for the progressive form. Stative verbs are unique in that while they are durative, they do not involve any action or change. As such, they are generally not used in the progressive form. However, stative verbs are a very large group with many subcategories, including emotion/attitude (e.g., *appreciate* and *desire*), mental perception (e.g., *believe* and *know*), and possession (e.g., *belong* to and *have*). Also, verbs in the stative group often function in more than one subcategory. For example, *have* can function as a possession verb ("I have a car") as well as an experience verb ("I'm having a hard time"/"I had a car accident" where *have* both mean *experience*). In short, understanding the lexical aspect of verbs can also help learners better grasp English tense and aspect. In fact, research (Bardovi-Harlig, 1998, 1999) has shown that lexical aspect plays a very important role in ESL/EFL acquisition of tense and aspect.

The fact that the progressive aspect and the perfect aspect each need an auxiliary (*be* for the progressive and *have* for the perfect forms) and the fact that different forms can be used to express the future make the English tense and aspect system very complex and hence difficult for L2 learners. In addition to complexity in form, the English tense and aspect system is also complicated in use due to the following three reasons: (1) the present tense may also be used to refer to the future (e.g., "The conference opens next Monday"/"We are meeting tomorrow at 9:00") or to the past (i.e., the use of the historical present to describe a past event to make it more vivid and lively); (2) the past tense can be used to refer to the present and the future for politeness or for expressing hypothetical/counter factual conditions (e.g., "If I had time, I would help you"); and (3) different tenses/aspects may sometimes be used to refer to the same event due to differences in speakers/writers' foci and perspectives, an issue that will be explored in detail below. Because of its complexity in form and use, the English tense/aspect system is extremely challenging for ESL/EFL learners, especially those whose L1 does not have tense and aspect inflections, as is the case in many Asian languages.

## 8.2 Established useful practices for describing/teaching tenses/aspects

1.  Use diagrams and/or other visual aids to help students better understand English tense and aspect, especially the differences among the various tense/aspect combinations. Azar and Hagen's (2009, 2011) series provides many excellent examples. A common diagramming method uses a linear horizontal line with a vertical line in the middle that symbolizes the present plus a mark or marks (in the form of a short vertical line, cross, triangular, etc.) in particular positions on the horizontal line to indicate the time or times being referred to, as is shown in the diagrams in Figure 8.2. The diagrams are usually accompanied by example sentences.

2.  In terms of teaching sequence, begin with the simple present tense/aspect, with "be" being the first verb taught, followed by regular verbs and then irregular verbs. Then teach the present progressive, followed by the simple past and the past progressive. Next continue either to the simple future and the future progressive or to the present perfect and the present perfect progressive followed by the past perfect and past perfect progressive. Typically end with the future perfect and the future perfect progressive. Also, after a new tense/aspect is introduced, a comparison/contrast will often be made between this new tense/aspect and the one or ones that have just been taught. This sequence plus the comparison review is obviously optimal because it basically follows the logical order of moving "from simpler to more complex" and "from more useful to less useful" in language learning.

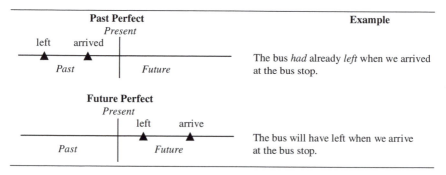

FIGURE 8.2 Examples of diagram for teaching tenses/aspect.

3.  Offer generalizations or rules of thumb, especially those that involve a comparison and contrast of two closely-related tenses/aspects. To recall, sound rules should be accurate, simple, and clear. However, because of the complexity of the English tense/aspect system, it is very difficult to come up with rules that are ideal in all of the three aspects. The rules offered in most existing textbooks are generally clear and fairly simple but sometimes not completely accurate. Here is an example: The simple present is used for stating facts and for talking about habits and routine activities, whereas the present progressive is employed for describing activities that are taking place at the moment and situations that are temporary in nature. This rule, though clear and simple, is not completely accurate because, as mentioned above, both the simple present and the present progressive can be used to refer to scheduled future events and other future conditions. Thus, some elaboration of the rule is necessary to make the rule accurate. In fact, such elaboration is necessary for quite a few of the English tenses/aspects.

Take the present perfect as an example. There are at least two complex issues that a clear rule about the use of this tense/aspect must cover. First, the present perfect may refer to three different situations related to time: (1) an action/event that occurred/completed in the past ("I've seen the movie"); (2) an action/event or state that began in the past but has continued to the present ("I've lived here for two years"); or (3) repeated actions in the past ("She has read the book three times"). Second, given that the present perfect can refer to an action/event that occurred in the past (the aforementioned number 1 and 3 uses), it is thus necessary to explain how this tense/aspect differs from the simple past, the tense/aspect used primarily for describing past actions/events/states. Generally, teachers and textbooks do a good job explaining the first issue (the three different situations the present perfect may refer to). However, the second issue (the difference between the simple past and the present perfect) is often inadequately addressed (sometimes with inaccuracies, an example of which will be discussed in Section 8.3 below). One explanation about the difference given by some textbooks is that the selection between the simple past and the present perfect in referring to a past action/event is based on whether it is relevant to the present: if it is relevant, the present perfect should be used; otherwise the simple past is the correct choice. Although such a short explanation is accurate and simple, it is not truly clear because it does not explain how the relevance of a past action/event to the present is determined. A more adequate explanation is needed to make the point clear, which will be given in Section 8.3 below during a discussion of how to explain the differences between these two tenses/aspects and also the differences between the present perfect and the present perfect progressive.

Besides the problem of some unclear rules in the existing descriptions of English tense/aspect, sometimes there is also the issue of failing to provide general rules that are true and useful for learners. For example, Willis (2003, pp. 100–101) points out two such generalizations that he believes should be taught to learners: (1) "all present tenses can be used to refer to the future" ("If it <u>rains tomorrow</u>, we'll cancel it"/"We'<u>re meeting tomorrow</u>"); and (2) past tense forms "do not always refer to past time" because we often used the past tense forms in the present in order to show politeness or express a hypothetical condition ("If I <u>had</u> time, I <u>would</u> help you <u>now</u>").

4.  Provide lists of time words or phrases (including those of frequency) that are typically used with certain tenses/aspects, such as *now* and *always/every-day/often* with the simple present; *right now* and *currently/presently* with the present progressive; *yesterday/last* + *time word/before* with the past; *since* + past time word and *for* + time length phrase with the perfect aspect. However, a word of caution is necessary regarding this practice because some of the time words may be used with more than one tense/aspect. For example, "now" may be used with both the simple present and present progressive. Also, *tomorrow* and *next* plus any other time word (*Monday/week*) can be used with the present tense (e.g., "Our first meeting is next Wednesday").

5.  Provide lists of types of verbs that are typically not used in certain tenses/aspects. The most common list is one of *state* verbs that are generally not used in the progressive form, e.g., *have/like/love*. However, such a list should be accompanied by an explanation of exceptions—something that many teachers and textbooks already do. There are two main causes of exceptions. First, some verbs can be used in two or more different subcategories, in one of which they can take the progressive form. Besides the aforementioned *have* example, *hold* is another, for it can be a durative verb ("He's holding her hand") and a stative verb ("The room holds 30 people"). Second, stative verbs that usually do not take the progressive form may do so in some special circumstances. For instance, a state verb may be used in the progressive form when the durative non-change state that it usually indicates becomes dynamic as shown in the following example (involving the verb "contain") given by Langacker (2001, p. 14): "The dam is containing the surging flood-waters." Similarly, if a durative state is being viewed as temporary, the progressive is perfectly acceptable: "Stop it! You're being rude." Knowing when non-progressive-compatible verbs may be used in the progressive form can help learners use them correctly and communicate more effectively.

Finally, it is important to note that teachers and material writers have now incorporated more and more contemporary linguistics theories and research findings (especially the role of discourse context and construal) in the description and teaching of the English tense/aspect system. For example, Celce-Murcia and Sokolik's (2007–2009) series provides many sound theory/research-based usage rules/patterns. Book 5 of the series gives two particularly good examples. The first is about the use of the past and then the historical present tense in story telling: "English-speakers often start a story in the past tense, but then switch to the present when telling the main part of the story" (p. 19). The second is the use of "being going to + verb" and "will" in narratives about future events: "the future form (***being going*** to + verb) is often used to introduce a topic or set the scene" and "English speakers may use ***will*** or its contracted form (I'll) in the rest of the narrative in the future context" (p. 25). These discourse analysis finding-based general rules are very helpful for learners to grasp how to use tense/aspect for effective communication. More of such rules and explanations should be incorporated because they will make the tense/aspect description clearer and more accurate and its teaching more effective. To illustrate the point, a few examples will be looked at below, which deal with some difficult tense/aspect usage issues.

## 8.3 Explaining/teaching challenging issues with new insights

This section explores how to use discourse and Cognitive linguistic theories (mainly *construal*) to help better describe and explain some tense/aspect issues that are particularly challenging for ESL/EFL learners.

### 8.3.1 Differentiating closely related tenses/aspects: simple past vs. present perfect and present perfect vs. present perfect progressive

As mentioned above, both the simple present and the present perfect may refer to an activity/event that was completed in the past, e.g., "I saw the movie last Friday; in other words, I've seen the movie." This fact makes it difficult to explain the difference between the two tenses/aspects. A similar problem also exists for the present perfect and the present perfect progressive, for both can refer to an activity/event that began in the past but has continued to the present, e.g., "He has worked here for years"/"He has been working here for years." Which tense/aspect in each pair to use in such cases depends largely on the discourse context and the speaker/writer's communicative purpose/viewpoint (construal). In the case of whether to use the simple present or the present perfect to refer to a past action/event, it depends on whether the speaker/writer considers the action/event is relevant to the present or not, a decision that is in turn determined by the discourse context and the speaker/writer's communicative purpose (what s/he wants to focus on and convey). For example, suppose that a person saw a movie last Friday and is being asked when and where s/he saw it, the answer will surely be in the simple past form: "I saw it last Friday." However, if s/he is being invited to see the movie but does not want to see it again, s/he will most likely reply by using the present perfect, "Thank you, but I've already seen it." Similarly, if this same person is making comments about the movie and wants to add validity to her/his comments, s/he would most likely use the present perfect by mentioning: "I've seen the movie so I know what I'm talking about."

Regarding whether to use the present perfect or the present perfect progressive to refer to an action/event that began in the past but continues to the present, the choice will depend on whether the action/event is expected to continue into the future and whether the speaker/writer wants to emphasize the continuous aspect of the action/event and its effect/implication. If there is no such emphasis is intended, the speaker/writer may opt for the present perfect. If such a focus or highlight is needed, then the present perfect progressive will be used. The following two examples (taken from COCA but edited for clarity/simplicity) help illustrate the point:

1. Psychologists <u>have studied</u> for years the effects of disasters on children. They <u>have produced</u> many important findings on the issue.
2. Scientists at the institute <u>have been studying</u> complex laboratory tests to decipher the patterns of resistance of the disease to treatment.

In example 1, even though psychologists are still and will almost surely continue to study the effects of disasters on children, the focus of the writer is on what the researchers have done rather than the continues aspect of the research. So the present perfect is used. In contrast, the focus in example 2 is on the continuous aspect of the research because it is ongoing and the scientists have not deciphered the patterns yet. Hence, the present perfect progressive is called for.

In most of the current textbooks, there has been little discussion of this nature (i.e., the discourse context and the speaker/writer's perspective) in the explanation of the difference between the two tenses/aspects in each pair. As a result, the rules/explanations are sometimes incomplete or inadequate, as can been seen in the following explanations taken from the comparison of the two pairs of tense/aspect given in Elbaum's book 3 (1996, p. 45). For lack of space, only the relevant paired contrasting points and examples are cited.

### Simple Past vs. Present Perfect

| We use the simple past with: | We use the present perfect with: |
|---|---|
| ... | ... |
| 2. A repeated past action that took place in a completed time period (yesterday, last month) | 2. A repeated past action that take place in a period that includes the present (today, this month) |
| He *sent* out three résumés last month. | He *has had* three interviews this month. |
| 3. An action that occurred at a specific time in the past | 3. A past action that does not mention a specific time |
| He *came* to the U.S. in 1984. | He *has* already *become* an American citizen. |

### Present Perfect vs. Present Perfect Continuous*

| We use the present perfect with: | We use the present perfect continuous with: |
|---|---|
| 1. A continuous state (nonaction verbs) | 1. A continuous action (action verbs) |
| Daniel *has been* in the U.S. for ten years. | Daniel *has been living* in the U.S. for ten years. |

*The term *continuous* is used in this cited textbook.

In this comparison, the explanations and examples make it appear that the two contrasting tenses/aspects in their given pair were each referring to actions/ states that differ in location of time and aspect. There is no mention of the fact that the two contrasting tenses/aspects can actually refer to the same action, although from different perspectives. As a result, there is also no mention of how discourse context and the speaker/writer's communicative purpose (viewpoint) may be really the difference that determines the choice between the two contrasting tenses/aspects in some cases. Let us look at the issue in the specific contrasting points in the comparison. First, the #2 use of the simple past states that it is for "a repeated past action that took place in a completed time period." The problem is that this same type of past action, including the very example listed, can actually also be referred to by using the present perfect when necessitated by context, such as when responding to a question like "What has he done with his job search?": "He *has sent* out three résumés so far." Also the #3 use of the present perfect (in comparison to the simple past) says it is for "a past action that does not mention a specific time," but the fact is that the same action can also be talked about using the simple past if we need to focus on when it actually happened: "He became an American citizen last year." Finally, the #1 use of the present perfect continuous form states that it is for "a continuous action (action verbs)," but, as noted above, a continuous action of this type can be described by simply using the present perfect, for, the very example given by the textbook "Daniel has been living in the U.S. for ten years" can be substituted with "Daniel has lived in the U.S. for ten years" without changing the meaning. In this case, the progressive part is not necessary unless, as noted above, one has a special focus.

In short, the above examples show that in order to provide learners with tense/aspect usage rules that are clearer and more accurate, greater attention should be paid to the role of discourse context and the speaker/writer's communicative purpose/viewpoint. A sound understanding of the issue will enable learners to make more appropriate tense/aspect choices. In fact, making the right choice of form for effective communication is all that grammar is about.

### 8.3.2 Tense/aspects in conditional clauses: unusual tense/aspect use 1

There are some unusual tense/aspect uses in English. The major ones include: (1) the use of past tense for present situations; (2) the use of the present for expressing future actions/events and past actions (the historical present); (3) tense/aspect in conditional clauses; and (4) the use of the progressive for showing temporariness or various effects. Because the first two unusual uses and their motivations have been discussed in some detail before (in Chapter 4, section 4.1, about the use of the past tense for politeness purposes and this chapter about the use of the present for future actions/events/states), they will not be addressed again. Only the second two uses will be discussed (#3 in this section and #4 in the next section), as they have only been mentioned in passing.

As shown in Table 8.3, English conditional sentences fall into three types based on the tenses/aspects used, although semantically they may be grouped into many more different categories than listed below (cf. Celce-Murcia & Larsen-Freeman, 1999, p. 548). There are two difficult questions concerning the use of tense/aspect in conditional sentences. The first relates to the use of the simple present in the conditional clause of the type I sentences. Many ESL/EFL learners have difficulty understanding why the simple present is used when the action/event referred to is actually in the future (if it happens). The answer appears to be that it is quite logical to use the simple present to talk about something as a condition because being a condition, it is uncertain whether and when the action/event may happen. Then, one may ask why the present is used to express scheduled future events. A likely sensible explanation is that the present is often used to talk about facts and a scheduled event may be viewed as a fact by the speaker.

The second difficult question concerns the difference between the future conditional and the hypothetical conditional: "If I have time tomorrow, I'll be there" vs. "If I had time tomorrow, I would be there." Obviously, the difference between the two lies in how the speaker views the possibility of having time tomorrow. In other words, the choice of which of the two is determined entirely by the speaker's viewpoint and intention. Furthermore, some learners may also find the forms for the hypothetical and counterfactual sentences convoluted and unnecessary, especially for learners with an L1 without verb tense/aspect inflections where conditionals are understood from context. For example, if someone actually said "if I am you," we would certainly understand it is counterfactual because the speaker *I* cannot really be the listener *you*. In this sense, the tense/aspect form variation used in the English conditional senses is

**TABLE 8.3** Tense/aspect in English conditional sentences

| Type | Tense/aspect used | | Major semantic category | Example |
|------|------|------|------|------|
| | Conditional clause | Main clause | | |
| I | Simple present | future | factual | If you heat ice, it will melt. |
| | | | future | If I've time tomorrow, I'll be there. |
| II | Past | would + simple | hypothetical | If I had time tomorrow, I would be there. |
| | | | counterfactual | If I were you, I would be there. |
| III | Past perfect | would + past perfect | counterfactual | If I had had time, I would have been there. |

redundant. An explanation to help these learners better understand the ration-ale for the unusual and convoluted tense/aspect forms for some of the condi-tionals is that it is actually the case in almost all languages that additional and often unusual forms are used to express different meanings. For example, English uses inversion and in some cases the auxiliary *do* to form questions. Similarly, in Chinese—a non-inflectional language—a question marker *ma* is often added to indicate an utterance as a question, and, also in Chinese, an action comple-tion marker "quo le" is used to indicate what is known as the perfect aspect in English.

### 8.3.3 *Progressive for temporariness/other effects: unusual tense/ aspect use 2*

As noted earlier, one major semantic function of the progressive is to indicate the temporariness of an action/event/state. This use of the progressive is motivated by one or a combination of following two scenarios. The speaker/writer either knows or perceives the action/event/state in question as being temporary; s/he wants to emphasize its temporary nature; and/or the listener/reader has some background knowledge about the event/state that makes it necessary for the speaker/writer to use the progressive. The following examples help illustrate the point.

3.  A: "What do you do?" B: "I'm selling furniture …"
4.  "Dad, now you're being mean."
5.  A: "How is Mike's job at the bank?" B: "Oh, he is selling cars now."

In example 3, the two interlocutors were likely meeting the first time and the B person clearly considered what s/he was doing as temporary and wanted the A person do know it. Otherwise, the B person should have said, "I sell fur-niture." In example 4, the child wanted to emphasize to her/his father what the latter was doing was mean, not that the latter was a mean person. In example 5, the two interlocutors were acquaintances; as such, the B person had to let A know that Mike changed his job and was selling his cars for the time being. Speakers also use the progressive with stative verbs to produce certain effects or to express unique meanings, including creating an intensifying effect and expressing change in state (Celce-Murcia & Larsen-Freeman, 1999, p. 121). The best example for the intensifying use of progressive stative verbs is the McDonald's TV commercial: "I'm lovin' it." The following quote from COCA offers an example of a progressive state verb for indicating change in state: "As the bulk of the garden is in place … I'm liking it more and more." Helping students understand the contexts and motivations for the special uses of the pro-gressive may enable them to better grasp them and to use them to communicate more effectively.

## 8.3.4 *Present or past tense? Difficult tense/aspect issues in academic writing*

In English academic writing, especially in writing empirical research articles, appropriate use of tense/aspect is a rather complex issue and often a challenge not only for nonnative speakers but also for native speakers. This is because academic writers have to reference and evaluate what other researchers have done and what their findings were as well as what they themselves did in the studies being reported on and what their own findings are. There are some general rules concerning the use of tense/aspect in academic writing, but these rules are not absolute and often require judgment calls on the part of the writer. In other words, the writer's interpretation and construal plays a key role. Here are two general rules, one for referencing and reporting on other scholars' research and one for discussing and reporting on one's own research.

In referencing and reporting on others' research, the general rule is to use the present tense (simple present or present perfect) to present what is considered to be general findings that are considered recent and still true or to give assessment of the study and its findings, but use the past tense to describe its methodology/ procedures used and detailed specific findings. The following are a few examples for illustrating the rule. They are taken from the author's published articles, but some editing of the examples was done for simplicity and clarity purposes. Also, the italicized words in brackets are added comments about what type of information the writer of the passage was presenting or what the writer was trying to do.

6. "Research <u>has shown</u> that synonyms <u>share</u> the same meaning at the course-grained level but <u>differ</u> in meaning at the fine-grained level (Edmons & Hirst, 2002)" [*general/recent findings*].
7. "Gardner and Davies's (2007) study <u>has</u> three limitations [*writer's assessment of the study*] … Gardner and Davies themselves explicitly <u>recommended</u> 'a reanalysis of the lists across major registers'" [*what the researchers actually did*].
8. "Using a 'lexical substitutability' test in a corpus study of near-synonyms, Church et al. (1994) <u>attained</u> basically the same finding [*what the researchers did*]: lexical items' 'textual substitutability' <u>is</u> a good indicator of their semantic similarity" [*general finding still considered true*].
9. "Master (1994) found that, whereas the ESL students who received systematic instruction on the use of articles significantly improved their performance on article usage, those who did not receive such instruction did not" [*specific findings*].

It is important to note that in reporting other researchers' findings, the verb in the main clause concerning what the research did should be in the past tense, but the verb in the object noun clause regarding the general findings that are considered recent and/or true) needs to be in the present tense (as in example sentence 8). A common way to avoid this inconsistency of the use of tense/ aspect in one sentence is to place the names and year of the cited study at the end of the sentence in parenthesis as shown below:

10. Lexical items' "textual substitutability" is a good indicator of their semantic similarity (Church, et al., 1994).

If the finding in the noun clause is, however, very specific or is out of date/ no longer considered true), the verb should be in the past tense just as the verb in the main clause (as in example sentence 9). Obviously, these criteria are somewhat subjective. Whether a finding is recent enough or still considered true may depend on the writer's interpretation.

Also useful to know is that the verbs that describe what the general findings or positions of the cited researchers are often either stance verbs (e.g., *advocate/ argues/contend/claim/posit*) or interpretive verbs (e.g., *exhibit/demonstrate/indicate/ show/suggest*). These verbs tend to be used in the present tense. On the other hand, verbs that describe what the cited researchers did are action verbs (e.g., *analyzed/ computed/examined/investigated/scrutinized*) and these verbs often appear in the past tense when used to report on other scholars' research.

As for describing and reporting on one's own study, the general rule is to use the present tense to describe the rationale, purpose, and the overall design of your study, and to discuss your interpretation of and the significance of the results of the study, but use the past tense to describe the methods and procedures used and the results of your study. Here are a few examples (again taken from the author's published journal articles) to illustrate the rule.

11. Given 1) the importance of synonymy, 2) the effectiveness of corpus/elicited data examination in the study of synonymy, and 3) the inadequate attention that synonymous nouns have received so far, this study aims to use both corpus and elicited data to examine the use of two sets of synonymous nouns [*rationale and purpose of the study*].

12. After we tabulated the results of the participants' performance, we calculated the mean of the missed obligatory uses of the article *the* ... We then conducted a MANOVA test with a post hoc Tukey's test ... the Tukey's test showed that the intermediate group's means in all categories were significantly lower ... [*procedures and results*].

13. The results in Table 6 show that ... Thus, native language does not appear to be a significant factor in ESL learners learning and use of the article *the* ... [interpretation of research results].

However, it is important to note that sometimes there is a fine line between reporting results and interpreting results. So it will be the writer's judgment call. There is another general practice that may be beneficial for learners to know:

writers often use the present perfect to refer to existing research and then use the simple present to introduce their current study. Here are two simplified generic examples of this practice:

14. Research <u>has shown</u> that X knowledge/skill is very important in learning Y. However, it <u>is</u> still not clear how this knowledge/skill <u>is</u> developed. It <u>is</u> thus the purpose of this study to investigate the process of the development of this knowledge/skill and the factors involved.

15. There <u>have been</u> many studies on the effects of L1 transfer in L2 learning. Yet no study <u>appears</u> to have examined the effect of transfer of the X aspect of L1, an important yet often overlooked issue. Against this backdrop, this study <u>aims</u> to examine this specific area of transfer.

To conclude this section and the chapter, it is necessary to repeat that these general rules are not absolute. They are simply guidelines for ESL/EFL students to follow as they learn to use tense/aspect appropriately. It is paramount that when giving students these general rules, we must provide them with many concrete examples. Besides examples to accompany the general rules, another important practice is to have students read many representative research papers and pay special attention to the use of tense/aspect.

## Suggested teaching activities

1. *Which tense/aspect to use?* This activity asks students to fill in the blanks by choosing between two closely related tenses/aspects based on the information and the contexts provided.
    1. Mary took the TOEFL test last Saturday.
        a. Now, she_____ (take) the TOEFL test.
        b. It was last Saturday when she_____ (take) the TOEFL test.
    2. John joined this golf club in 2001.
        a. John_____ (be/become) a golf club member for more than ten years.
        b. John_____ (be/become) a golf club member more than ten years ago.
    3. Tom started to live in Chicago in 2006 and he is still living in Chicago.
        a. Tom_____ (live) in Chicago since 2006. (*Not sure if he'll continue living there*)
        b. Tom_____ (live) in Chicago since 2006. (*You need to emphasize that he'll continue living there*)
2. *What time does it refer too?* This activity is designed to help learners understand the special uses of English tense/aspect (i.e., tenses/aspects do not refer to the time they normally do). Give students a list of sentences or

passages and ask them what time (past, present, or future) each is actually referring to. The following is a list of some examples.

   a.   Our flight departs at 5 this afternoon.

   b.   Could you please tell me how to get to the train station?

   c.   If I were you, I would go home and rest.

   d.   At that moment, I see a deer running across the road and it's too late for me to stop the car, so I start screaming, "Oh, No …!"

3.  *"Be going to" or "will"?* This activity is designed to help students learn the typical tense/aspect use in expressing a series of connected future actions (which typically begins with "be going to" followed by "will") or a series of connected habitual past actions (which usually begins with "used to" followed by "would"). Give students a list of planned activities (an example given below) and ask them to write and tell about their planned activities. Here is an example:

   1.   Go to New York this Thursday;

   2.   visit Empire State building and Broadway Friday;

   3.   visit Central Park and Wall Street Saturday;

   4.   fly back Sunday.

4.  *Tell a vivid story.* Ask students to write/tell a story or past event that they remember well. Tell them that they have to begin the story/event by using the past tense to provide all the general background information. Then they need to use the historical present tense to describe the main actions involved to make them sound more vivid. Provide students with an example if necessary.

5.  *Why is the tense/aspect shifted?* Give students passages that involve tense/aspect shifting. Ask them to first identify the different tenses/aspects used and the places where a tense/aspect shifting occurs. Then have them determine and explain why the shifts are necessary. The following is an example of a short passage. It is from ABC's Nightline program (taken from COCA).

> I had a general feeling that it was doing a good job, but I wanted to be very clear with myself. And <u>I've done my homework</u>, and I have to say I am absolutely astounded at the persistence of this debate, and about what I consider to be a rather false issue.

Ask students to note where the tense/aspect shifted and explain particularly why the speaker used the present perfect in "I've done my homework" rather than the simple past "I did my homework." (The present perfect here serves two purposes: 1) to move from a description of past thoughts to a discussion of the points the speakers wants to make; 2) to help provide credibility to what the speaker would say.)

# 9
# ARTICLES

The English article system is another important but very difficult aspect of grammar for ESL/EFL learners. English articles are important because they constitute a crucial part of the English system for information referencing and identification—a key function of language. Their importance is best evidenced by the fact that corpus data have repeatedly shown that *the* and *a/an*, key articles in English, are among the first few most frequent words in English: *the* is the most frequent word in both the one billion-word Oxford English Corpus and the 100 million-word BNC while *a/an* is the sixth and fourth most frequent word in the two corpora, respectively. The difficulty of learning the use of articles in ESL/EFL has been well reported in research (Liu & Gleason, 2002; Master, 1997). To address this important and challenging topic, this chapter begins with an overview of the English article system followed by a brief mention of some common practices for describing and teaching English articles. It concludes with a discussion of some practices for describing/teaching a few specific aspects of article use.

## 9.1 The English article system: an overview

### 9.1.1 English articles and their semantic functions

In discussing the English article system, the first issue concerns what it consists of. For many, it is composed of two articles: *a/an* (known as the *indefinite article*) and *the* (the *definite article*). However, this simple description overlooks the fact that many English nouns are often used without an article. Therefore, many grammarians (Celce-Murcia & Larsen-Freeman, 1999; Chesterman, 1991; Master, 1997; Yule, 1998) believe that a complete description of the English article system should address the use of what they label as the *zero* article.[1] Some (e.g., Celce-Murcia & Larsen-Freeman, 1999, p. 271) also include *some* as an article when it is "unstressed" before a noun. Table 9.1 offers a summary of the English articles (including *some* and the *zero* article) and their major semantic functions. While some student textbooks do not include *some* and the *zero*

**TABLE 9.1** The English article system

| Article | Semantic type | Sub-type | Example |
|---------|---------------|----------|---------|
| **Zero** | *Generic* | Count noun | Ø <u>Giraffes</u> are large animals with a long neck. |
| | | Non-count | Ø <u>Air</u> is essential for human survival. |
| | *Non-generic* | Count noun | Ø <u>Giraffes</u> are needed in this zoo. |
| | | Non-count | Giraffes need to drink Ø <u>water</u>. |
| **A/An** | *Generic* | | <u>A giraffe</u> is a large animal with a long neck. |
| | *Non-generic* | *Non-specific* | I need <u>a dog</u>. |
| | | *Specific* | I saw <u>a dog</u> behind the building. |
| **Some** | *Non-generic* | Count noun | We need <u>some</u> pens. |
| | | Non-count | I need <u>some</u> water. |
| **The** | *Generic* | | <u>The giraffe</u> is a large animal with a long neck. |
| | *Non-generic* | *Cultural* | <u>The sun</u> rises in the East. |
| | | *Situational* | Please give me <u>the salt</u>. |
| | | *Structural* | <u>The students at the university</u> are mostly female. |
| | | *Textual* | I just saw a dog and a cat there. <u>The dog</u> was small. |

article in their discussion of the English articles, some do. It is up to the teacher whether to include them. Also, the table lists four sub-semantic functions of the non-generic use of *the* based on Liu and Gleason's (2002) classification model, which will be discussed later.

To understand the use and the semantic functions of the English articles, it is necessary to briefly define a few concepts related to the use of articles and nouns, including the *generic* and *non-generic* use. The *generic* use of a noun refers to a species, race, or a human invention (e.g., *computer/internet*). In English, the generic use of noun may appear in the following three different forms (some examples already given in Table 9.1):

1.  (*the + singular noun*): The whale is a large sea mammal.
2.  (*a + singular noun*): A whale is a large sea mammal.
3.  (*Ø Plural noun*): Whales are large sea mammals.

It is important to note that some grammarians (e.g., Celce-Murcia & Larsen-Freeman, 1999, p. 283) suggest that the *definite article + plural noun* form can also be used in the generic sense when referring to a race or the people of a nation, e.g., *The Germans are good musicians*. Also, while all of the three forms can convey the generic sense, they often occur in different contexts with the first form (*the + a singular noun*) being most formal and most abstract (used mainly in academic/technical writing), followed by the *Ø plural noun* form, and then the *a + singular noun* form, the least formal as it a common colloquial and concrete manner for expressing the generic sense (Celce-Murcia & Larsen-Freeman).

**TABLE 9.2** Articles and the semantic types of nouns they each modify

|  |  |  | Definite | Indefinite |
|---|---|---|---|---|
| **Common** | Count | Singular | the (the book I wrote) | a/an (I need a spoon) |
|  |  | Plural | the (the books I've read) | Ø (I need spoons) |
|  | Non-count |  | the (the water I bought) | Ø (I need water) |
| **Proper** | In general |  | Ø (Mike/Miami) | *N/A* |
|  | Special cases |  | the (the Rocky Mountains/the Joes) |  |

In contrast to the *generic* use, the *non-generic* use of a noun refers to one or more members in a species, etc., as shown below.

4. The giraffe we saw at the zoo yesterday is sick.
5. A giraffe at the zoo is sick.

It is important to note that the non-generic accounts for the majority use of nouns. Besides the concepts of *generic/non-generic*, there are two other important pairs of concepts relevant to the use of articles: 1) *common nouns* (those that do not name a specific person, place, etc., such as *book* and *student*) vs. *proper nouns* (those that name a specific person, place, etc., such as *George Bush* and *Japan*); 2) *count* vs. *non-count nouns* (this contrastive pair has already been explored in Chapter 6). The next section explains how these concepts and other issues affect the use of articles.

### 9.1.2 Type of noun and the use of article

Whether a noun is common or proper and whether it is count or non-count are two important factors in deciding which article (*a/an, the* or *zero*) the noun should occur with. Of course, an even more important determining factor is whether the noun is definite (i.e., having a specific referent) or indefinite (i.e., having a non-specific referent). If a noun is specific, whether singular or plural, the article *the* is used except for proper nouns (e.g., not *the Boston, although there are some cases where a proper noun takes the article *the*: the Smiths and the Mississippi River). The reason that proper nouns generally do not take the definite article is that they are by nature already specific/definite. If a noun is non-specific and count/singular, then the article *a/an* is used; if it is non-specific but count/plural or non-count, the *zero (Ø)* article is called for. Table 9.2 above summarizes this general rule regarding which article to use based on the semantic type of noun.

While this general rule appears to be simple, its application in practice is much more complicated due to the difficulty involved in determining the specific/non-specific and sometimes the count/non-count status of a noun. There are various

**TABLE 9.3** Scenarios for article use based on noun specificity

| Scenario | Article to use | Example |
|---|---|---|
| Non-specific to both parties | *a/an* | I need a dog. |
| Non-specific to the speaker/writer but specific to the listener/reader | *a/an* | I understand you have a dog. |
| Specific to the speaker/writer but non-specific to the listener/reader | *a/an* | I used to have a dog. |
| Specific to both parties | *the* | Have you seen the dog? (One spouse asking another about their only dog) |

factors that may affect how these determinations are made. Furthermore, there are also exceptional usages to deal with, such as the aforementioned use of *the* with proper nouns. Some of the major difficult issues are explored below.

### 9.1.3 Specific or non-specific: the crucial complex question in article use

As stated above, whether a noun is specific or non-specific is crucial in deciding whether to use the indefinite or the definite article. The issue is complex because we need to know to whom the noun is specific, i.e., to the speaker/writer, the listener/reader, or both parties. Based on Brown (1973) analysis, Table 9.3 summarizes the four possible scenarios concerning the issue and the article that is called for in each scenario.

It is clear from the table that the only scenario that calls for the use of *the* is when the noun is specific to both parties. Then how and when can the speaker/writer know that the listener/reader knows the referent being mentioned? In some cases, the answer to the question is fairly simple, such as the examples given in Table 9.3. However, the question can be difficult in many other cases (especially from ESL/EFL learners' perspective), such as the use of *the* in the *Mississippi River*/the *sun* but not in *\*the Lake Michigan/\*the Mars*. Some grammarians (Halliday & Hasan, 1976; Hawkins, 1978) have studied this question closely by exploring the types of contexts or conditions in which English speakers/writers can assume that the noun in question is specific to the listener/reader and the definite article can be used. In other words, they tried to systematically identify the types of conditions that license the non-generic use of *the*.

Halliday and Hasan's (1976) research suggests that the licensing conditions may be found in four areas: *language structure, situation, text,* and *culture,* although they did not elaborate how. Drawing on the work of grammarians before him, Hawkins (1978, pp. 106–149) successfully identified eight types of non-generic use of *the*. While Hawkins description offers a comprehensive coverage of the different semantic functions of the non-generic use of *the,* it is too complex and too detailed for language learners, given that simplicity is a key principle for pedagogical language description. Furthermore, some of Hawkins's different uses are actually very similar and can be combined. Using Halliday and Hasan's theory as a guide, Liu and Gleason (2002) simplified Hawkins's eight non-generic uses of *the* to four: *situational*, *textual*, *structural*, and *cultural*, which are described below in a separate section.

### 9.1.4 *The four major non-generic uses of the*

This description of the four major non-generic uses of *the* is drawn largely from Liu and Gleason (2002, p. 7). The two most common uses are *situational* and *textual*. Situational use refers to cases where *the* is used with a first-mention noun whose referent can be sensed directly or indirectly by the interlocutors (e.g., *Open the door/Pass me the sugar, please*) or the referent is known by the members in a local community, such as the only dog in a family or the only bank in a small town (e.g., at my university, the big quad at the center of the campus is known and called *the quad*).

Textual use is the use of *the* with a noun that has been previously referred to or is related to a previously mentioned noun. Here is an example of the latter: "We observed a class today; the teacher was really energetic." In this example, even though the word *teacher* is a first-mention, *the* is warranted because the word *class* mentioned in the first sentence already makes clear which teacher is being discussed here.

*Structural use* is the use of *the* with a first-mention noun that has an identifying or specifying modifier, e.g., the employees of Google/the person who was injured yesterday and the first person to finish the race. It is necessary to emphasize that the modifier must be one that identifies or specifies the noun, not one that classifies the noun. Nouns with a classifying modifier take the *zero* rather than the definite article: "Ø Children with attention deficit disorder can now be helped by medication." In this example, the prepositional post-noun modifier does not identify actual individuals, so the *zero* article is used.

*Cultural use* refers to cases where *the* is used with a noun that is unique and well-known referent in the English speech community (e.g., *the sun/the White House*) or *the* is used in an idiomatic expression with no clear motivation for it (e.g., *right on the money* = right on target). *Cultural use* is not listed as a type by Hawkins (1978), but it is mentioned in his *large situational use* category where *the* is used because the referent is considered general knowledge known to all the people in a country or in the world. Compared with Hawkins's term *large situational use*, *cultural use* is a more appropriate term because many of the cases in this category are conventional cultural practices, such as the use of *the* before mountain ranges and rivers but not before lakes, and its use before the musical instruments we play (*play the violin/the piano*) but not before the sports we play (*\*play the basketball*). Of course, the use of *the* in these circumstances is not completely arbitrary but often governed by rules, an issue that will be addressed below in discussing how to teach the use of articles. Still, as Liu and Gleason's (2002) study shows, of the four types of non-generic use of *the*, *cultural use* is the most difficult for ESL/EFL learners to grasp due to its complexity and the arbitrariness involved with some of the specific uses in this category.

## 9.2 Established useful practices in describing/teaching English articles

In discussing common practices for teaching English articles, it is necessary to first note that due to the complexity of the English article system, some educators suggest that for beginning ESL/EFL learners, no "sustained attention" should be directed to articles, but teachers still should use any available opportunity to highlight the use of the indefinite article before singular count nouns and to contrast the nouns used with *a/an* with those with non-count nouns , e.g., *an apple* vs. *water* and *a book* vs. *paper* (Master, 1997. p. 226). In fact, tying the use of the indefinite article to count indefinite nouns is the typical way teachers and grammar books begin introducing the English article system.

So, the first common practice in the teaching of English articles is to teach them together with the introduction of the types of nouns (*common* vs. *proper* nouns and *count* vs. *non-count* nouns). Typically, it begins by introducing the indefinite article *a* with a singular countable noun (e.g., *a/an book/apple*) and the *zero article* plural and the *zero article* proper nouns as shown in Ø *Apples are sweet; I like phones made by Ø Apple* (the electronics maker). Often real objects are used to help learners better understand the concepts. Later, the definite article *the* is taught along with the conceptual distinction between indefinite/non-specific and definite/specific, i.e., the distinction between *a/an* and *the*. In teaching the "specific vs. non-specific" distinction, many teachers and textbooks do a good job by focusing on the distinction between whether the listener knows the referent of the noun in question. Usually, the teaching is accompanied by a lot of fill-in-the blank questions in context in which students are asked to fill in the blanks with either *a/an, the,* or the *zero* article (in some exercises, only two choices: *a/an* or *the*), as shown in the following example:

I'm telling you_____ story.___ story is about_____ Jackie Chan.

Finally, teachers and textbooks often offer general article usage rules based on the examples taught. Here are two such rules: *never use a singular noun without an article or another determiner; use the definite article if your listener knows or is thinking about the same referent you are mentioning* (summarized from Azar & Hagen, 2011, pp. 306–307, Celce-Murcia & Sokolik, 2009, Book 5, pp. 43–46).

Another common teaching practice is to list marked errors related to article use, such as missing articles or unnecessary articles: I have car > *I have a car;* Give *me an advice* > *Give me some advice.* In this practice, it is best to work on actual errors made by one's students. The teacher can collect errors and then present them to students (typically embedded in utterances). Often, the teacher asks students not only to identify the errors but also explore their causes and article usage rules that the errors violated. Having students identify and explore the sources of the problems provides them with a great opportunity to learn and reinforce the rules they have learned. Of course, sometimes students do not know why their particular usage is erroneous, often due to inter-lingual differences. For example, students who say "an advice" often believe that the word is a count noun. It is thus important for the teacher to help students correctly identify all the problems.

One more common practice is to teach articles (mainly the definite article) with the phrases they are in, i.e., to teach them as fixed expressions, such as *the USA/at the beginning/on the contrary/on the surface/in the end*. To make it more effective, the teacher can have students contrast these expressions with those with Ø article, such as *America/for example/in contrast/in comparison/on average*. This practice is particularly useful for learning idioms (e.g., *bite <u>the</u> bullet/drop <u>the</u> ball/kick <u>the</u> bucket*). More importantly, empirical research has shown that this lexicogrammatical approach to article instruction is often more effective than a purely grammatical or syntactical approach (Master, 1997).

## 9.3 Explaining/teaching challenging issues with new insights

### 9.3.1 Tailoring the explanation of the generic use of articles to learner needs

As mentioned in Chapters 1 and 4, often students with different L1s may have different levels and/or different types of difficulty with a particular L2 lexico-grammatical structure. Studies (Ionin & Montrul, 2010; Ionin, Montrul, Kim, & Philippov, 2011) have shown that while ESL/EFL learners whose L1 does not have articles (such as Korean/Japanese/Russian) often experience serious difficulty in understanding/using the *the + singular noun* as a generic noun (e.g., *The tiger is an endangered animal*), Spanish-speaking ESL/EFL learners often have great difficulty understanding and using the bare (Ø) plural nouns in the generic sense (e.g., *Tigers are endangered animals/Spaniards are very athletic*) as well as difficulty with the non-generic definite article-plural noun uses (e.g., *The tigers are large*). The difficulty experienced by ESL/EFL learners with an article-less L1 was caused largely by the lack of articles in their L1, a fact that makes it difficult for these learners to understand that the definite article *the* used with a singular noun can refer to the entire species, race, etc. The Spanish-speaking EFL/ESL learners' difficulty has resulted from the fact that in Spanish a bare plural noun cannot be used to express a generality; instead, the definite article must be added to a plural noun to do so. These Spanish article/noun usages differ completely from those in English.

Clearly, due to the different types of difficulty the two different groups of ESL/EFL learners face, we need to teach them differently by focusing on different aspects/areas of the generic use of English articles. For ESL/EFL learners with an article-less L1, we should highlight how English frequently uses the definite singular in formal context to refer to an entire category, including not only species and race but also human inventions such as *the computer/internet/phone*, as shown in <u>*The computer*</u> *has become indispensable in contemporary life.* These students should also be given a lot of input and exercises to distinguish the *the + generic singular* and the *the + non-generic singular* uses (e.g., *The tiger is a large animal* vs. *The tiger (a specific one) is small*). For Spanish-speaking (and many other Romance language) learners of English, it would behoove the teacher to contrast and highlight the differences between their L1 and English in the generic use of plurals nouns. They should also be given ample opportunity to use bare plural nouns in the generic sense.

### 9.3.2 Teaching the non-generic uses of the with the right sequence/strategies

As noted above, the non-generic use of the definite article *the* falls into four major semantic types: *cultural, situational, structural*, and *textual*. Research (Liu & Gleason, 2002) has shown that the four types of use present different levels of difficulty to ESL/EFL learners with *situational* being the easiest (i.e., being the first to be acquired), followed by *structural/textual uses*, and finally *cultural* use. In fact, this is also the order native English speakers follow in acquiring the non-generic use of *the*, as reported by Liu and Gleason based on previous research. Given this acquisition order, it would make sense in the teaching of the non-generic use of *the* to begin with *situational* use. There is in fact another important motivation to do so: it can be done even with low-level students by using real objects and the TPR method. The teacher and the students can give and follow commands by employing things readily available in the classroom or things that can be brought to class easily. Here are a few examples: *Come to <u>the</u> board/door; give me <u>the</u> chalk/chalk eraser; turn on <u>the</u> light/computer.* Furthermore, the teacher can use such TPR activities to help students reinforce their understanding of the difference between *a/an* and *the* by mixing commands that contain *the* with commands that contain *a/an*: *Give me a book* vs. *give me the eraser* and *find me an eraser* vs. *find me the chalk eraser.*

After students have developed a basic understanding of situational use of *the*, we can move on to *structural* and *textual* uses. With both use types, the rules are quite simple and clear (see Section 9.1.4 above). However, students need an enormous amount of input and practice before they can use them correctly most of the time. This is especially true for learners with an article-less L1. As for the teaching of *cultural use*, the task is very challenging because of the reasons already mentioned above. However, there are some general rules and patterns that will be very useful for learners to know. There are also motivations for some seemingly arbitrary usages, and it would be helpful for students to understand these motivations. Here are a few examples. The first relates to patterns in the article use with geographical names: Oceans, rivers, seas, and mountain ranges always take the definite article. Mountains in singular form and lakes in general do not take any article, e.g., Mount Everest and Lake Michigan. However, names of lakes ending in a plural may take the definite article, such as The Great Lakes. The second rule relates to disease names: Except for a few contagious diseases that take the definite article (e.g., *the flu/the plague*), most ailments take the indefinite *a/an* (*a cold/headache*), but a few in the plural form may either take *the* or *zero* article (e.g., *Ø/the measles/mumps*). All formal disease names take the *zero* article, e.g., *cancer/pneumonia*. Let us look at one example of motivations for unusual usages: the use of *the* in *the earth/sun/moon* but not in *Mars/Jupiter*. The reason *the* is used with *earth/sun* is that they each have other meanings: *earth* can refer to land/soil and *sun* to sunlight or sunshine. Furthermore, *sun* also means star and there is more than one sun in the universe; similarly, *moon* also means *satellite* and there is more than one moon in the solar system. Because of these reasons, *the* is needed before each of these words when used as the name of the particular star, planet, or satellite it signifies. In contrast to these three nouns, Mars, Jupiter, Venus, etc. are proper names; as such, they cannot take *the*. Finally, it is important to note that there are many more other cultural uses that are difficult to describe and explain. A few more are discussed in the next section.

### 9.3.3 Explaining the motivations of cultural and unusual uses of articles

It is first important to note that while some unusual article uses can be explained fairly easily, some are more difficult. An example of the former is the use of *a/an* before non-count nouns modified by an adjective, e.g., *a good education/knowledge* and *a hard/soft wood* (as in *Oak is a hard wood*). The rationale for the use of *a/an* is that in such cases the speaker is referring to a particular type of the concept that the non-count noun expresses. In other words, the speaker is framing an unbounded concept as a bounded one, making the use of *a/an* possible. An example of difficult-to-explain uses relates to the issue that while there are some common expressions that contain a count noun with no article used (e.g., *go to church/court/school*), there are many more that involve a count noun with the definite article used when the listener may not actually know the referent (e.g., *go to the beach/doctor/hospital/store*). It seems that the best explanation is that in both cases (i.e., no article use and the use of *the*), the focus is not the particular place one is going to, but the activity involved, e.g., *going to school* = studying; *going to the store* = shopping where *the store*, as Celce-Murcia and Larsen-Freeman (1999) suggest, is used in the generic sense meaning the place where one shops. This theory of the unusual use of articles as being motivated by a focus on activity may actually be supported indirectly by a difference between American and British English: while Americans typically use *go to the hospital/be in the hospital*, the British prefer no article in these expressions, especially in the case of *in hospital*. Furthermore, some Americans also do not use *the* in these cases.

Explaining the reasons for the usual article uses can help students better understand such usages. Another useful practice for learning these unusual usages is to memorize them as fixed structures. There are some other phrases that should be learned this way, including *take the bus/train/subway*, *listen to the radio*, and *use the phone/internet* (all with *the*) and *go to bed/college/prison/town, play + any sport*, and *watch TV* (all without an article).

### 9.3.4 Corpus and discourse-based approach to a/an vs. the

As noted above, when a count, non-specific noun is first mentioned, the indefinite article is used, but when it is mentioned again, the definite article is called for. So discourse plays a key role in the use of articles. To help students better understand the important role of discourse in article use and/or to reinforce their understanding regarding this issue, we can have students do a corpus search of *there [be] a [noun]* and *there [be] the [noun]* sentences and a search of *a [noun] [be]* and *the [noun] [be]* sentences. To make the search more manageable, we can have them place a specific noun in the search, e.g. *there [be] a book*. For low-level students, the teacher can do the query with the students in class or do the query before the class and show the results.

Table 9.4 lists the results of the queries of COCA for *there be a book/boy* vs. *there be the book/boy* and *a book/boy be* vs. *the book/boy be* sentences. The results show that the frequency of *there is/was a book/boy* is more than ten times that of *there is/was the book/boy*. The teacher can ask students to explore why. With some guidance, students should recall or know that the "There be …" sentence structure is used to introduce new information, i.e., the noun in this sentence structure is always new information to the listener/reader. This explains the predominant

**TABLE 9.4** COCA query results of two pairs of contrastive sentences

| Sentence | Total tokens in COCA | Ratio |
|---|---|---|
| There is/was *a* book… | 156 | 10:1 |
| There is/was *the* book… (The book was in sight) | 15 | |
| There is/was *a* boy… | 91 | 11:1 |
| There is/was *the* boy… (The boy was in sight) | 9 | |
| *A* book is/was … | 18 | 2:100 |
| *The* book is/was… (The book already mentioned) | 856 | |
| *A* boy is/was… | 25 | 6:100 |
| *The* boy is/was | 409 | |

use of *an/an* in this sentence structure. Concerning the few "There is/was <u>the</u> [noun]" tokens, the students should be able to find out by reading the tokens that in these cases the noun being mentioned was either identified or could be sensed by the listener, e.g., "And of course, there is the book he has written." In contrast to the frequency disparity between *there be a book/boy* and *there be the book/boy*, the frequency of *A book/boy is/was* is only 2 or 6 percent of that of *The book/ boy is/was*. An exploration of the reasons for the disparity in this pair should help students understand that the extremely low frequency of a sentence beginning with *a + noun is/was* is due to the fact that we usually do not start a sentence with new information (if we need to start with new information, we use the *there be* sentence structure). The high frequency of sentences beginning with *the book/ boy is/was* structure is that we often begin a sentence with old information. The use of *the* in *The book/boy* means the noun has been mentioned previously. This corpus/discourse-based teaching activity should help students better grasp the use of not only the articles *a/an* and *the* but also the *there be [noun]* sentence structure in context. Also, going through the corpus sentence examples exposes students to authentic language input about the grammatical forms in question.

### 9.3.5 Treating the English articles as a binary system

This is not really a practice for teaching a particular aspect of the article system. Instead, it deals with the teaching of the entire article system. Developed by Master (1997), this approach treats the English articles as a binary system that serves to either classify or identify nouns/referents. The indefinite article *a/an* along with the *zero* article performs the function of classification; the definite article *the* serves the purpose of identification. Indeed, when *an/an* or the *zero* article is used, it helps to classify the noun/referent in question. For example, when a person says, "I have <u>a</u> car," it tells us, among other things, that what the speaker has is a car, not something else (classification). Yet if a person states, "This is <u>the</u> book that I recently bought," the utterance essentially identifies the book, setting it apart from any other books. This binary approach simplifies the complex article system to only two choices. Essentially, when deciding which article to use for a given noun, a person simply asks whether s/he needs to tell what it is that is being mentioned or which one it is. For the former, *a/an* or the *zero* article is used; for the latter, *the* is called for. Empirical studies reported in Master (1997) showed that this binary approach was effective in helping students more systematically grasp the use of English articles.

### Suggested teaching activities

1. *Telling what you see or what you and your family have.* This activity is meant to help low to lower-intermediate level students practice the use of articles. It may take different forms. One is to give students a picture of a room full of

various things (including both count and non-count things) and have them talk about/write down what things are in the picture. Another is to have students talk about/write down the possessions they or their families have. One more option is to have students come up with a shopping list that must include groceries. The teacher should provide feedback and explain any common problems found in the students' work.

2. *Filling in the missing articles.* Give students a passage of 150–300 words, depending on students' level. In the passage, all the articles have been removed. Ask students to add in articles wherever necessary. As an alternative (especially for lower level students), the teacher can first give students the passage with the articles still in it and have students identify all the articles. Then collect the passage and give them a version of the passage with the articles removed and have them add in the missing article.

3. *Story telling with "Once upon a time."* This activity helps students practice article usage rules, especially the rule that we use *a/an* for the first mention of a count noun and *the* for its subsequent mentions. Ask students to tell a story they are familiar with by beginning the story with the following sentence: "Once/Once upon a time, there was a/an ..."

4. *"In spring" or "in the spring."* This corpus-based activity is intended to help students learn that the names of the four seasons may be used with or without the definite article and to find out which of the two forms is more common. Ask students to do a corpus query (using COCA if possible) for both *in + a season name* and *in the + a season name* for each of the four seasons and report the frequency. Alternatively, the teacher can do the query with the class or simply provide students the query results (for low-level students). For upper-intermediate/advanced students, the teacher can ask them to read through some of the concordance lines to see if they can find any difference in meaning/usage between the two forms of the expression.

5. *"Are you eating a chicken" or "Are you eating chicken?"* This activity aims to help students reinforce their understanding that some nouns can be used either as count (preceded by *a/an*) or non-count. Give students a list of such words and ask them to make two sentences using each word. In one sentence, the word should be a count noun and in the other it should be a non-count noun. Here are some examples: art, chicken, life, paper, school, science, watermelon, wood.

## Note

1 Master (1997) actually argues that there are two *zero* articles, one alternating with *a/an* and the other alternating with *the* which he calls the *null* article. This classification is interesting and important for linguistic study, but it does not appear to be very useful for language-learning purposes.

# 10

# PREPOSITIONS, PREPOSITIONAL ADJECTIVES/ADVERBS, AND PARTICLES

To begin with, it is necessary to differentiate among *prepositions*, *prepositional adjectives/adverbs* (hereafter referred to as *adpreps*[1]), and *particles*. A preposition is a word that connects a noun or pronoun with another word or structure—typically a noun, verb, or adjective—for example, *governor of Florida*, *depends on*, and *happy about*. An adprep is a preposition that is used in the function of an adjective or adverb, i.e., without a noun phrase after it, as shown in *The light/search is still on*. A particle is an adverb or a preposition used as an adverb together with a verb to form a phrasal verb, such as *give up something* and *take on something*. (The issue of particles and phrasal verbs will be discussed again in detail in Chapter 14.) The reason that adpreps and particles are discussed together with prepositions in this chapter is that they are closely related to prepositions both in form and meaning. As far as form is concerned, most adpreps and particles are prepositions in origin and thus identical in form with them. Semantically, the adpreps and particles derive their meanings largely from the prepositions whose form they share. Equally importantly, they all express essentially spatial relations, literally or metaphorically.

This chapter is devoted to these three closely related lexical/syntactic categories because they serve very important functions in English but simultaneously they are notoriously difficult for ESFL/EFL learners, a point that will be elaborate on below. For the sake of simplicity, hereafter "prepositions" will be used to mean all the three lexical categories, with the other two terms used only when necessary for clarity. Specifically, this chapter will begin with a brief overview of English prepositions, their importance, and the difficulties they present to EFL/ESL learners. It will then offer a summary of common useful practices for teaching prepositions followed by examples of how contemporary linguistic theory and research-inspired teaching practices may help learners better grasp the semantic and usage patterns of prepositions and deal with difficult usage issues.

## 10.1 Overview: basic information, importance, and difficulties

Although small in number,[2] English prepositions are a key part of speech used for expressing and understanding both literal and figurative relations, especially spatial and temporal relations, in the physical world we human beings inhabit. The importance of prepositions is perhaps best evidenced by their extremely high frequency and ubiquity in English. Based on findings from the two billion-word OEC and the 425 million-word COCA, twelve prepositions are among the fifty most common words in the English language, including *of, to, in, for, on, with, at, by, from, out, up,* and *about*. In fact, *of, to,* and *in* are three of the ten most frequently-used words. As an example of their ubiquity, there is at least one preposition in every sentence in this chapter so far.

While prepositions are important, they are also very challenging for ESL/EFL learners. There are several reasons why prepositions are difficult to learn. First, some prepositions are multi-functional, i.e., they are also used as adpreps and particles, as has already been shown. Second and more importantly, many prepositions are polysemous. Take *over* as an example. It has over a dozen different meanings (Tyler & Evans, 2003, pp. 64–106). Here are some of them:

1. They decide to hang the picture <u>over</u> the fireplace. (Above)
2. Mary put a tablecloth <u>over</u> the desk. (Above with contact = covering)
3. The Governor has direct authority <u>over</u> this department. (In control of)
4. The thief jumped <u>over</u> the back fence to get in. (Across from one side to the other)
5. They talked <u>over</u> what to do next. (About/regarding)
6. John chose basketball <u>over</u> football. (Preference)

Third, many of the use meanings of prepositions are figurative or extended from their core prototypical meanings. For instance, *over* used in sentences 3, 5, and 6 fall into this category. Of course, if learners are made fully aware of the motivations behind such figurative or extended uses, they would not find such uses as challenging, a point that will be discussed below. However, not enough has been done by teachers in this regard. The fourth cause of difficulty is that sometimes more than one preposition may be used to express the same meaning, e.g., *a love of books* vs. *a love for books* and *rush <u>for</u> the exits* vs. *rush <u>to</u> the exits*. In other words, in some cases, the use of prepositions may vary from speaker to speaker and from one English variety to another, adding to the confusion of ESL/EFL learners. In addition to these inherent difficulties in the use of prepositions, there are also challenges arising out of language differences. As Celce-Murcia and Larsen-Freeman (2009, p. 401) point out, the work of the English prepositions "is often performed in other languages, such as German, Russian, and Latin, through inflections," especially those prepositions used to indicate role relationships, such as *by/to/for* whom. Such relationships are shown in the noun inflections in many other languages. Furthermore, the use of preposition often varies from language to language: for instance, *John is <u>at</u> home* becomes *Johann ist zu* (=*to*) *Hause* in German.

## 10.2 Established useful practices for describing and teaching prepositions

Because of the aforementioned difficulties, prepositions have always been a challenging issue for language learners and teachers alike. Teachers and material writers have developed various useful strategies and techniques for teaching prepositions. The following are a few of the most common useful practices according to findings from class observations and the survey of the grammar textbooks mentioned in Chapter 7:

1.  Use pictures and picture maps to introduce and show the basic spatial meanings of prepositions. Frequently used pictures include a/an person, animal, or object being *in* a place (e.g., a room/bird nest) or *on* something (a table/floor); a/an person/animal moving *into/out of* a place or moving *up/down* something (a stairway/tree). Picture maps are also often used because they can make preposition teaching more meaningful. Using maps, the teacher can have students talk about where they plan to go and how to get there based on the information on the map. It enables students to use prepositions in their narration, such as *walk to/toward x place, turn left on Y street*, and *arrive at* X. Physical actions are also useful for teaching prepositions, especially prepositions of location and direction (e.g., *to/from/toward*). For example, the teacher or a student can walk into/out the classroom, away from and toward the chalk board, etc. and have students describe what the person is doing. The visuals and physical actions are effective for learning/teaching prepositions because it capitalizes on students' embodied experience, the very human experience upon which the meanings of prepositions are based.

2.  List and provide the different meanings of a preposition, often with illustrative examples. For example, Celce-Murcia and Sokolik's book 5 (2009, p. 215) lists the following four meanings of *through*: "a. duration; b. pervasive quality; all over; c. by means of; d. enduring; tolerating."

3.  Have students learn, memorize, and repeatedly use fixed prepositional phrases, especially those *verb + preposition* and *adjective + preposition* phrases, such as *(be) absent from, adjust to, (be) afraid of, agree with, argue about (something) with (someone), consist of,* and *be capable of.* Such a practice is supported by the linguistic theory that language is made up of many prefabricated/semi-prefabricated expressions and by the learning theory that memorization and frequent use facilitate vocabulary and language learning (Nation, 2001). In other words, learning and using these fixed prepositional phrases help students improve their accuracy and fluency in the use of preposition, which in turn should enhance their overall language proficiency.

4.  Have students do a lot of preposition-focused exercises in which the prepositions in a sentence or passage are removed and the students are asked to

provide the missing prepositions. It is very important that such exercises are given in a meaningful way, such as having students look at a picture(s) or listen/read a story first and then fill in the missing prepositions based on the pictures or the story.

While these common teaching activities are helpful and effective to a degree, especially when used with beginning and low-level students, they become inadequate as learners' English proficiency increases. Their inadequacy appears to be in two main areas: (1) a lack of systematic exploration of the usage patterns of prepositions (especially when they are used figuratively) and of the motivations for such usage patterns; and (2) little discussion of difficult and confusing usages issues. For example, in the student textbooks that list/present fixed prepositional phrases, there is no discussion about why these phrases are used the way they are, i.e., why a specific preposition is used in a given fixed phrase. An understanding of the usage patterns and the difficult usages issue as well as the motivations behind them can help students grasp prepositions more effectively. Contemporary linguistic theories (especially those of Cognitive Linguistics) and research findings have offered many new insights that can help us more effectively enhance students' understanding in this regard. For example, according to Cognitive Linguistics, prepositions and their meanings, like language and meaning in general, are conceptual in nature and based on our embodied experience (Tyler & Evans, 2003). Furthermore, empirical studies (Cho, 2010; Tyler, 2012) have shown that understanding the embodied conceptualizations that underline the meanings of prepositions can help learners see the motivations behind the semantic/usage patterns of prepositions, which in turn enables learners to more effectively grasp these usage patterns. Below is a discussion of how this can be done with concrete examples.

## 10.3 Explaining/teaching challenging issues with new insights

### 10.3.1 At/on/in: Their usage/motivations as spatial/temporal location terms

*At*, *on*, and *in* are prepositions used first and foremost for expressing location in space. However, they are often also used to indicate a specific point or period in time thanks to our conceptualization of time in spatial terms as shown in *before/after* this week, *in* the past/future, look *forward to* the future/*back at* the past. The conceptualization of time as spatial is also evidenced by the fact that we often use the past tense in the present to create distance and appear less imposing (or more polite), as shown in *Could you help me?* The three prepositions in question are each used to reference different spatial and temporal locations, i.e., they are often not interchangeable. For example, in spatial reference, we generally say that a person lives *at* a given address *on* a given street *in* a given city, not the other

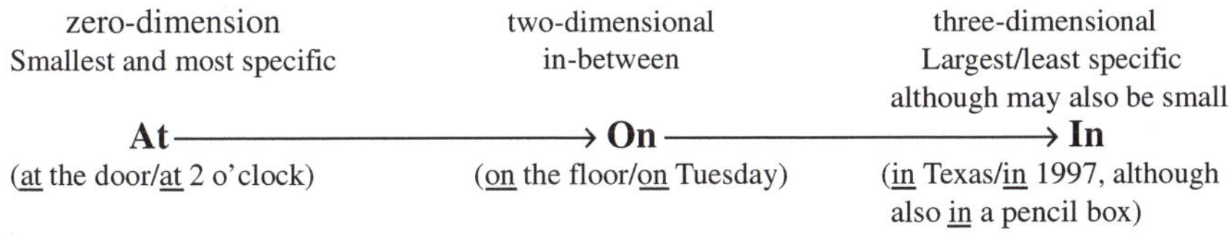

| zero-dimension | two-dimensional | three-dimensional |
|---|---|---|
| Smallest and most specific | in-between | Largest/least specific |
| | | although may also be small |

**At** ———————————————→ **On** ————————————→ **In**

(at the door/at 2 o'clock)  (on the floor/on Tuesday)  (in Texas/in 1997, although
                                                         also in a pencil box)

**FIGURE 10.1** Semantic and usage differences among *at/on/in*.

way around. Similarly, in temporal reference, we usually say that a meeting is held *at* a given hour/minute *on* a given day *in* a given month/year, not reversely. The general semantic differences among the three prepositions are summarized and illustrated in a diagram in Figure 10.1. So far, many teachers and textbooks merely present to learners these general usage patterns (i.e., *at* an address or an hour but *on* a street or day) without drawing students' attention to the bigger picture or the broad semantic and usage differences among of the three prepositions summarized and illustrated in the above diagram. Even those that do point out the general pattern differences (e.g., Celce-Murcia & Sokolik, 2008, book 2, p. 39; Keith, 2010, book 1, p. 269) often do not give and explore the reasons or motivations behind the differences.

The semantic and usage pattern differences among the three prepositions are motivated by their different prototypical meanings. *At* typically refers to a point where two lines or objects (literal or figurative) meet, e.g., *at* a junction/juncture; because a point is not even one dimensional, the space that *at* refers to is generally small. In comparison, *on* usually refers to a surface area, as shown in the common expression *on the surface of*; given that a surface is two dimensional, the space that *on* signifies is larger than that indicated by *at*. *In* suggests a three dimensional space; as such, it can be either small (e.g., *in a pencil box*) or enormously large (e.g., *in the universe*). Although the space that *on* refers to can also be very large, e.g., *on* earth, it cannot surpass the size of the space that *in* can refer to, such as the universe shown in the aforementioned *in the universe* phrase. This semantic patterning of the three prepositions can help us easily explain why we say *at home/school* but *in a city/country*. This also helps explain why *finish something on time* refers to a much more specific time (usually at the designated time) than *finish in time* (any time before the designated or designed time). Of course, given that *in* can also refer to a very small three-dimensional space, sometimes it is also used to refer to small amount of time as shown in the expression *in a minute*.

It is also important to note there are some cases where the use of the three location prepositions does not appear to comfort to the patterns described above. The first is the set phrase *at night*. Unlike *at noon* which typically refers to 12:00 at midday, *at night* usually refers to the entire night. Thus, *at* in *at night* does not refer to a very specific time. At the present, there is no known reason for this unique use of *at*. A probable reason is that night is the time for sleeping (at least for most of us) and people have no consciousness during sleep. Hence this period of time of unconsciousness is construed as being very short. Another example of usage that does not conform to the general patterns is that while we say *on the morning/afternoon/evening of a specific day*, we also say *in the morning/afternoon/evening*, e.g., "He likes to work early in the morning and in the evening." Also, while we generally treat a town/city as a three-dimensional place and talk about being *in* it, we sometimes may also use *on* and *at* as shown in the following examples from Yule (1998, p. 162):

7.   The sun is shining <u>on</u> Baton Rouge [a town in Louisiana] this morning
8.   Flight 410 to Nashville has one stop *at* Baton Rouge.

How can we explain these uses? The answer lies in the difference in construal or perspective as well as the conceptual process of metonymy. Concerning the difference between <u>on</u> and <u>in</u> *the morning/afternoon/evening*, the choice of *on* typically indicates treating the time (the morning or afternoon) in reference as a specific unit of time different from the morning or afternoon of another day, while the selection of *in* usually reflects thinking of the time in question as "an extended period of time (like a container) available" (Yule, 1998, p. 164). That is why generally whenever the date or day of the morning/afternoon/evening is specified, we use *on*: *on Wednesday morning/on the morning of January 9*. When the reference is to a habitual non-specific morning/afternoon/evening, we usually use *in*: "He likes to read *in* the morning." Regarding the use of *on* and *at* with a city, when we look down at a city from up in the air, it can be viewed as "a kind of surface with sunshine on it" as in sentence 7; and "if that city is treated as one point in a journey, essentially having no relevant dimension, then stop at it" as shown in sentence 8 (Yule, 1998, p. 162). Of course, another explanation for the use of *at* here is that the name of the city Baton Rouge is actually used metonymically to refer to its airport (a *whole for part* metonym), for when an reference is an airport (a much smaller space than a city), *at* is the usual preposition to use.

Another case that does not appear to follow the aforementioned *at/on/in* semantic usage pattern concerns the fact that all three can be used with the noun *corner*: *at/on/in the corner*. Yet a close look at these three usages will show they each refer to a different aspect or type of corner, as is shown in the drawings in Figure 10.2.

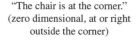  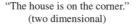

"The chair is at the corner." "The house is on the corner." "The chair is in the corner."
(zero dimensional, at or right (two dimensional) (three dimensional, inside
outside the corner) the corner)

**FIGURE 10.2** Visual illustrations of *at/on/in* the corner.

When we say *at the corner*, we typically mean the point where two lines (roads/ streets) meet, hence the common expression "I'll meet you at the corner of ..." *On the corner* is two dimensional and refers to the surface where the two roads/streets meet, hence the expression "The house/store is on the corner of ..." In contrast, *in the corner* refers to the inside of a three-dimensional corner, hence the common expression "He likes to sit in the corner."

## 10.3.2 Closely related and contrasting pairs of prepositions: pattern finding

Pattern finding will be shown by examining one pair of closely related prepositions (*after* and *behind*) and one pair of contrasting prepositions (*on* vs. *off*). Regarding *after* and *behind*, while they are often defined by dictionaries as synonyms, they are rarely synonymous in actual usage, as can be seen in the following examples:

9.  She is immediately <u>after</u> her in the race.
10. Keep moving. I'm right <u>behind</u> you.
11. I'll leave <u>after</u> nine.
12. She sits <u>behind</u> Mike.
13. The drywall is quite strong as it has solid wood <u>behind</u> it in its entirety.
14. The police are <u>after</u> him.
15. They left their past <u>behind</u> them.
16. The government is going <u>after</u> those who evade taxes by having foreign bank accounts.
17. The committee is fully <u>behind</u> her.

To guide students in finding the semantic and usage patterns of the two prepositions, we can have them examine examples like the above; for students of intermediate or advanced level, we can instead have them do a corpus query of examples by themselves. In examining the examples, the teacher can work with the whole class in doing the following: (1) determining the meaning of each sentence; (2) deciding whether the preposition in each case can be substituted by the other in the pair; and (3) identifying the semantic and usage patterns of each preposition. The teacher can also have students do the activity in pairs or groups, but the teacher should be ready to provide guidance and assistance whenever necessary.

It is clear that except in the first two sentences (9 and 10), the two prepositions are not interchangeable, especially in sentences 14 through 17 where the prepositions are used in the metaphorical senses noted by Tyler & Evans (2003, pp. 169–76). Exploring why they are not interchangeable helps understand their semantic and usage differences. The fact that only *after* can be used in sentence 11 tells us that *behind* cannot be used in reference to time or temporal sequence. On the other hand, the fact that only *behind* can be used in sentences 12 and 13 suggests that *after* cannot be used to indicate a stationary position (as sitting or being built behind something is a stationery position). In other words, these examples indicate that while *after* can refer to both spatial and temporal positions, *behind* can refer mostly to spatial ones. In contrast, while *behind* can refer to both moving and stationary spatial positions, *after* is used typically for expression moving positions. These semantic differences help account for the differences in their metaphorical usages, too. For example, the stationary or non-moving position sense of *behind* enables it to be used to mean *support* as shown in sentences 13 and 17. On the other hand, the on-the-move spatial position sense of *after* and our encyclopedic knowledge about the chase that law-enforcement officers often engage in for tracking down criminals help create the use of *be/go after* to mean to chase and track down someone. With the above exploration, we can have a clear understanding about the semantic and usage differences between *after* and *behind*.[3]

Concerning the contrasting pair *on* vs. *off* the prototypical meaning of *on* is being *in contact with/supported by*. The prototypical meaning of *off* is the opposite of *on*: being *no longer on/no longer attached to* or *away from*. Most of the extended or metaphorical meanings of each proposition are derived from its prototypical meaning. Therefore, like their core meanings, the extended meanings of the two prepositions also form a contrastive pattern. A good teaching practice is to have students examine examples of expressions (corpus-based if possible) that involve the two prepositions. Ask students to determine the meanings of the examples and find the semantic patterns of the two prepositions. The following are some examples from COCA. While the two prepositions in these example sentences are all used in the extended or figurative sense, those in the first four (18–21) are much more transparent than the rest of them.

| | | | |
|---|---|---|---|
| 18a. | Mike's comment is right <u>on target</u>. | 18b. | The outcome is entirely <u>off target</u>. |
| 19a. | The meeting is still <u>on schedule</u>. | 19b. | Everything seems to be <u>off schedule</u> recently. |
| 20a. | Let's <u>stay on topic</u>. | 20b. | The essay <u>is off topic</u>. |
| 21a. | Our economy is now <u>back on track</u>. | 21b. | High oil prices could <u>set the economic recovery off track</u>. |
| 22a. | Our record <u>on balance</u> is very good. | 22b. | This will <u>keep the militants off balance</u>. |

23.  Despite this, life <u>goes on</u>.
24.  Your accusation is completely <u>off base</u>.
25.  This proposal will <u>bring on</u> a meaningful debate about health insurance.
26.  The two carried <u>on</u> a lengthy conversation.
27.  He's <u>come off</u> the drug for three months now.
28.  Kevin <u>took off</u> on his snow board.
29.  It may <u>come off</u> as insincere.

Bearing in mind the core meanings of the two prepositions and using their embodied experience, students should be able to correctly determine the meanings of most of the sentences. If students have difficulty with some of the less transparent examples, such as *on/off track/base*, the teacher can use pictures (for *on/off railway tracks/a base*) and body actions (for *being balanced/unbalanced*) to help them understand the meanings. Then ask students to identify any semantic patterns. Based on these examples, *on* has the following meanings: (1) being/doing as desired/intended/planned; (2) doing/working in a continuous fashion (*go on/carry on*); and (3) in existence/operation (*bring on*; *turn on a computer*). In contrast, *off* carries the following meanings: (1) not being/doing as desired/intended/planned; (2) stopped (*come off the drug*; *turn off the computer*); (3) left abruptly and/or quickly (*take off*); and (4) appear differently from reality (*come off as insincere*).

### 10.3.3 Using embodied experience/construal to explain difficult usage issues

When a preposition (including its adpreps and particle) is used in the prototypical meaning, it is usually easy to understand. For example, in the case of *up*, *go up a hill*, *hang/put up a banner*, and "Oil prices are up (or have gone up)" are easy because these expressions are based on the prototypical meaning of *up* being higher and more. However, usages based on the extended or metaphorical meanings of a preposition are often more difficult to understand if one does not know how the extended meanings have derived from the prototypical meaning. Examples of such usages include *brush up one's second language* and *shut up (a) shop/a window*. The difficulty in such usages becomes more challenging when two prepositions of opposite meanings are used to mean basically the same thing, e.g., *shut up* and *shut down* something (both meaning "to close," although the situations we use each may differ). However, if we understand how the extended meanings of a preposition have actually derived from its prototypical meaning via our embodied experience, then it will be much easier to grasp them. Let us take *up* and *down* as examples.

The two major extended meanings of *up* are *betterment/improvement* and *completion*. Both senses, as Tyler and Evans (2003) convincingly show, are clearly derived from the prototypical meanings of the word: *higher/more*. Concerning its betterment sense, based on our embodied experience, *up* is generally better than *down* and having more of something "often implicates improvement or betterment" (Tyler & Evans, 2003, p. 139). For instance, when we have more energy, we generally feel better. It is this *higher/more = better* experience that gives the betterment meaning to expressions like *brush up*, *cheer up*, and *dress up*. The completion meaning of *up* is based on our experience of filling a container, especially liquid containers. When a container, such as a bottle, is filled up to its limit, it is completely full, hence the sense of completion. This explains the use of *up* in *charge up*, *finish up*, and *stock up*. As for the preposition *down*, its two major extended meanings are *worse/inferior* and *completion* and both senses are derived from its prototypical *lower/less* senses (Tyler & Evans, 2003). It is our experience that a decrease in something often leaves it in a worse and inferior position. This experience motivates expressions such as *[be] down in the dumps, look down upon,* and *put someone down.* Regarding the completion sense of *down,* when something is decreased to zero/none, it is completely gone, hence its completion sense. This sense helps account for expressions such as *burn down, close down,* and *run down* (e.g., *a supply runs down*).

The following are few more examples about how difficult-to-explain usages can be better understood based on our experience and construal/viewpoint. The first deals with why we generally say *in a/the car* but *on a bus/plane/ship/train.* This is because a car is so small that we can only sit *in* it, i.e., we cannot easily move around in it. In contrast, a bus/plane/ship/train is much larger and we can move around *on* its deck. Then one wonders why sometimes we can also say that someone or something is *in* a/the bus/plane/train. The answer is that when we use *in,* it is typically when we are looking at and talking about people or things in a stationary bus/plane/train, for example, "I still see some people <u>in</u> the train" and "The lights <u>in</u> the train have just gone out." The following two examples help further illustrate how the outside vs. inside perspectives may influence the speaker's choice of *in* or *on* in such cases:

30. "Stay in the train. I'll get you there in a few second." (Speaker outside the train)
31. "We're just making a short stop. Everyone please stay on the train." (Speaker inside)

Another example relates to *go down* vs. *go up* a road/street. We often hear both used. Learners often ask which one to use. There are several factors that may influence a speaker's choice and these factors are again tied to the speaker's physical location and perspective. Typically, if the speaker is standing at the lower point of the street (e.g., the bottom of a slope) and the direction of the road/street he/she is looking or pointing at is higher, *go up* would be the choice. If the situation is the opposite (e.g., the speaker is at the top of a slope), *go down* will be used. Also, if the street numbers in the direction you are going are becoming larger, we would tend to use *go up*; otherwise, we would use *go down.* The other factor is whether the direction one is headed is north or south. If it is north, we generally opt for *up*; if it is south, we would choose *down.* A related example concerns the use of <u>*at/on/in*</u> *a/the street* as shown in the following examples:

32. I'm now at 12th street.
33. There're a lot of people on the street.
34. We are now dancing in the street in Pittsburgh.

It is important to note that based on COCA data *on the street* is by far the most common followed by *in the street*. *At* is used mostly in *at X street*. Which one to use is again determined by the speaker's perspective or construal (Tyler & Evans, 2003). *At* is used when in referencing the point where two streets meet. For instance, in sentence 32 when the speaker made the utterance, s/he must have been walking or driving on a street and just arrived at 12th street. The choice of *on the street* is typically made when the speaker is viewing the street as a surface (two dimensional) whereas the selection of *in the street* is usually the result of the speaker looking at the street as a three-dimensional entity with the buildings on the two sides of the street clearly in view.

The final examples deals with why *go through* is positive whereas *fall through* is negative when both phrases contain the same adprep *through*. Although the question may not be an issue for native speakers of English, it is often puzzling for ESL/EFL learners. As we know, *go through* means "become accepted or approved" while *fall through* means "fail." It is much easier to understand the positive meaning of *go through* because "through" indicates the completion of a process and go is intentional and purposeful; if an intended action is completed, it is certainly positive from the perspective of the intender. On the other hand, with *fall through*, the verb *fall* dictates its negative meaning. This is because generally no one would intentionally fall (except for committing suicide or some other unusual purposes). If someone or something indeed fell and *fell through* (meaning a completed fall), it would mean the thing was either totally destroyed or seriously damaged: hence the meaning of failure. It is necessary to note that *through* can also mean "in one side and out of the other" and this meaning is used metaphorically in the *fall through the cracks* idiom, which means becoming lost/unnoticed and unattended to.

## Suggested teaching activities

1. *Is it to fill* in *or fill* out *a form?* This activity aims to help students understand how the use of prepositions or prepositional particles is affected by construal. Tell students that in American English, to complete a form is to *fill out* a form, but in British English it is to *fill in* a form. Ask students to explore and explain why American speakers use *out* whereas British speakers use *in*. Ask them to think what image they have for the act of *filling in* a form or anything for that matter and what image they have for *filling out* a form. This should lead them to the understanding that *fill in* focuses on the act of putting in information in the vacant spaces in the form while *fill out* concentrates on the result of the spaces being filled up/out. In other words, the Americans and the British construe the act of completing a form differently.

2. *Finding the meanings of* in *and* out of. This a corpus-based deductive learning activity in which students try to find examples for the semantic patterns of *in* and *out of* used in the "state" sense (i.e., being in or out of a state such as

danger or love)—one of the key meanings of *in* and *out of*. Before doing the activity, students should have learned that when used in the "state" sense, the two prepositional phrases can refer to (1) emotional/mental state (e.g., *in/ out of love/misery/mourning*), (2) physical state (*in/out of jail/repair/shape*), or (3) some abstract state or condition (*in/out of danger/luck/operation/ service/ session/sync*), as well as (4) the profession or trade one is engaged in (*in banking/education/medicine*). In this activity, students need to find at least five examples for each of the four types of state. Students may work individually or in pairs/groups. After the students are finished, ask them to share their examples and explain why they classify the state type of each of the examples the way they did.

3.  *Checking out <u>above</u> vs. <u>over</u> and <u>below</u> vs. <u>under</u>.* This is a two-part activity for teaching the differences between *above* and *over* and between *below* and *under* (the reason for teaching the two pairs together is that they mirror each other in meaning and use). The teacher may choose to teach just one pair. The first part of the activity is especially suited for low-level students. The second part may be more appropriate for students of at least a lower-intermediate level proficiency.

    In part 1, the teacher can use pictures, diagrams, and/or everyday objects to help students understand visually and conceptually the similarity and difference between the two prepositions. For example, the teacher can have pictures showing a flat TV *above/over* a fireplace, a tablecloth *over* a desk, and the moon in the sky *above* a landscape on earth. Ask students to describe the pictures/diagrams by using the right prepositions. Then have them determine and summarize the semantic and usage differences between the two prepositions. With visuals as an aid, the students should uncover and learn the following two key differences: (1) anything said to be *above* another thing or person cannot be in contact with the latter (this differentiates it from *over*); and (2) anything over another thing has to be either in contact with the latter or within the latter's potential reach, i.e., it cannot be too high above the latter; otherwise the preposition *above* should be used (see Tyler & Evans, 2003, pp. 110–121 for more details on this issue). The semantic differences between *below* and *under* are essentially identical to those between *above* and *over*. So, the teaching activity and procedure can be the same.

    In part 2, have students read and understand the following sentences that contain the preposition *above*. Tell them that the preposition in each sentence cannot be substituted with *over*. Ask them to think about why this is the case, keeping in mind the key differences between the two prepositions.

    1.  The CEO said his conduct was above suspicion.
    2.  Many believe that the Pope's character is above criticism (reproach).
    3.  His performance was above expectations.

Sentences 1 and 2 try to convey the sense that the CEO's behavior and the Pope's character were clearly superior beyond any suspicion/criticism. *Over* will thus be inappropriate because it would imply that the CEO and the Pope were close to being suspicious or reproachable. In sentence 3, *over* will not be very appropriate because it would suggest that the person's performance was just slightly above expectation.

4. *Be aware of the difference between to and at when used after verbs.* Give students the following two pairs of sentences that involve the use of the prepositions *to* and *at*:

| | |
|---|---|
| 1a. Tom threw the book to John. | 1b. Tom threw the book at John. |
| 2a. The manager went to Mike. | 2b. The manager went at Mike. |

Have them identify any semantic difference between the two sentences in each pair. If students have difficulty, tell them to focus on the two prepositions. Provide some assistance if necessary. After the differences are identified, ask students to explore and explain the reason for the semantic difference. Again tell them to think about the prototypical meanings of the two propositions. At the end of the activity, students should understand that *to* simply indicates the goal of an action, but *at*, due to its prototypical meaning of a sharp focus and the strong intensity that comes with a sharp focus, typically conjures up the image of a target that one tries to hit (see Tyler, 2012, pp. 152–154 for more detail). This difference should help explain why "throw an object *at* someone" means to try to hit someone with it and why "go *at* someone" means to tensely or relentlessly criticize someone.

5. *Is it made of or from wood?* This activity is designed to help students better grasp the use of *made of* and *made from*, a difficult topic for some ESL/EFL students. For low-level students, give them some sentence examples like those below (taken/adapted from COCA). For students of intermediate-level, have them do a corpus search of both structures.

1. The desk is made of wood.
2. The sculpture is made of glass.
3. The door is made of steel.
4. The fabric is made from wood (pulp).
5. Pesticides are made from oil.
6. This charcoal is made from wood.

Then ask them to examine the examples closely to uncover the general principles for choosing one of the two phrases. Tell students to think of the prototypical meanings of the two prepositions and try to identify any differences between the proto sentences. If they have difficulty, explain that both have the material source sense but which indicates a more close/

direct relation between the thing and the source. Students should not have much difficulty in determining that *of* conveys a more close/direct relation than *from*, a preposition highlight a distance *from* a source to a target. This helps explain that if the source from which something is made is no longer clearly observable, *from* should be used, as shown in examples 4–5.

## Notes

1  This term has been used by Tyler and Evans (2003) to refer to the same type of use of prepositions as adverbials to be defined.
2  While the exact number of prepositions in English is difficult to determine, especially if we include complex prepositions (those made up of two or more words), it is generally believed to be no more than 150 in total.
3  It is important to note that there are some cases where two prepositions are entirely synonymous and their only difference lies in register or style, e.g., *act/depend on* vs. *act/depend upon* and *different from* vs. *different than*. In such cases, we can have students do cross-register corpus queries to learn their register difference.

# 11

## STRUCTURAL ALTERNATION

### English Object Placement, Subject/Object Deletion, and the Passive Voice

This chapter covers three interesting but challenging English structural alternation issues: object placement, subject/object omission, and the passive voice. Structural alternation means the alternate forms that a given structure may assume, as will be shown below. Structural alternation issues are challenging because ESL/EFL learners often do not know when and why an alternate form of a given structure is used or selected and what semantic implications its selection has. Helping ESL/EFL learners understand these questions are essential for them to correctly grasp of the usages of the alternate forms.

## 11.1 Explaining/teaching object placement with new insights

There are two difficult object placement issues in English. One concerns the issue of the placement of the direct and indirect objects used with ditranstive verbs. The other involves the placement of the single object in a phrasal verb with a separable particle (e.g., turn *down the offer*/turn *the offer down*). The two issues are looked at in detail below.

### 11.1.1 Placement of the direct and indirect objects

As mentioned above, the indirect object of many ditransitive verbs may appear directly after the verb before the direct object or after the direct object in a *to/ for* prepositional phrase:

1a. *Mary gave Tom the idea.*            1b. *Mary gave the idea to Tom.*

In other words, the position of the direct object and the position of the indirect object may alternate. However, not all two-object verbs allow this alternation. For example, for verbs such as *donate*, *contribute*, *explain*, and *suggest*, we allow only the prepositional structure for the indirect object. We cannot say:

2.  *\*Mary donated/contributed the school money.*
3.  *\*Mary explained/suggested Tom the idea.*

Furthermore, some verbs that usually permit the alternation of the direct/ indirect object positions may disallow it in certain cases:

4a. *Give me a hug.*                    4b. \**Give a hug to me.*

In addition, when the direct object is in the form of a pronoun, then it cannot be placed after the indirect object; e.g., we cannot say:

5. \*Mary gave Tom it [the idea.].

While some textbooks and teachers have included these object placement usage issues/rules in their teaching, there was not much exploration about the motivations for the usage rules until the 1990s, when linguists began to use Cognitive linguistic and discourse analyses to examine the topic (e.g., Goldberg, 1995, 2006; Tyler, 2012; Yule, 1998). So far, Cognitive linguistic and discourse analyses have offered us interesting insights into the motivations of these usage rules. These insights should be incorporated into teaching. If we recall the discussion in Chapter 4, language, according to Cognitive Linguistics, is composed of symbolic units or constructions, which are pairings of form and meaning. Hence, constructions, including unfilled schematic ones, are meaningful. The V + N + N ditransitive construction (but not including its alternative V + N + prep structure) has the meaning of Cause-to-Receive. The following example shows that only the V + N + N ditransitive construction has the Cause-to-Receive meaning. When we say "X bought something for Y," it can mean either that X bought it and gave it to Y" or that X bought it on Y's behalf. However, when we say "X bought Y something," it can only mean that X bought it and gave it to Y due to the meaning of this construction. The reason that only the V + N + N ditransitive has the Cause-to-Receive meaning is due to our conceptualization that "the proximity of form correlates with closeness (inherence) of meaning (or strength of effect)" (Kövecses, 2006, pp. 361–362). In other words, it reflects our embodied experience that the closer the two entities, the stronger the bond or transmission between the two if transmission is attempted. This explains why "She taught the children to draw" and "She taught drawing to the children" do not convey exactly the same meaning. The former sentence implies the children learned to draw, but the latter does not have this implication, because the learners in the latter sentence structure are much farther away from the verb than they are in the first sentence. Because the V + N + N ditransitive construction has the Cause-to-Receive meaning, verbs that do not have this meaning (e.g., *cook/knit/open*) automatically inherit it when used in this construction, as shown in "Tom cooked Mary a dinner;" "Jean knitted John a sweater;" "Mike opened Joe a beer."

Based on the above explanation, expressions that contradict this Cause-to-Receive meaning are not allowed in this construction. For example, as Goldberg

(1995) explains, while we say *sent Tom a book*, we do not say *send Canada a book* because, based on our world knowledge and experience, only a person can be a natural recipient of a book. It is not natural for a place to be a recipient. Similarly, we can say *open someone a beer* but not *open someone a door* because, when opening a door, we usually do not and cannot give it to the person we open it for. Our world knowledge also helps us understand why *give someone a hug/kiss* is natural but *give a hug/kiss to someone* is not: it is impossible to physically give a kiss to a person not adjacent to you (a meaning expressed by *\*give a kiss to someone* where the recipient is away as indicated by the preposition *to*). This also explains why both *blow someone a kiss* and *blow a kiss to someone* sound natural: it is possible to blow a kiss to a person not adjacent to you.

It is also important to know that the Cause-to-Receive meaning and usage of the ditransitive construction "originated in Old Germanic [Old English]; it was not part of Latin and Latinate languages" (Tyler, 2012, p. 180). This helps explain why verbs with a Romance language origin cannot be used this way even though they do carry the Cause-to-Receive meaning, such as the verbs *donate*, *contribute*, *explain*, and *suggest* mentioned above. Verbs of a Romance language origin are fairly easy to detect: they usually consist of more than one syllable. In contrast, verbs with Old Germanic origin are short, usually made up of one syllable: *buy/get/give/show/tell*.

Regarding the rule that a direct object in the pronoun form must be placed before the indirect object, it is based on the general discourse rule that rheme (old information) should be given first and new information (theme) or information that should be emphasized should be placed at the end of an utterance. When we use a pronoun *it/them* to refer to a direct object, it must be the case that the direct object has already been mentioned, e.g.,

6.  A: Could you lend me *your biology textbook?*
    B: I've given *it* to Mike.

It would violate the aforementioned discourse rule to say *\*I've given Mike it*.

### 11.1.2 Placement of the object in separable phrasal verbs

The same discourse rule that accounts for the usage patterns of the placement of the direct/indirect object positions also helps explain the position alternations of the object used in the transitive phrasal verb structure with a separate particle. Celce-Murcia and Olshtain (2000) offer an excellent explanation on this issue using examples like the following.

7.  Tom shut down *his shop*.
8.  Tom shut *his shop* down.

Based on a pure sentence-level grammatical analysis, the two sentences are semantically equivalent. However, based on a functional-discourse analysis using the concept of given vs. new information, the two sentences are not truly equivalent, for the variation of the object is motivated by discourse context. The word order shown in sentence 7 "would be preferred in contexts where the direct object … was truly new or specially emphasized information," whereas the word order shown in sentence 8 "would be preferred where the direct object had already mentioned but was not sufficiently recent or well established as old information to justify the use of the pronoun [it]" as in "Tom shut it down." (Celce-Murcia & Olshtain, 2000, pp. 56–57). In other words, concerning where the object should be placed in a separable transitive phrasal verb structure, there are three options. The first is to place the object after both the verb and the particle as in "Tom shut down *his shop*." This option is typically chosen when the object is new information or information that needs to be emphasized, e.g., when responding to the question "What did Tom shut down?" The second option is to change the object from the noun form to the form of a pronoun and place it between the verb and the particle as in "Tom shut *it* down." This option is used only when the object is old information, e.g., when answering the question "What did Tom do with his shop?" The third option is to place the object noun directly between the verb and the particle as in "Tom shut *his shop* down." This option is typically used when the object is neither completely new nor completely old information, e.g., when responding to a question that involves an earlier mention of the object—one like the following: "I've heard Tom's shop is not doing well. That's a shame, but it's sort of understandable in this recession. Do you know what Tom plans to do?"

The fact that a direct object in the pronoun form as old information must be placed before the particle is again motivated by the discourse rule that old information should be provided first. In summary, the placement of an object is determined by three key factors: conceptual meaning, discourse, and purpose/focus of communication. Exploring and understanding the reasons for the object position alternation patterns should help ESL/EFL students more effectively grasp them.

## 11.2 Explaining/teaching subject/object deletion with new insights[1]

### 11.2.1 Patterns of permissible subject/object omissions in English

English has been classified as a non **pro-drop language**, i.e., a language that does not allow subject/objection omissions (as reported in Liu, 2008a, 2008b; White, 1985, 1989). This classification is made largely in comparison with many other languages that allow extensive subject and/or object deletions, including most Romance languages (e.g., Spanish/Italian/Portuguese, which permit a broad dropping of the subject) and some Asian languages (e.g., Chinese/

Japanese, which allow an extensive omission of both the subject and the object). Research has shown that ESL/EFL learners with a pro-drop L1 tend to transfer L1 subject/object omissions into English (Liu, 2008b; White, 1985, 1989; Yuan 1997). For a long time, researchers who dealt with the issue focused exclusively on English as a non-pro-drop language and on the difference between English and learners' L1. However, recent corpus studies and cognitive analysis (Liu, 2008a, 2008b; Goldberg, 2005) have shown that English actually also allow some subject and object deletions, as can be seen in the following examples:

 9. "[It] Sounds good."
10. "[I] Hope you like it."
11. "The football coach gives [money] to charity regularly"
12. "Not everyone is like that." "I know [that/it]."
13. "Gently wash and drain [core cabbage]; place [it] in a deep jar." [Instruction]

To avoid repetition, the exact extent and the contexts in which such omissions occur will be described below when discussing how to help learners accurately grasp the issue.

The fact that subject/object omissions occur in English has important pedagogical implications. Seeing such omissions, ESL/EFL learners with a pro-drop L1 may incorrectly view them as positive evidence for licensing a transfer of the broad subject/object omissions from their L1 into English. What further complicates the issue is that empirical studies cited in Liu (2008b) have shown that while Spanish/Italian speakers commit only non-permissible English subject omissions (i.e., they do not omit objects), Chinese/Japanese speakers commit mostly non-permissible object deletions, i.e., they seldom omit subjects, even though their L1 also allows a broad use of null-subject. How do we explain this? Liu (2008b) argues that this difference between the two L1 groups must have resulted from different L1 influences on the way they interpret the subject/object omissions in English. It is well known that L2 learners often "misanalyse the L2 data they are exposed to, in order to make it confirm as far possible to the parameter values imposed by the L1" (Towell & Hawkins, 1994, p. 117). It is thus logical for Spanish/Italian-speaking ESL/EFL learners and the Chinese/Japanese-speaking ESL/EFL learners to misinterpret the data differently.

For Spanish/Italian-speaking ESL/EFL learners, the presence of null subjects plus the subject–verb agreement features in English (third-person singular and the inflected *be*) may constitute enough "positive" evidence for assuming that, as in their L1, it is the subject–verb agreement inflection for verbs that licenses subject omissions in English. This is because when these learners hear subjectless English utterances, they are likely to note two important features. First, there are no subjects in these English sentences. Second, subject–verb agreement is required in English as shown in the verb inflections in the subject omission examples (e.g., the third-person singular *-s* in *Sounds good* and its absence in first-person subject omission as in *Hope you like it*). As these two grammatical features (null subjects and verb inflections) match those of their L1, it would be very natural for Spanish/Italian speakers to assume that their L1 pro-drop rule also applies in English, resulting in a wide use of null subjects in their English. The reason that there is no transfer of null objects by these speakers is that, as indicated earlier, languages such as Spanish and Italian do not license object omission and, furthermore, there is no verb–object agreement in English. These two factors help prevent Spanish/Italian ESL/EFL learners from seeing the occurrence of null object utterances in English as a license for null objects.

In contrast, English subject/object omissions may lead to a very different response from Chinese/Japanese ESL learners. First, Chinese and Japanese are non-inflectional language (i.e., there is no verb inflection for indicating subject–verb agreement). So, when these learners notice the subject–verb agreement inflections in subject-less English utterance (*Sounds good*), it works as a block preventing Chinese/Japanese speakers from transferring null subjects (Liu, 2008b; Yuan, 1997). In other words, the third-person singular *-s* and the inflection of the verb *to be* may remind them of the difference between English and their native language, causing them to provide the subject in order to help them generate the correct verb form. On the other hand, the lack of agreement between verb and object in English (as in Chinese and Japanese) and the presence of English null objects may work as a catalyst prodding them to transfer null objects from their L1.

Because of the aforementioned problems, it is important for teachers to help ESL/EFL learners avoid the trap of mistaking permissible subject/object deletions in English as positive evidence for extensive use of null subjects/objects in English. Learners need to understand how the use of null subjects/objects in English differs from the pro-drop practice in their L1. Empirical studies reviewed by Liu (2008b) have shown that instruction can help L2 students significantly reduce the use of non-permissible null subjects/objects. However, given that ESL/EFL learners from different pro-drop L1 backgrounds face different challenges in learning non-null subjects/objects, it will be necessary to develop language descriptions and instructions tailored to the different needs of the students of different L1 groups. With the established knowledge that speakers of Romance pro-drop languages only have problems of using non-permissible null subjects (i.e., they do not have any problem of using non-permissible null objects), instruction for ESL learners from such an L1 background should concentrate exclusively on helping them avoid null subjects. In contrast, for Chinese/Japanese (also other languages that allow extensive object omissions), instruction should focus on helping them prevent non-permissible null objects. Below is a discussion of how to help each of the two groups separately. Before proceeding, however, it is important to note that regardless of your students' L1, when helping students learn to avoid non-permissible subject/object omissions, first tell them that generally they should not omit any subject or object because it is always correct to supply it. When students reach a higher proficiency and are familiar with the contexts where subject/object omissions are permitted, then they can begin cautiously using acceptable null subjects/objects.

## 11.2.2 Teaching subject-deletion to Spanish ESL/EFL learners

For Spanish (and similar Romance language) speaking EFL/ESL learners, teaching materials and instructions for unlearning impermissible subject-deletions should highlight the differences in the use of null subjects in English and their L1. Language description and learning activities should aim to help the students figure out that null subjects in English are not licensed in the way they are in their L1. Instead, the use of null-subjects in English is confined to only certain verbs in sentence initial positions and limited mostly to singular first person *I* and third person *it* used in face-to-face interactions. We can present students with pairs of sentences to compare and contrast the null-subject use between the English and their L1, as shown in the following examples between English and Spanish (any acceptable null subject in the examples is placed in a parenthesis):

| English | Spanish |
|---|---|
| 14a. "(It) sounds good." | 14b. "(Eso) tiene sentido [(It) has sense]." |
| 15a. "(I) hope you're right." | 15b. "(Yo) espero que (tú) tengas razón [(I) hope you have reason]." |
| 16a. "I watched it." | 16b. "(Yo) lo mire [(I) it watched]." |
| 17a. "He watched it." | 17b. "(Él) lo miró [(He) it watched]." |
| 18a. "We watched it." | 18b. "(Nosotros) lo miramos [(We) it watched]." |
| 19a. "They watched it." | 19b. "(Ellos) lo miraron [(They) it watched]." |

It is clear from these examples that while all the subjects in the Spanish sentences can be deleted, only two in English can (14a and 15a). This contrastive knowledge should help prevent students from viewing the limited occurrence of null subjects in English as evidence for allowing a broad agreement-based subject deletion.

## 11.2.3 Teaching object-deletion to Chinese ESL/EFL learners

Helping Chinese (also Korean/Japanese) ESL/EFL learners in dealing with English object deletions is a much more challenging task due to the fact that there are several contexts/situations in which an object may be omitted in English. Generally, it is not a good idea to first present to these learners a complete description of the contexts because it would give them an unnecessary learning burden and cause more confusion. It is best to first emphasize that, in comparison with the broad use of null objects in their L1, the use of null objects in English is quite limited. The teacher can present students with pairs of sentences for a comparison and contrast, as shown in the following English vs. Chinese examples.

| **English** | **Chinese** |
|---|---|
| 20a. "There's no class today." | 20b. "jintian mei ke [today no class]". |
| "I know (that)." | "(wo) zidao [(I) know]." |
| 21a. "Do you like the book?" | 21b. "ni xihuan zhe ben shu ma? [You like this book question marker?]" |
| "Yes, I like it" (or "Yes, I do.") | "(wo) xihuan [(I) like]." |
| 22a. "Please give me Tom's address if you have it." | 22b. "qin ge wo Li de dizi ruguo ni you [Please give me Li's address if you have]." |
| 23a. "If you buy a car, I'll buy one, too." | 23b. "ruguo ni mai che, we ye mai [If you buy car, I also buy]." |

From these examples, one can see that object deletion is very limited in English (only in example 20a). One can deduce that object deletion in English is not allowed for most verbs, as evidenced by 21a, 22a, and 23a, even though the objects in these examples could be easily recovered from the discourse context. In contrast with English, null objects in Chinese are always permitted as long as a deleted object is identifiable from the contextual information. This difference is fully understandable because, as explained in Chapter 3, Chinese culture (as well as Korean/Japanese cultures) is high context where meanings are not explicitly expressed but are drawn from context; in contrast, American/British cultures are low context where things must be spelt out. Giving students this information should also help them better understand the differences in subject/object omissions between English and their L1.

There is another point that we need to draw Chinese ESL/EFL students' attention to when teaching object deletion: the common use of an auxiliary alone (such as "do" and "have") in English as a response to a question. For example, in 21a, the typical response to "Do you like the book?" is not really "Yes, I like it" but "Yes, I do" where *do* stands for the verb *like* and the object pronoun *it*. In other words, both the verb and the object are deleted. Such use of an auxiliary with the verb and object deleted may be mistaken by Chinese ESL/EFL learners as evidence for object deletion. Given that auxiliary-based substitutions and omissions are very common in speech, it is extremely important to make sure these learners understand that whenever an auxiliary is used in such a case, both the verb and the object are omitted. In other words, it is not a case of object deletion. In fact, no object deletion alone is allowed in such cases in English, as can be seen in:

24. "Do you play golf?" "Yes, I do." (But *not* "I do play.")
25. "Have you seen the movie?" "Yes, I have." (But *not* "I've seen.")

After learners are made aware of the differences between English and their L1 in the use of null objects, we may gradually explain to them the extent and the contexts in which object deletion is allowed in English, as it will help them gain a better understanding of the issue. There are essentially three types of null-object use (Liu, 2008b). The first is the discourse-context warranted use (mostly in face-to-face conversation) as shown in the exchange:

26a. "You have to work hard to pass the course."     26b. "I know [it]."

Verbs can be used in this manner include *explain, find out, know, promise, see,* and *understand*. Some dictionaries list these verbs as intransitive when used without an object, but such a classification is incorrect. True intransitive verbs can be used without any discourse context, e.g., "Tom *ate* last night" where *ate* is intransitive and the meaning is clear. Yet we cannot say, "Tom *explained/knew* last night." Listeners/readers will need to know what Tom explained/knew for the utterance to be truly meaningful. In face-to-face interactions, the deleted object is recoverable or known by the listener.

The second use of object omission is situation-warranted, such as in instructions on warning signs or product manuals as shown below:

27.   Bake for 45 minutes … (instruction on a cake mix box)
28.   Shake well before use. (instruction on medicine bottle)
29.   Don't touch! (a sign near a newly painted area)

The third type of object omission is what (Goldberg, 2005) calls "the implicit/de-profiled theme [object]" construction where the object of a transitive verb is omitted, as shown in the following examples taken from Goldberg (2005) and Liu (2008a):

30.   Tom blew/sneezed into the paper bag.
31.   John gives to charity regularly.
32.   Tigers only kill at night.
33.   We all have to give and take.

According to Goldberg, there are two major reasons for omitting the object in these cases. First, the object is something unpleasant/inappropriate to mention, as in sentence 30 where what Tom blew/sneezed into the paper bag was obviously some bodily fluid—something unpleasant—and in sentence 31 where what John gives to charity must be money, and it is often considered inappropriate in the West to mention how much money one gives to charity. Second, the object is not the focus of the utterance, as in sentences 32 and 33 where the focus is on the activity (e.g., killing/giving/taking), not the object. Understanding the motivations for de-profiling/omitting the theme/object should enable students to better understand when and where the object can be deleted.

Finally, it is important to note that the discussion in this section highlights two important issues in lexicogrammatical description/explanation. First, vocabulary and grammar are inseparable, for subject/object deletions are often verb-specific. Second, a more accurate description of a grammatical structure and its usage rules can lead to more informed instruction tailored to the unique needs of learners from different L1 backgrounds. By exploring the rules/patterns of permissible subject/object deletions in English (rather than treating it simply as a non-pro-drop language), we are able to provide accurate usage rules targeted specifically to help ESL learners with different L1s based on their unique learning difficulties.

## 11.3 Explaining/teaching the passive voice with new insights

Although some linguists and language educators advise against the use of the passive voice, this sentence structure actually plays an important and sometimes indispensable role in effective communication (*Merriam-Webster dictionary of English usage*, 1994). For example, in some cases, the theme (object), rather than the agent (subject), of an action is the focus in a communication event. In some other cases, the agent of an action is unknown. The following passage from an online Wikipedia article about "gunpowder" (2012) can help illustrate both points (the passive voice structures in the quote are italicized):

> Gunpowder *is classified* as a low explosive because of its relatively slow decomposition rate and consequently low brisance … Gunpowder is thus less suitable for shattering rock or fortifications. Gunpowder *was widely used* to fill artillery shells and in mining and civil engineering to blast rock roughly until the second half of the 19th century, when the first high explosives (nitro-explosives) were discovered. Gunpowder *is no longer used* in modern explosive military warheads, *nor is it used* as main explosive in mining operations due to its cost relative to that of newer alternatives such as ammonium nitrate/fuel.

It is clear that in this piece, gunpowder is the focus, not who has made or used it. As a result, the passive voice is used extensively in this passage. Existing textbooks all seem to do a good job in mentioning/explaining this and its related reasons as our main motivation for using the passive. They often provide a list of such reasons for using the passive without mentioning the agent, such as the following given in Elbaum's book 3 (1996, p. 53):

> We do not know who performed the action or it is not important to say who performed the action.
> The performer of the action is obvious.
> We make a general statement.

We want to avoid mentioning the performer.

We want to give an impersonal tone, especially in scientific and technical writing.

However, no textbook appears to have mentioned discourse context as another important motivation for the use of the passive. As noted previously, in English, we typically begin a sentence with given or old information. If the given information happens to be the object of the action in the new sentence, then the passive voice becomes a more natural and preferable choice, as can be seen in the following excerpts from a brief online article on the history of wild turkeys by Mayntz (2012):

> Wild turkeys are instantly recognizable game birds, and while they *are often seen* as gullible and comical, they have a noble history in their native North America.

> … Turkeys *were revered* in ancient Aztec and Mayan civilizations. The Aztecs honored the wild turkey – huexolotlin – with religious festivals twice a year, and believed turkeys to be a bird manifestation of Tezcatlipoca, a trickster god. Because of that spiritual connection, the feathers of turkeys *were frequently used* to adorn necklaces, jewelry and clothing…

> Even while turkeys *were honored* by ancient civilizations, they *were also recognized* as an important food source…

Because the topic of the article is *wild turkeys*, eight of the nine clauses (verbs) have *wild turkeys* as the subject (the given information). More importantly, five of the verbs are in the passive voice due not only to the need of keeping *wild turkeys* as the focus but also the need to ensure discourse flow of the article (the old-to-new information flow). The only different subject in the passage is in the sentence that begins with "The Aztecs honored the wild turkey …," but its use is due to the fact that Aztec has been mentioned in the previous sentence, i.e., it is not new information. In language teaching, we can help learners understand the need or value of using the passive voice in such context by showing them that if we replace the passive voice structures, it would make the passage choppy, as can be seen if we reword the above passage in the following way (the passive to active voice changes are underlined):

> Wild turkeys are instantly recognizable game birds, and while <u>people often see them</u> as gullible and comical, they have a noble history in their native North America.

> … <u>Ancient Aztecs and Mayans revered</u> turkeys. The Aztecs honored the wild turkey – huexolotlin – with religious festivals twice a year, and

believed turkeys to be a bird manifestation of Tezcatlipoca, a trickster god. Because of that spiritual connection, the Aztecs used the feathers of turkeys to adorn necklaces, jewelry and clothing …

Even while ancient people honored turkeys, they also recognized them as an important food source …

In short, it is very important for the teacher to help students understand the key factors that influence our choice of the active or passive voice as well as the typical contexts in which the passive voice is preferred. There are basically two key factors: (1) the speaker/writer's purpose/construal; and (2) discourse context. The typical contexts in which the passive is preferred or needed include: (1) the object of the action is the focus or the speaker/writer does not want the subject of the action to be known (as in the case of President Clinton's answer mentioned in Chapter 4); (2) the subject of the action is unknown; (3) the object of the action is old/given information; and (4) the genre in which one writes calls for the passive such as scientific/technical writing.

## Suggested teaching activities

1. *Finding and correctly placing the misplaced objects.* Give students sentences, some of which contain misplaced objects. Have students find and correctly place them as well as explain the source(s) of the problems. Here are a few examples:
   1. Please communicate us your suggestions.
   2. I've heard you bought a new laptop. Could you show me it?
   3. Please confirm me your receipt of my application.
   4. They grant her the opportunity. (no error)
2. *Where to place the object?* Give students a series of dialogues in which two alternate ways of placing the object are provided. Ask them to select one option and explain the rationale for their choices. The following is an example.
   A: Could you [show *me* your new iPad/show your new iPad to *me*]?
   B: Sorry, I [lent *Tom* it/lent *it to Tom*], and he [messed *it* up/messed *up it*]. I'm very upset.
3. *Recovering the non-permissible null subjects/objects.* Give students sentences which contain either non-permissible subject deletions (for learners with a Roman language that allows wide subject-deletions) or non-permissible object deletions (for learners with an Asian language that allows broad object deletions). Ask students to identify and supply the deleted subjects or objects. Here are two sample sentences.
   1a. How about renting this movie?    1b. No like it.
   2. Do you have Professor Smith's email address? Please give me if you have.

4. *Why are these null objects permissible?* Give students sentences or passages which contain permissible null objects. Ask students to identify them and explain the reason for omitting each. Here are three sample sentences:

    1. We deliver. (A note on a restaurant menu)

    2a. Why were you late?              2b. Let me explain.

    3. The janitor comes in and cleans at night.

    Note: The first reason students usually come up with is that the deleted objects were all clearly implied and recoverable (which is a main rationale for object deletion in their L1). However, being recoverable alone does not warrant object deletion in English. For example, the deletion of it "Could give me John's email address if you have [it]?" is not acceptable even though it is clear the deleted object "it" refers to John's email address.

5. *Why is the passive used?* Give students a paragraph or two from a published article in which the passive voice is used extensively (such as the two examples given above in Section 11.3.) Ask them to identify all the instances of the use of the passive and then give the rationales for each use. Be ready to answer/discuss any questions the students may have regarding the rationales.

## Note

1 A substantial portion of this section is taken from my (Liu, 2008b) article.

# 12

# WORD MEANING AND USAGE

## Polysemy, synonymy, and other challenging issues

Word meaning and usage constitute arguably the most important and difficult aspect of vocabulary learning. The difficulty lies mainly in the fact that while many words have more than one meaning (a phenomenon called **polysemy**), often several words may have essentially the same meaning (a phenomenon called **synonymy**). Furthermore, some words have loaded connotations or special cultural meanings— words which Lado (1972, p. 286) calls "**culturally-loaded**." Additionally, many words are register-specific, i.e., they are appropriate only for certain registers. Thus, polysemy, synonymy, culturally-loaded words, and register-appropriate use of words are very challenging issues in vocabulary learning and teaching (Laufer, 1997; Nation, 2001). This chapter attempts to address these issues, one by one.

## 12.1 Polysemy

It is important to note that while some individuals use the term polysemy to cover all of the words that have more than one meaning, many linguists insist that polysemy refers only to words with more than one <u>related</u> meaning, such as the word *deposit*, which can mean something deposited naturally at the bottom of a sea or money/valuables deposited into a bank. This latter position differentiates polysemy from homonymy, which designates words that are spelled the same but have different unrelated meanings, such as the word *bank*, which can mean the land at the edge along a river or a monetary institution. However, it is not always easy to determine whether the different meanings of a word are related. If one is not sure whether a word is a homonym or polyseme, s/he can check a dictionary. It is an established practice in lexicography to list a homonym as separate words (i.e., separate entries), as in the case of *bank*. In contrast, a polyseme is listed as one word (one entry) with its various meanings numbered and spelt out one by one. Concerning the difficulty of polysemy for ESL/EFL learners, here is an example (a real sentence from an ESL freshman composition) to help illustrate the point. "Convicted murderers should be sentenced to death because murder is a <u>great</u> crime." It is clear that by "<u>great</u> crime," the student writer meant "huge crime." The problem was that the student did not know that *great* does not mean *huge/large* in a neutral sense. Instead, it typically conveys the meaning of *large* in the sense of *magnificent/wonderful*—the key extended meaning of the adjective as shown in phrases, such as *a great idea/achievement*.

## 12.1.1 Core meaning and extended meanings in polysemy

The different meanings of a polyseme are often related to or derived from its core meaning, i.e., it primary meaning. The other senses of the word are the extended meanings, some of which can be peripheral due to their low frequency of use. To illustrate the point, the core meaning of the verb *run* is *to go by moving the feet rapidly* (intransitive)/*perform as by running* (transitive). Its extended meanings in English are very wide, including *to compete* (*run for an office*), *to operate/test* (*run a computer program*), and *to manage* (*run an organization*). The core meaning of a word is usually the same across languages, but its extended meanings often vary from language to language. For example, the core meaning of *run* in both English and Chinese (pronounced *pao*) is the same, but the extended meanings of the word in English are much wider than those in Chinese, i.e., *run* is semantically mapped much more broadly in English than in Chinese. For instance, its English meanings of *operate/test* and *manage* do not exist in Chinese. Similarly, the verb *open* has the same core meaning in both Chinese (pronounced *kai*) and English: *to cause to become open/to unfold* as shown in *open the door/a book*. Yet its extended meanings in the two languages differ noticeably. *Open* boasts a much more broad semantic mapping in Chinese (and some other Asian languages such as Korean and Japanese) than in English. In Chinese, *open* can mean *to turn on* something (*open the computer/light/TV*) and *to operate* (*open a machine including a car*), meanings that are absent in English.

Not knowing such L1 and L2 differences in polysemous words can cause problems in L2 vocabulary learning. For instance, many low-level Chinese ESL learners make mistakes such as "*Open* the light/TV, please." Similarly, many Asian students often ask their professors what classes the school will *open* when they actually mean what classes the school will *offer*. They do so because they do not know that in English open a class has a totally different meaning: to let more students in a closed class where the enrollment has reached its cap. It is therefore necessary to draw learners' attention to such L1 and L2 semantic mapping differences in polysemous words.

## 12.1.2 Figurative meanings in polysemy: the role of metaphorical process

The extended meanings of a polyseme are often derived via the cognitive process of metaphor based on our embodied conceptualization. For example, the adjective *bright* has the literal core meaning of *having a strong shine or glow*. Then based on our embodied experience that bright light/color makes things look clear and good, we have the derived figurative meanings of *lively/vivid/cheerful* and *intelligent*. Historically, metaphorical use of language has not received adequate attention in linguistics or in language teaching (Liu, 2007). This should be changed, for, as discussed in Chapter 4, metaphor is fundamental not only in language but in thought itself. It is imperative that we attach more importance to metaphor in the teaching of polysemous words. The reason is twofold. First, many of the meanings of polysemous words, including many prepositions, are figurative rather than literal, as can be seen in utterances such as "The predictions are right <u>on</u> *target*/entirely <u>off</u> *target*" and "It's <u>beside</u> *the point*." Second, understanding figurative meanings can be challenging. While many figurative meanings of words are based on universally-shared embodied experience (e.g., *bright* = lively/cheerful/intelligent, whereas *dark* = gloomy/evil/ignorant), some are based on cultural experiences peculiar to the speakers of a particular language. For example, the use of the verb *buy* in English to mean *believe as true*, as in "I don't <u>buy your story</u>" and the use of *eat* in Chinese to mean *experience* as in "He's <u>eating fragrance</u>," which means that the person *he* is enjoying great popularity and the privileges that come with it (Liu, 2002).

The two different types (sources) of figurative meanings will need to be attended differently in vocabulary teaching. For those figurative meanings based on universally shared experience, the teacher can encourage learners to resort to their own embodied experience to enhance their understanding. For those with figurative meanings that have arisen out of unique L2 cultural experience, it is important to help learners understand the unique cultural experience. For instance, as Liu (2002) has argued, the aforementioned use of *buy* to mean *accept as true* is motivated by the conceptual metaphor *life is business*, a dominant metaphor deeply rooted in the psyche of the people of the English-speaking countries (considering the fact that Britain was one of the first capitalist countries and the U.S. is the largest capitalist country in the world). One does not need to go far to find many more figurative use of English words based on the *life as business* metaphor: *personal* <u>business</u> (=personal matters), <u>cash</u> *in* (= take advantage of), <u>budget</u> *one's time* (= plan one's time), *get* <u>shortchanged</u> (= get treated unfairly), <u>sell</u> *an agenda/idea* (= promote an agenda/idea). Exploring and understanding the cultural background of the figurative meanings of words should make the learning and teaching of lexical items more interesting and in turn help learners better understand and retain them. This issue will be revisited in Chapter 14.

## 12.2 Synonymy[1]

Synonymy refers to words that share the same meaning. However, true synonyms are rare unless we take cross-dialect synonyms (e.g., *sofa* and *couch*) into account (Stubbs, 2001). Thus, all synonyms are actually near-synonyms. However, for the sake of simplicity, the term *synonymy* will be used. To understand synonymy, it is important to know that while synonyms express basically the same concept, they often do so in different fashions, for different contexts, and/or from different perspectives. In other words, synonyms are often not entirely identical in meaning and hence not completely interchangeable. As such, synonyms are a challenging and simultaneously important lexical category because they are essential for expressing shades of meaning to help us convey our ideas and feelings precisely for effective communication (Liu, 2010b). For ESL/EFL learners, synonyms are particularly challenging. As Swan (1994, pp. 47–48) notes, English learners "often have enormous difficulty in distinguishing close synonyms such as *evil* and *wicked* ... *begin* and *start*. Dictionary definitions do not usually help ... ordinary dictionaries are not designed to settle demarcation disputes between synonyms." As an example of ESL/EFL problems with synonyms, there once was a dance performance in China developed to <u>glorify</u> the Chinese Communist Party and the government, but in the English version of the program, the performance was listed as one to <u>eulogize</u> the Party and the government. Obviously the translator did not know the difference between *glorify* and *eulogize*. The reason may be that many dictionaries list the two adjectives as synonyms.

## 12.2.1 Differentiating synonyms

Because synonyms are not entirely interchangeable, it is thus important to know and describe how a given set of synonyms differ in meaning and usage. Yet the fact that synonyms share essentially the same meaning has made the task of accurately differentiating synonyms very difficult. As a result, there was not much research on synonymy until the 1990s when advancements in computer technology and corpus linguistics began to enable researchers to examine the typical usage patterns of lexical items in mega-sized corpora. Guided by Firth/Halliday/Sinclair's lexical semantic theory that the meaning of a word is largely contextual, influenced by its co-occurring words, researchers (Gries, 2001; Gries & Otani, 2010; Hanks, 1996; Liu, 2010b, 2013; Liu & Espino, 2012) have studied the semantic and usage patterns of various sets of English synonyms by focusing on the distributional patterns of the synonyms. Specifically, they identified and analyzed the immediate collocates and grammatical structures that each of the synonyms in a set typically occurs with. In doing so, they uncovered the behavioral profile of each synonym. This corpus-based behavioral-profile research approach has enabled researchers to successfully identify the fine-grained semantic and usage differences among the synonyms being examined.

For example, in a study of five synonymous adjectives: *chief, main, major, primary,* and *principal,* Liu (2010b) identified the types of nouns that each of the adjectives typically modifies in COCA, and, in doing so, he was able to determine the semantic similarity and differences among the adjectives. While all of the five adjectives often modify abstract nouns (e.g., a *chief/main/major/primary/principal concern/issue/objective*), they differ in the other types of nouns they each typically modify. For example, *chief* and *principal* are the two in the set that are used mainly to modify job titles, but they differ in that the job titles modified by *chief* are all of power (*chief executive/justice/operating officer*) whereas the titles modified by *principal* are all those about shares of contribution or ownership (*principal investigator/owner/sponsor*). As for *primary*, due to its core meaning of being first in order of sequence, it often collocates with nouns to form noun compounds that mean things first in sequence (*primary care/election/school*). Regarding *main*, it is is the only adjective in the set that is often used to modify concrete nouns (*main building/dish/gate/lobby*). The study also looked at the frequency with which each of the adjectives is used with the definite article *the* (e.g., *the chief reason/the main purpose*) vs. the frequency it is used with the indefinite article *a/an* (e.g., *a major concern/a primary goal*). The rationale for this analysis was that a definite singular issue unequivocally indicates a higher degree of importance than an indefinite singular issue, as shown in the following two examples:

1.  *A major reason* for the Chargers' turnaround is QB [quarterback] Drew Brees.
2.  Poverty was *the main reason* these people left their home country.

While in example 1, the quarterback was merely one of the major reasons for the Charger's turnaround, in example 2, poverty was the only main reason why the people left their home country. Liu's analysis on this issue indicates that, of the five adjectives, *main* boasts the highest frequency (percentage-wise) in the definite-singular use while *major* registers the lowest, suggesting *main* conveys the highest degree of importance and *major* the lowest.

Liu and Espino's (2012) study of four adverbs: *actually, genuinely, really,* and *truly* provides another example regarding how corpus-based behavioral-profile study can effectively differentiate synonyms. In this study, besides examining the collocates of the adverbs (i.e., the adjectives/adverbs/verbs that each of the adverbs typically modifies), the researchers also investigated the sentence positions in which each adverb typically occurs. The reason for doing the latter was that often the meaning of an adverb may vary depending on where it is located in a sentence as shown below:

3.  *Strangely*, he answered the question.
4.  He answered the question *strangely*.

In sentence 3, *strange* is located sentence initially as a sentence modifier (a disjunct); consequently, the sentence means that "it is strange that he answered the questions." In sentence 4, *strangely* is located right after the verb phrase "answered the questions," serving as its modifier of manner; hence the sentence means that "He answered the questions in a strange manner." The results of the analyses of the various distributional patterns of the four adverbs show that while they all may function as adverbials in the meaning of *in fact/in truth* (e.g., "He is *actually/genuinely/really/truly* interested in the offer"), the extent of their use in this sense varies from adverb to adverb, with *genuinely* and *truly* being the only two in the set that are used mainly in this sense. *Actually* and *really* each differ noticeably from the rest. *Actually* is used much more often than the others as a sentence modifier. Furthermore, as a sentence modifier, it often functions as a contrastive linking adverb to contradict what has been said or believed to be, as shown in the following utterance: "She said she didn't know why he left. *Actually*, she did." As for *really*, it is also often used as a sentence modifier, but its function, unlike that of *actually*, is to assert the truthfulness of a statement and for emphasis only, as can be seen in the following example: "Don't tell me about your last date. *Really*, I don't want to hear about it." Moreover, *really* also differs from the other adverbs in that it is frequently used as an intensifier/emphasizer, e.g., "He *really* did it" and "She is *really*, *really* nice." The above examples clearly show that corpus-based analysis of the collocates of the synonyms in a set can effectively differentiate their semantic and usage patterns.

## 12.2.2 Conventional usage and construal: key factors in synonym use

While corpus-based behavioral-profile analysis can help us accurately determine the semantic and usage differences among synonyms, it has one weakness: corpora cannot allow the researchers to ask the speakers/writers who produced the data why they chose to use a given synonym rather than its alternatives. This latter information is very important for a complete understanding of the use of synonyms. Liu's (2013) corpus analysis of the use of two sets of synonymous nouns (*authority/power/right* and *duty/obligation/responsibility*) finds that while speaker/writers generally use established collocations or usage patterns in their synonym selections, sometimes they do not. For example, while *the* right *to vote* is the well-established expression (i.e., we all generally view *voting* as a *right* rather than an *authority* or *power*), there were some tokens of *power to vote* in COCA, as shown in the following example when the writer of a short letter to *Ebonics* (an African-American magazine) referred to voting as a power rather than a right: "… our ancestors fought so hard and died to give us the *power to vote*. Let's not let them down. VOTE!!" By choosing this rare collocation, the writer must have construed (i.e., framed) voting as an issue of *power* rather than *right*, i.e., s/he viewed voting as an act of power that could shape the government and policies in America and change the lives of African-Americans. Similarly, we generally consider the question of whether the U.S. President or Congress can declare war an issue of *power* or *authority* (i.e., whether the President or Congress has been given the *power/authority* to declare war). However, in the COCA data, some politicians and journalists chose the word *right* in the debate about the issue. Obviously, these individuals construed the act to declare war as an issue of *right* rather than *authority/power*.

To investigate how and why speakers/writers make synonym choices the way they do, Liu (2013) included, in addition to a corpus-based behavioral analysis, a survey study in which the subjects had to not only fill in the deleted synonymous nouns but also explain the rationales of their selections. A sample question is given below:

> It is the_____of the government to protect the people in this country.
> A. duty    B. obligation    C. responsibility

The results of this part of the study reveal that conventional usage and construal are two key factors that affect speakers/writers' synonym selection decision. Conventional usage refers to the most frequently used or well-established expressions, such as the aforementioned *right to vote* as opposed to the unconventional *power to vote* usage. Generally, a speaker/writer would use the conventional usage unless s/he determines that the given context evokes a concept that is not expressed by the conventional usage. In such a case, the speaker/writer will select an unconventional usage whose meaning s/he decides better expresses the concept in the given context, just as the aforementioned *power to vote* selection by the writer of the letter to *Ebonics*. This finding about the two key factors in synonym use has an important implication for L2 synonym teaching: focusing on teaching the established usages, but, after students developed adequate English fluency, they should be made aware they may opt for non-conventional usages to more accurately express their ideas/views.

There is another finding from Liu's (2013) study that has important pedagogical implications. Usually, in a synonym set, there is one dominant member (in some cases two). For example, *right* is the dominant member in the *authority/ power/right* set and *responsibility* is the dominant member in the *duty/obligation/ responsibility* set. The COCA data also show an increased and broadened use of the dominant members in the contexts (collocations) where traditionally a non-dominant member has been typically used. For example, traditionally, to fire a person, the individual who does the firing must have been given the *authority* or *power* to do so. Yet in COCA, *right to fire* is the most common usage. Similarly, although *civic duty* has been considered the more conventional usage, COCA shows almost an equal number of tokens of *civic duty* and *civic responsibility*. Given this finding, it appears that it would make sense in synonym teaching to begin by introducing the dominant member in a set. After students become familiar with the dominant member, the teacher can move onto the non-dominant members.

## 12.3 Established useful practices for teaching polysemes and synonyms

### 12.3.1 Practices for teaching polysemes

The first practice is explaining and teaching polysemes in context. One specific example of this practice is to have students read sentences with a given polyseme used in different meanings (the target words can be marked to draw students' attention) and then ask them to determine (i.e., guess from context) the different senses of the word. Here are two sample sentences concerning the polyseme *fork*: "John put down his knife and <u>fork</u> on the table and started talking" vs. "The accident happened at the <u>fork</u> of a country road." In the process, the teacher should ask students to explore how the two meanings are related. It is also very important to teach students how to look for information in context to help guess word meanings. Often, the meaning of a difficult word (especially a technical word) is defined when or after it is mentioned, e.g., "Tom Jones is an <u>avid</u> reader, <u>who reads two to three books a week</u>." Sometimes the meaning of a word can be inferred from causal or contrasting relationships shown in context, e.g., "The huge snow storm prevented people from getting out of their homes, <u>so</u> the whole city was <u>paralyzed</u>" (causal) and "Mike was very active before the accident, <u>but now</u> he's become almost like a <u>paralyzed</u> person" (contrastive).

The second practice, one that typically accompanies the first, is using definitions, especially dictionary definitions, to assist students in the understanding of the different meanings of the polyseme being learned. As mentioned above, in dictionaries, a polyseme is listed as one entry. The different meanings are numbered and given separately in a sequential order that usually begins with the core meaning. The teacher can ask students to check a dictionary for the polyseme they encountered in reading or listening. Or the teacher can have students guess the meaning and then summarize their responses. The summarized definition can be based on dictionary definitions. It is important that the definitions given are simple and clear, using easy vocabulary (Nation, 2001). A useful free online source for definitions of meanings of polysemy is WordNet, a website provided by Princeton University: wordnetweb.princeton.edu/perl/webwn. The site provides, for each word, a thorough list of its meanings, definitions, and illustrating examples. Also, for students with a homogeneous L1, the teacher may use L1 definitions to explain difficult-to-explain meanings (Liu et al., 2004; Nation, 2001).

The third practice is focusing on the core meaning first and then expanding to the extended, metaphorical meanings. Such a practice enables students to see better how the extended meanings are related to the core meaning. However, not many textbooks seem to systematically examine the metaphorical meanings of polysemes. Section 12.4.1 below will explore how to do this.

The fourth practice is employing pictures, diagrams, and other visuals to help students better understand both the core and the extended meanings of a polyseme, especially the various meanings of a polysemous preposition, as has been shown in Chapter 10. One such visual activity is semantic mapping, which illustrates the relations between the core meaning of a word and its extended meanings, as well as the relations among the extended meanings. Figure 12.1 offers a simplified semantic map of *run*.

The fifth practice is comparing/contrasting the semantic mappings of a word between L1 and L2 when teaching students with a homogeneous L1. It can help prevent L1 interference, particularly in cases where there is a polyseme in

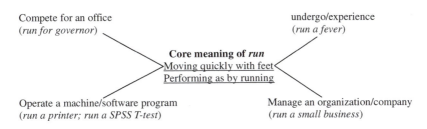

Compete for an office
(*run for governor*)

undergo/experience
(*run a fever*)

**Core meaning of *run***
Moving quickly with feet
Performing as by running

Operate a machine/software program
(*run a printer; run a SPSS T-test*)

Manage an organization/company
(*run a small business*)

**FIGURE 12.1**   Simplified semantic mapping of the verb *run*

learners' L1 but not in the target language. In such a case, the different meanings of the L1 polyseme are expressed by different words in L2. For example, *hot* is a polyseme in English as it can mean both *temperature hot* and *spicy hot*, but in many other languages, there is one word for each meaning. So, when English speakers learn one of the latter type of language, it is often difficult for them to know and remember which of the two target words should be used for *hot*. The teacher should also help enhance students' awareness of culture-bound connotation differences, an issue that will be addressed below in Section 12.4.3.

### 12.3.2  Practices for teaching synonyms

Just as is the case in teaching polysemes, the first practice is explaining and teaching synonyms in context, i.e., having students encounter synonyms and determine their meanings in reading and listing passages. However, given the aforementioned corpus research finding that the distributional/collocational patterns of the synonyms in a set can most effectively show their semantic and usage differences, teachers should include corpus-based examinations of the collocations of synonyms in context-based synonym learning. Section 12.4.2 below will discuss how to incorporate such corpus analyses.

The second practice is using dictionaries, especially thesauruses and synonym dictionaries. It is important to note, though, that while thesauruses can help us find the synonyms of a word, they usually do not provide definitions or explanations about the differences among the synonyms. Synonym dictionaries are a much better tool because they not only list synonyms but also offer explanations.

The third practice is teaching synonyms one at a time rather than teaching them simultaneously. The rationale for teaching one synonym at a time is that teaching a set of synonyms all together simultaneously will cause more confusion than learning (Nation, 2001). Thus, only after one synonym in a set has been taught and learned should a new one be introduced. As noted above, according to Liu's (2013) research findings, it is best to first teach the dominant member in a synonym set.

The fourth practice is doing semantic and functional feature analysis (Nation, 2001), as shown in the following analysis of *authority/power/right* (Table 12.1)

**TABLE 12.1** Semantic/functional analysis of *authority/power/right*

| | Source of Power/Right | | | | Nature of Power/Right | | |
| --- | --- | --- | --- | --- | --- | --- | --- |
| | Constitution Law | Office | Knowledge Prestige | Birth | Official | Individual | Natural Prerogative |
| Authority | x | x | x | | x | | |
| Power | x | x | x | | x | x | |
| Right | x | | | x | | x | x |

based on Liu's (2013) study. However, this type of analysis should be used only after students have learned all the synonyms in the set. Otherwise, it may cause confusion. Also, whenever possible, the teacher should use pictures or diagrams to help illustrate the relations among the synonyms to help learners visualize and hence better understand them.

Finally, there are also various types of exercises for helping students practice learned synonyms, including matching synonyms with definitions and filling in blanks in a sentence with the right synonyms. Some examples will be introduced in the Suggested Teaching Activities section below.

## 12.4 Explaining/teaching challenging issues with new insights: polysemy, synonymy, culturally-loaded words, and register

### 12.4.1 Cognitive analysis of metaphorical bases in polysemy learning

As an example of cognitive analysis of polysemes, we can look the word *head* because many nouns of body parts have extended figurative meanings. We can give students phrases composed of the word *head* that are used in different meanings: *head of a person, head of an organization, head of a nail, head of a river,* and also *head* as an intransitive verb meaning *to move* toward a given direction/destination (*She's heading/was headed to school*) as well as a transitive verb meaning to *lead* an organization (*She heads a large firm*). First ask students to explain the various meanings of the word and then explore how the meanings are related to one another based on our embodied experience with the functions of a *head*. Students should have little difficulty in uncovering the relations. Even with the phrase *head/be headed to*, students should be able to figure out that it is based on our experience that when a person or animal moves towards a place, it is usually the head first. Similar exploration may be done with other names of body parts, such as *back, foot,* and *eye*. Besides body parts, there are many other groups of polysemes that can be explored this way, such as temperature words used to describe atmosphere, emotions, and personalities (e.g., *a* <u>heated</u> *debate/a* <u>hot</u> *star/a* <u>cold</u> *person*) and furniture/housing structure words used as verbs (*a program* <u>housed</u> *in x department/a person* <u>chairing</u> *a department/a room* <u>seating</u> *100 people*).

## 12.4.2 Corpus-based analysis and other practices in synonym learning

Doing corpus queries of the collocational patterns of synonyms not only enables students to uncover the latter's semantic/usage patterns but also allows them to accomplish it through discovery learning. In addition, it simultaneously exposes them to a large amount of input. For lower-level students, the teacher can provide them with corpus search (concordance) results and have them analyze the results to uncover the semantic/usage patterns of the synonyms in question. Let us look at the example of finding the difference between the two common verbs *begin* and *start*. To differentiate verbs, the best collocates to investigate are their complements or objects. So the teacher can have students query the typical nouns used after the two verbs, then have them analyze the results and identify any systematic differences. The analysis can be done individually or by the whole class with the concordance lines projected onto a screen. The analysis should reveal that while both verbs can take abstract and activity nouns as their objects (e.g., *begin/start a class/meeting/process*), only *start* takes concrete nouns (e.g., *start a/ an car/engine/fire/machine*).

After the typical collocations of a synonym are identified, ask students to memorize them as established usages. As mentioned above (Liu, 2013), even native speakers rely mainly on conventional usage in their synonym selections. Finally, in teaching students with a homogeneous L1, it is helpful to draw their attention to L1/L2 differences in the collocates of a word and in the use of synonyms in general, especially in cases where there is one word in L1 that conveys meanings that are expressed by two or more synonyms in L2. For example, English has *inaccurately/incorrectly/mistakenly/wrongly* as a set of synonyms, but there is only one Chinese word, *cuowu de*, for these English synonyms. While these English adverbs are often interchangeable, only *wrongly* can mean *unjustly/ unethically/illegally*, e.g., *wrongly convicted/imprisoned* and *acted wrongly*. It is difficult for Chinese-speaking ESL/EFL learners to understand this difference. Thus, making students aware of the difference can help them use the synonyms more appropriately.

## 12.4.3 Culturally-loaded words

Besides having a denotative meaning (the basic definitional meaning found in dictionaries) a word may also have a connotative meaning (the affective association(s) the word conjures up). Take the noun *sunshine*, for example. Its denotation is *the light and heat from the sun*, but it has the connotative meaning of *cheerfulness and happiness* because we often associate sunshine in this positive manner. The denotative meaning of a word is often (not always) the same across languages, but its connotative meaning may vary, sometimes significantly. For example, the word *propaganda*, whose denotation is *wide public promotion of ideas*, etc., has a very negative connotation (often meaning an act of brainwashing) in the West. However, in China and many current and former communist countries, the word does not have this negative connotation. In fact, it is even part of the name of a very important department of the government and government-owned institutions and companies: the *Department of Propaganda*, a department at every level of the government in China. One can find this department so named on some Chinese government and organizations' websites. In a recent email from the Chinese Students Association at a large U.S. university announcing the organization's elected leaders, there was one person listed as the "Head of Propaganda." As mentioned above, Lado (1972, p. 286) labeled such words "culturally-loaded words" and defined them as lexical items that "are similar in primary meaning but different in connotation." He gave the word "fat" as an example. While the word is pejorative in American English, suggesting being overweight and unhealthy, in Spanish, it is often complimentary, signifying good health.

Obviously, if L2 speakers are not aware of such connotative differences, it can lead to serious communication breakdowns or even conflict. Here is a true example. One of my graduate students once was invited to a professor's home for a Thanksgiving dinner. After the dinner, the professor's wife, who was in her early sixties, was stepping on a ladder for Christmas decoration. Seeing that, my student wanted to help and said to the professor's wife, "You're old and let me do it for you." The professor's wife became livid, yelling at the student, "You think I'm old?" The problem was that the student did not know that the word *old* in English has a very negative meaning and does not have the positive meaning that it sometimes has in the Chinese language. In fact, *old* plus name is a common address form for someone older than you in Chinese. Also, last name plus *old* is a very honorable address form reserved only for very accomplished senior political leaders and scholars. Traditionally, language teachers focus mostly on the denotative meanings in vocabulary teaching, overlooking connotations. Research (e.g., Liu & Zhong, 1999) has shown that ESL/EFL learners, especially EFL learners, are often unaware of cross-language connotation difference in lexical items. It is thus very important for teachers to include connotative differences in vocabulary description. For language teachers teaching students of a homogeneous L1, it would be a good idea to identify L2 words with connotations that may cause problems for students due to influences from their shared L1 and present this information to the students. For these teachers, it may also be helpful to make students aware of words that have a very negative connotation in the L1 but do not in English so they would be willing and able to use these words in English. Here are two examples of such words: *hostess* is a euphemist term for prostitute in Korean and *motel* in Taiwan is synonymous with a place where people meet to have an affair. For native English-speaking teachers teaching students of different L1s, it is advisable to help students learn as much as possible about the English words that have unique connotations. These words can be divided into two groups: those that have a negative connotation in English but not so in other languages and those that have a positive connotation that may be absent in other languages. As an example of the former type, the word *boy* in American English has a patronizing connotation, especially for Afro-Americans. As an example of the latter type, *individualism* often has a positive connotation in English due to the fact of Western culture being primarily an individualist culture. Yet *individualism* often has a very negative meaning in collectivist cultures such as Chinese and Japanese.

### 12.4.4 Register-appropriate use of words

As mentioned in Chapter 3, register refers to a style of language used in a given social or situational context. There are formal and informal registers as well as various professional registers such as legal and academic writing. The knowledge about the register(s) in which a word is usually used is very important but also difficult for L2 learners, for very often L2 learners are found to use words in a register-inappropriate fashion (Laufer, 1997). For example, many ESL/EFL students use very informal words in their academic research papers, producing sentences such as "The study got great results" and "The issue is really a big deal." Language educators and material writers have become more and more aware of the importance of teaching register, and many learner dictionaries now provide such information. While offering students such information is helpful for language learners, it is often not enough. There are a few different learning reinforcement activities that can be useful. One is a corpus-based activity. We can ask students to do a corpus query of the frequencies of a word of interest in various registers of a corpus. It can be easily and quickly done because many online corpora provide this query capability. Students can get instant results and hence information about the register information about the word. An even more helpful practice is to have students do a corpus-based synonym use comparison in which they compare the frequency distributions of a word and its synonyms with different degrees of formality, for instance, *get* vs. *obtain/acquire*. This activity is especially useful because it allows students to enlarge their vocabulary while they learn about register. As we know, a major reason that L2 learners use informal words in formal contexts is that they have a limited vocabulary, i.e., they do not know the formal synonyms of a common but usually informal word.

### Suggested teaching activities

1. *Differentiating the related meanings of a word by cognitive analysis.* Any polyseme can be used in this activity. As an example, ask students to think how the two meanings of *great* are related: "large in size/number" vs. "excellent/wonderful." If students have difficulty, ask them how people generally feel about something that is very large in size or quantity (e.g., a building or mountain) as compared to the same thing but much smaller in size. In fact, it is generally a universal conceptualization that the larger something is, the more

magnificent it is considered to be. An example in point is the fact that in Chinese, *da ren* (= a large person) is an honorable person while *xiao ren* (=a small person) means an evil person. Another word that can be used as an example for this type activity is the adjective *slow* (its meanings of not fast in motion/speed, not intelligent, poor business, etc.).

2. *Corpus-based collocation analysis.* A simple example for this activity is to query for the noun collocates of *big* and *large* so as to differentiate the two synonymous adjectives. After students completed the query, have them analyze and group the typical nouns they modify and then identify the differences: while both adjectives can modify concrete nouns (e.g., *a big/large bowl/building/city*), they differ in two important ways: (1) *big* is used much more frequently and semantically broadly than *large;* (2) *big* modifies abstract nouns such as *a big problem/question* much more often than *large*, whereas *large* modifies, more than *big* does, nouns about number/quantity: *a large number/quantity/portion*.

3. *Filling in blanks or substituting the underlined words with the right words.* This type of activity can be used for practicing either polysemy or synonymy. Besides filling in the blanks or substitute the words with the right one, students can be asked to explain their choices in order to help them better understand and retain the words. The fill-in the blanks examples here deal with the aforementioned synonymous adverbs *incorrectly* or *wrongly* (tell them that in some cases either one works), while the substitution examples concern the use of *authority, power,* and *right.*

   1. John pronounced this word _____. (incorrectly)
   2. Some of them have been _____ charged with child abuse. (wrongly)
   3. He answered most of the questions _____. (incorrectly)
   4. The Congressman acted _____ in taking this vacation paid entirely by lobbyists. (wrongly)
   5. In the U.S., all citizens have the <u>privilege</u> of getting Medicare when they reach 65. (right)
   6. She thinks woman should have the <u>freedom</u> to decide whether to continue a pregnancy. (right)
   7. They believe they now have the <u>ability/force</u> to influence government decisions. (power)
   8. The committee has been granted the <u>ability</u> to hire the next manager. (authority)

4. *Error correction.* In this activity, besides correcting the error, students should also explain what the problem was in each sentence. The examples below relate to three different sets of synonyms (*authority/power/right, effective/efficient,* and *feasible/practical*).

   1. No individual has the <u>power</u> to take a person's life under these circumstances. (right)
   2. Such cars are too small, so they may not be <u>feasible</u>, especially for people with families. (practical)

3. Can wiping out poverty in the world ever be a <u>practical</u> achievement? (feasible)
4. All citizens are encouraged to exercise their <u>authority</u> to vote. (right)
5. There has not been any study demonstrating that car alarms are <u>efficient</u> at preventing theft. (effective)
6. *Surprised or amazed: Using the word with the right connotation.* This activity aims to help learners of intermediate level and above to understand the importance to use words with the right connotation. In the first part of the activity, tell students that the following was taken from an email sent by an Asian student to a professor meant as compliment, but the word "surprised" used in the email briefly confused the professor: "Dear Dr. X, I would to thank you for being a very good teacher … We were all <u>surprised</u> that you were able to answer all of our questions…" Ask students to think and discuss (in pairs or groups) (1) why "surprised" was not appropriate and which word would be more appropriate in this context, and (2) what might have been the reason(s) for this inappropriate choice of word. Ask students to consider the issue of L1 and L2 differences in the core vs. peripheral meanings as well as the denotative vs. connotative meanings of the word. The discussion should lead to the conclusion that *amazed* instead of *surprised* should be used in this context and that the likely reasons could be that unlike in English where there are several related words for expressing *surprised* (e.g., *amazed* and *shocked*), there might be just one word in the learners' L1 and that the L1 equivalent of *surprised* has no negative meaning. Afterwards, ask students do a comparative corpus study of the use of *amazed/astounded/shocked/surprised* (either as a whole class, small groups, or in pairs). Finally, have them make sentences using each of the words at least twice. The second part of the activity is to ask students to think of and explain to the class or their partners any words that they used inappropriately because they did not know their connotations.

## Note

1 Portions of this section are taken from the author's (Liu, 2010b, 2013; Liu & Espino, 2012) articles on synonym studies.

# 13
# WORD COLLOCATIONS

Collocations are very important but also challenging for language learners. They are important because language knowledge is essentially "collocational knowledge" (Nation, 2001, p. 321). To speak/write fluently and idiomatically in a language, one has to know how its words collocate. Collocations are difficult for L2 learners due to inter-lingual differences and the amount of effort needed to grasp them, as has been shown in research (Keshavarz & Salimi, 2007; Nesselhauf, 2003). To address this important and challenging aspect of language, this chapter first offers an overview of collocations, including issues such as what constitutes a collocation and whether collocations are generally arbitrary or motivated semantically.[1] Then, it discusses the existing common practices in collocation teaching. It ends with an exploration of how to incorporate corpus-based cognitive analysis to make collocation learning/teaching more engaging and effective.

## 13.1 Overview of collocations

### 13.1.1 What constitutes a collocation?

The word *collocation* has two major meanings in language description. First, as a non-count noun, it means the tendency for certain words to occur together "within a short space of each other in a text" (Sinclair, 1991, p. 170). For example, *classroom* and *students* tend to occur in the same context. Second, as a count noun, collocation refers to specific habitual combinations of two words that are often viewed as lexical items or units, such as *heavy rain* and *make a decision*. Longer combinations of words (three words or more) are called **formulae/formulaic sequences** or **lexical bundles**, and they will be discussed in the next chapter. This chapter deals with only two-word collocations, mainly the *verb–noun* and the *adjective–noun* types.

One point worth mentioning regarding collocations is that linguists and language educators do not have a consensus on what types of habitual combinations may be considered collocations. While some (Nation, 2001; Palmer, 1933) entertain a broad view of collocation that includes idioms, others (Fernando, 1996; Liu, 2010a, Moon, 1998; Nesselhauf, 2003) hold a narrower view, excluding idioms from collocations. This book adopts the latter view because collocations differ from idioms in two important aspects: degree of structural fixedness and degree of semantic transparency. First, while idioms are generally fixed in structure (e.g., *by and large* and *kick the bucket*), collocations usually allow some restricted variations (e.g., <u>*heavy*</u> or <u>*pouring*</u> rain and <u>*make*</u> or <u>*reach*</u> a decision). Second, whereas idioms are often opaque in meaning, collocations are generally transparent. (As a separate linguistic feature, idioms will be discussed in Chapter 14.)

It is necessary to note, though, that collocations themselves may also vary somewhat in structural fixedness and semantic transparency. Some allow little variation in structure (e.g., *do homework* where *do* appears to be the only verb that would work in the context). Others permit some degree of variation (e.g., <u>*have*</u>/<u>*suffer*</u>/<u>*experience*</u> a heart attack). Hence, some scholars believe that collocations can be divided into scaled subcategories based on their degree of structural fixedness and/or semantic transparency: "fixed," "strong," and "weak" (O'Dell & McCarthy, 2008, p. 8).

## 13.1.2 Collocations are generally motivated: a new finding

Traditionally, collocations have been considered primarily arbitrary (Benson, 1989; Chan & Liou, 2005; Lewis, 2000; Smadja & McKeown, 1991). There have been two major reasons for this view. The first is that collocations often vary from one language to another. For example, in English, one *does homework* but in German one *makes homework*. We will call this reason "inter-lingual difference." The second reason is that the meanings of collocations cannot be derived from the words in the collocation, i.e., collocations are unpredictable and hence unmotivated. As Smadja and McKeown (1991, p. 230) put it, "A collocation is arbitrary because it cannot be predicted by syntactic or semantic rules." Classical examples used to support this position include contrastive pairs such as *strong tea*/*powerful car* and *heavy rain*/*strong wind* (Firth, 1957; Keshavarz & Salimi, 2007). We will call this reason intra-lingual unmotivatedness. Because of these two reasons, some language educators (e.g., Lewis, 2000) have advocated teaching collocations as fixed chunks. According to Lewis, "the first task of the language teacher [in teaching collocations] is to ensure that they are not unnecessarily taken apart in the classroom" (p. 132).

However, results of recent corpus-based cognitive analyses of collocations suggest that, if examined intra-lingually, collocations are generally motivated rather than arbitrary, including even those collocations that have been used as classic examples to illustrate the arbitrariness of collocations (Liu, 2010a; Walker, 2011). The reason we need to look at the arbitrariness issue in intra-lingual rather than inter-lingual terms is that while it is valid to use inter-lingual contrastive analysis to draw L2 learners and teachers' attention to the differences between L1 and L2 collocations, it is not valid to use inter-lingual differences as evidence for viewing collocations as arbitrary. Such a practice overlooks two important facts. The first is that often a lexical item "does not have a single, fixed meaning but rather an array of senses related in principled ways to its proto-typical value" (Langacker, 2008b, p. 72). So a lexical item in a collocation that may appear strange based on its prototypical meaning may be entirely sensible viewed in one of its related senses. The second fact is that a lexical item may be semantically mapped differently in different languages, as shown in the previous chapter (Section 12.1.1) in the examples of *run* and *open*. While *running* an organization is possible in English, it is not in Chinese; in contrast, while *opening* (=turning on) a light is possible in Chinese, it is not in English. Thus, the collocations in the target language that appear arbitrary from the perspective of a learner's L1 can be completely sensible based on the semantic networks of the lexical items in the target language.

Liu's (2010a) corpus-based cognitive analysis of a series of collocations demonstrated this point clearly. Using COCA and BNC as data, Liu analyzed several well-known "arbitrary" collocations, such as *make/take/have/do a trip*, *strong tea* vs. *powerful car*, and *heavy rain* vs. *strong wind*. The results showed that these collocations were actually all motivated. For example, the closely related *make/take/ have/do a trip* collocations are not semantically interchangeable as many have assumed them to be. More importantly, they each have a quite distinctive meaning motivated by the verb involved. *Make a trip* often suggests a business trip; *take a trip* usually refers to a leisure trip; *have a trip* typically means "experience a trip" as shown in *have a great/nice trip*; *do a trip* (a collocation that has the lowest frequency among the four and usually appears in the past-tense form—*did a trip*) is used mainly to mean *completed a trip*, often in the sense of an accomplishment, as shown in the COCA example "We just *did a trip* to Central America." The different meanings of the four collocations are clearly motivated by their respective verbs. *Make* means to create and it is hence a more purposeful and effortful action than *take*. This explains the semantic difference between *make* and *take a trip*. As for *have a trip*, the verb *have*, as already explained in Chapter 8, has the meaning of *experience*, thus accounting for the collocation's meaning of "experience a trip." Regarding *did a trip*, a key meaning of the verb *do*, according *OED* only, is to accomplish, complete, finish, bring to a conclusion, a meaning of the verb perhaps best shown in the popular utterance: "We *did it!*" It is thus clear that the *make/take/have/do a trip* collocations are not arbitrary but semantically motivated.

Concerning *strong tea* vs. *powerful car*, Liu's corpus-based analysis has uncovered the motivations for why we typically say *strong tea* and *powerful car* rather than vice versa. First, Liu's corpus queries of the tokens of the two collocations revealed that there were actually also tokens of *powerful tea* and *strong car*, but they each were used to express a different meaning from that conveyed by their counterpart. When speakers say *strong tea*, they refer to its smell and taste, for which *strong* is a perfect adjective, as can be seen in the following COCA example: "The heady odor of *strong tea* filled the kitchen." When speakers say *powerful tea*, they are talking about the powerful health effects of tea, as shown in this COCA example: "Poppy pod tea has been used as an old time *powerful tea with many medical purposes*." *Powerful* is a natural adjective for effects. When speakers say *powerful car*, they refer to the physical power or force of the car (or its engine to be exact), as shown in the following COCA example: "Only a *powerful car* can race uphill or overtake another without the gas pedal being fully depressed." When speakers mention a *strong car*, they refer to a car which is solidly-built and can last and endure difficult driving conditions, as is shown in an article talking about how a new type of plastic can now be used to build *strong* cars (Liu, 2010a). Thus, the adjective used in each of these collocations is motived, rather than arbitrary. In fact, the semantically motivated use of *powerful/strong* can also be seen in the corpus research finding reported by Church and Mercer (1993) regarding the use of *powerful supporters* vs. *strong supporters*: while *strong supporters* refers to those "who are enthusiastic, convinced, vociferous, etc.", *powerful supporters* typically means those "who will bring others with them" (p. 20). The reason for the difference is not difficult to see because to be a *powerful supporter*, one has to have *power* (be it political, economic, or other power) in order to bring money and other supporters along. It is now clear that the *powerful car* and *strong tea* collocations, which have been widely believed to be arbitrary, are, after all, semantically motivated.

Similarly, according to Liu's (2010a) analysis, *strong wind* vs. *heavy rain*, another widely cited example pair for showing the arbitrariness of collocations, are not really arbitrary, either. Rain is made up of water, which has weight. Therefore, the use of *heavy* to modify it makes perfect sense. In contrast, wind has basically no weight, but it has force. Hence, the use of *strong* to describe it is entirely logical. In other words, the two collocations are clearly based on our embodied experience. In short, all the above analyses indicate that most collocations are motivated. Such a finding is in line with cognitive linguists' argument that "linguistic structure is a direct reflex of cognition in the sense that a particular linguistic expression is associated with a particular way of conceptualizing a given situation" (Lee, 2001, p. 1).

## 13.2 Established useful practices in collocation teaching

### 13.2.1 Noticing and memorizing

Liu's (2010a) survey of professional books and students textbooks related to collocation teaching suggests that collocations are currently taught primarily as fixed units, using mainly activities that are focused on noticing and memorization. The professional book discussions surveyed include (Hills, Lewis, & Lewis,

2000; Lewis, 2000; Nation, 2001; Willis, 2003). The most widely used activities include having students do the following:

1.  Identify and mark collocations in a passage or in a collocation dictionary. Typically students mark those collocations that they find unique either from an inter-lingual or intra-lingual perspective. It is thus important for the teacher to check the students' work as it helps the teacher learn what collocations call for more attention in teaching.
2.  Read passages with collocations that are highlighted/marked. This activity is essentially the reverse of the previous activity. Here the teacher highlights collocations believed important but also difficult for students to notice/learn.
3.  Fill in the blanks with the right word in a collocation. In this activity, the teacher may delete a key word in any type of collocations that are the focus of instruction, such as the verb in a verb–noun collocation or the preposition in an adjective or verb plus preposition collocation.
4.  Match collocates. Typically students are given two columns of words from scrambled verb–noun or adjective–noun collocations, with one column listing verbs/adjectives and the other listing nouns. Then they have to match the right collocates.
5.  Translate collocations from L2 back into L1 or vice versa. While the activity may involve collocations that appear identical in both L1 and L2, the focus is usually on those that are different between the two languages, e.g., *make homework* in German vs. *do homework* in English and *give a step* in Spanish vs. *take a step* in English.
6.  Memorize collocations by repetition or rehearsal. Rehearsal refers to writing up and practice scripts with target collocations before presenting them in class.

## 13.2.2 Pattern finding

A few experts (e.g., Nation, 2001; Willis, 2003, Zimmerman, 2009) recommend some useful pattern finding and organizing activities that may help students more effectively learn collocations. One of them is to identify and organize the collocations of a polysemous word. As we know, many words are polysemous. It is thus very important to learn their different meanings and the typical collocations used in each meaning. One example, adapted from Zimmerman (2009, p. 38), is to give students or have students find a series of nouns that are modified by the adjective *hard*: *hard chair, hard criticism, hard evidence, hard hat, hard heart, hard person,* and *hard test.* Then have students identify the major meanings shown in the collocations and group the collocations by meaning. Students should be allowed to use dictionary or corpus data to complete the task. In the end, students should be able to learn that, based on the collocations, *hard* has three major meanings: (1) difficult, (2) firm/solid, and (2) unfeeling/harsh. To help students reinforce their understanding of these meanings, the teacher can have students find the adjectives of the opposite meaning (antonyms) for the collocations, e.g., *soft chair/hat* against *hard chair/hat*, *easy test* against *hard test*, *weak evidence* against *hard evidence*, *gentle heart/person* against *hard heart/person*. Willis (2003, p. 156) offers another example of such semantic pattern finding for collocations. It involves students in classifying the *verb + for* collocations. The teacher first gives students a series of *verb–for* collocations, such as *apply for, battle for, fight for, look for, play for, search for*, and *work for*. Through discussion and exploration, students should learn that the *verb–for* collocations fall roughly into three semantic groups: (1) do something for a person/organization (*play/work for*), (2) work hard for or support/help a person/organization/cause (*battle/fight for*), and (3) try to find or obtain something (*apply/look/search for*).

Another type of pattern finding involves finding the metaphors that underlie many collocations (Willis, 2003; Zimmerman, 2009). As mentioned before, human language is largely metaphorical. Collocations are no exception. For example, from the literal *bright daylight*, we have *bright future/students* based on the metaphor "being bright means being clear and good." Also based on the metaphor "life/time is money," we say *budget/spend/save one's time*. This learning strategy helps explore the motivations of collocations. It is a practice that should be encouraged and used more, an issue that will be explored in greater depth in Section 13.3 below.

Finally, based on my own learning and teaching experience, there is one other area in collocation learning where pattern finding is helpful: register difference. Often, a noun may take more than one adjective or more than one verb as its collocates, e.g., for adjectives modifying the noun *increase*, we can use *big/enormous/large*, etc., and for verbs that collocate with the noun *agreement*, we can say *reach/have/come to an agreement*. However, the different adjectives or verbs involved usually vary in their degree of formality. For example, *enormous/tremendous increases* are more formal than *big/huge increases*. Similarly, *conduct research* is more formal than *do research*. It is very important that EFL/ESL students learn when to use which. Therefore, it will be a useful practice to have students group collocations by register so they will be able to use them in the right context.

## 13.3 Explaining/teaching collocations and collostructions with new insights

### 13.3.1 Using corpus queries for effective learning

With their increasing accessibility, corpora have been used more and more to help students learn collocations and research has shown it is an effective practice (Chan & Liou, 2005; Liu, 2010a; McCarthy & O'Dell's, 2005; Sun & Wang, 2003; Willis, 2003). In fact, corpus concordance can help effectively identify the collocation patterns of almost any lexical item, be it an individual word or a phrase. For example, if students are not sure which particular verb(s) collocate with the noun *progress*, they can simply do a corpus query, which will allow them to instantly learn that it is the verb *make*. If students want to learn which adverbs typically modify the adjective prepositional phrase *dependent on*, a quick corpus query will immediately provide them the information, as can be seen in the following ten most frequent adverbs that modify this adjective-prepositional phrase in COCA (shown in order of frequency with the phrase): *heavily, highly, totally, too, increasingly, entirely, completely, largely, very,* and *wholly*. Such information can help students to learn and produce idiomatic collocations.

However, although corpus queries can help learners quickly identify the typical collocation(s) they are interested in learning, corpus query results do not explain why the lexical items in a collocation are collocated the way they are. Incorporating an exploration of the motivations of the identified collocations would make the corpus-based learning more helpful and engaging.

### 13.3.2 Using cognitive analysis in exploring motivations in collocations

So far, this chapter has shown that while collocations are generally not arbitrary, they are still taught mostly as prefabricated chunks using primarily a noticing/memorization approach. While it is certainly necessary for students to notice, memorize, and repeatedly practice in collocation learning, such an approach is inadequate because it not only overlooks the motivated nature of most collocations but also, more importantly, takes away from the study of collocations any cognitive and linguistic analysis, a very important and useful part of the language acquisition process. This is a problem that Wray (2000) has identified in the lexical approach to the teaching of formulae: it does not allow students to generalize what they learn. Cognitive linguists have been very critical of the traditional practice of treating language primarily as an arbitrary system:

> [L]anguage has traditionally been understood as operating under its own set of rules and properties, most of which have been assumed to be largely arbitrary, idiosyncratic, and mysterious … Lexical items with multiple meanings are presented as homophones, with virtually no attempt to demonstrate any motivated connections among the meanings.
>
> *(Tyler, 2008, p. 458)*

This criticism is especially valid for the current collocation teaching practice. Liu's (2010a) examination of the existing reference and teaching materials on collocation found only one instance in which a textbook tried to draw learners' attention to the motivations of collocations. In a unit that focuses on a comparison between the "make" collocations and the "do" collocations, McCarthy and O'Dell (2005, p. 18) write, "If you remember that the basic meaning of *make* is about producing something and the basic meaning of *do* is about performing an action, then the collocations on this page may seem more logical." Such an explanation should help students better understand the collocations of the two verbs. Unfortunately, this quote appears to be all that the two authors offered about the motivations behind the collocations in their two-volume textbook series. There was no discussion at all about the issue of motivations behind any of the collocations of the other verbs in the series. In other words, McCarthy and O'Dell's discussion about the motivations of collocations was an isolated rather than a systematic effort. This might be because they believe that most of the collocations in their series are "surprising" or unpredictable (2005, p. 22), although, as shown, such a belief is somewhat ill-founded.

In short, it is important that we try to incorporate in collocation teaching an exploration of the motivations behind the collocations students are learning. Furthermore, empirical studies (e.g., Boers, 2000; Kövecses & Szabó, 1996; Tyler, 2012) have shown that understanding the conceptual motivations of figurative idioms, phrasal verbs, modal verbs, and prepositions significantly enhances students' grasp of these lexical items (an issue that will be discussed in the next chapter). It can thus be assumed that understanding the motivations of collocations can also help students learn these lexical units more effectively. The issue that still remains is how to help learners explore and understand the motivations of collocations. Below are three examples to help illustrate how it may be done.

### 13.3.3 Exploring motivations of four everyday verb–noun collocations

The first example relates to the explanation and teaching of the verb–noun collocations composed of *do/have/make/take*, such as *do chores/have an accident/make a decision/take a break*. The reason to use these common or what McCarthy and O'Dell (2005) call *everyday* verb collocations as our first example is that these collocations have been considered to be largely "unmotivated" and the verbs involved have been labeled *de-lexicalized* or *light verbs* (cf. Chan & Liou, 2005, pp. 235–236). However, a close cognitive analysis will help students learn that these collocations are in fact usually motivated. In practice, the teacher can provide students with a list of the most common collocations composed of each of the four verbs and place them in a table for comparison, just as shown in Table 13.1. The collocations in the table are based on a query of COCA.

Then meaningful analysis based on students' encyclopedic knowledge (knowledge based on life experience and learning) can be done to help students to understand the semantic motivations of the collocations of each verb and to differentiate the semantic and usage patterns among the collocations of the four verbs. For example, we can ask students to discuss which verb's collocations (i.e., the actions they express) involve more initiation, planning, and effort. It should not be difficult for them to figure out that the collocations of *make* do,

**TABLE 13.1** Typical collocations of everyday verbs

| Make | Take | Do | Have |
|---|---|---|---|
| Make a case | Take a bath | Do business | Have an affair |
| Make a change | Take a break | Do chores | Have an accident |
| Make a choice | Take a bus/taxi | Do dishes | Have an argument |
| Make a commitment | Take a chance | Do drugs | Have a conversation |
| Make a contribution | Take a look | Do errands | Have difficulty |
| Make a decision | Take a nap | Do exercises | Have a dream |
| Make a difference | Take an offer | Do harm | Have experience |
| Make an effort | Take a rest | Do homework | Have a feeling |
| Make a living | Take a phone call | Do laundry | Have fun/a good time |
| Make a mistake | Take a shower | Do research | Have a look |
| Make a phone call | Take a test | Do things | Have a problem |
| Make progress | Take a walk | Do work | Have trouble |

for we all know that generally *making a/an change/commitment/decision/effort*, etc. entails more initiation, planning, and effort than *doing chores/dishes/errands/home-work* and *taking a break/bus/chance/nap*, etc. Furthermore, the actions expressed by the *do* collocations are much more routine, with many being daily activities. In the process, the teacher can then ask students to examine the core meanings of the verbs and to determine how the core meanings of the verbs affect and contribute to the meanings of their collocations. The teacher will also need to draw students' attention to the *have* collocations, which differ quite noticeably from the collocations of the other three verbs. The teacher should help students understand that the key meaning of the verb in its collocations is *experience*. S/he can do so by asking students the question: "What does the verb *have* really mean in these collocations?" Students should not have too much difficulty answering it. They should also in turn understand that essentially the verb *have* can be replaced by the verb *experience* in most of the *have* collocations without any change of meaning, e.g., *experience* (instead of *have*) *a/an accident/break/difficulty/ dream/feeling/fun/problem*. In short, the semantic analysis should help learners better grasp the semantic patterns of the collocations of the four verbs, which in turn should enable them to use the correct verb-noun collocations.

### 13.3.4 Exploring motivations in verb–preposition collocations

Let us now see how a cognitive analysis may help students better grasp the use of *be/get on* (not *at/in*) *the phone*, a "verb + preposition+noun" colloca-tion. The reason for choosing this collocation is that many ESL/EFL students have difficulty understanding why we say *on the phone*, not *\*at/in the phone*. It seems rather arbitrary to them. To help students understand that this is really a motivated usage, we can first have students conduct a corpus search of the prepositions used in the phrase, i.e., used in the "*be/get + preposition + the phone*" structure. The results should show that the only prepositions used systematically in the given collocations are *on* and *off*, i.e., they are either *be/get on the phone* or *be/get off the phone*. Then we can ask students to compare the meanings of the four different collocations, especially the meaning of *on the phone* vs. that of *off the phone*. The students can fairly easily determine that *be on the phone* means "be in the process of having a phone conversation" and *get on the phone* means "pick up the phone to start a conversation," while *be/get off the phone* conveys the opposite meaning. Then we should ask the students to think why *on* and *off* help convey opposite meanings based on their experience and their understanding of the basic meanings of the two prepositions. It should help them see that the basic meaning of *on* (e.g., *A is on B*) is in contact while *off* is no contact or being separated from contact. Then they can extend the *in-contact* meaning of *on* to the meaning of being *in operation/use* and the *not-in-contact* meaning of *off* to the *not being in operation/use* meaning. This analysis process should enable the students to see the motivations for the two opposite collocations involved.

When appropriate, it would also be a good practice to examine the motivations of collocations in comparison/contrast with their counterparts in learners' L1 (especially when learners have a homogeneous L1). For example, we say *take medicine* in English, but it is *eat medicine* in Chinese and *drink medicine* in Japanese. It is very important that we help students understand that the use of *take* in this English collocation results from the broad semantic mapping of the verb *take* in English and its extended meaning of "to receive into one's body by eating, drinking, and swallowing," e.g., *take food, nutrition*, etc. (*OED online*, 2012). In contrast, the counterpart Chinese and Japanese collocations focus on the act of putting medicine into a person's mouth, just as one does with food and drink.

### 13.3.5 Exploring motivations in collostructions

Besides collocations, corpus-based cognitive analysis can also be used to more effectively teach other collostructions (lexical/grammatical constructions as explained in Chapter 5). One example relates to the teaching of the usage patterns of the following two pairs of constructions: *come + adjective* vs. *go + adjective* (e.g., *come true/alive* vs. *go bankrupt/crazy*) and *keep + something+adj* vs. *leave + something+adj* (e.g., *kept us healthy/warm* vs. *left us hungry/injured*). The teacher can have students do a query of the two collostructions in each pair or the teacher can do it with the students and show the results (a screenshot of the result of such a query for *come + adjective* in COCA is given in Figure 13.1). Then the teacher can ask students whether they notice any patterns regarding the two contrasting collostructions in each pair. With some prodding by the teacher, students should be able to notice that the *come/keep–adj* tokens in each pair typically express a positive meaning whereas the *go/leave–adj* tokens usually convey a negative meaning. Then the teacher can ask students to think, based

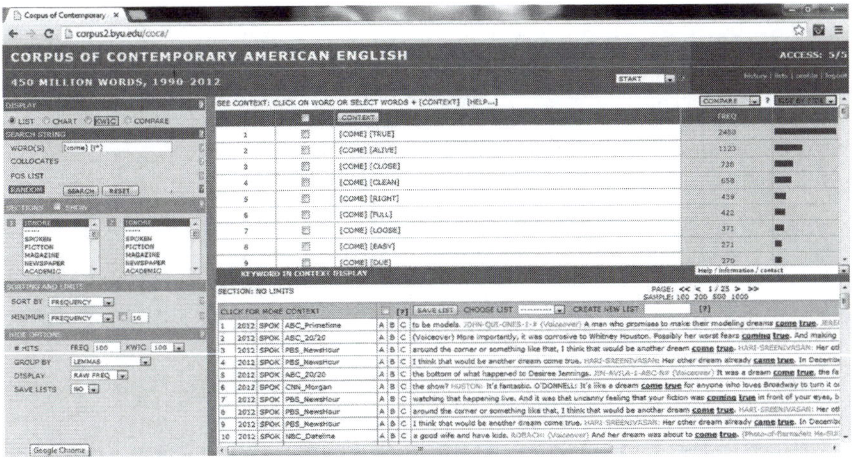

**FIGURE 13.1**   Most common "come + adjective" expressions in COCA.

on their experience, why this is the case. An exploration of the question should help students uncover the motivations of the patterns—what we want to come to us and keep are things desirable and what we want to go away from us or leave behind are things undesirable.

### 13.3.6  Caveats and challenges

It is paramount to note, however, that there are caveats and challenges in the use of corpus-based cognitive analyses in collocation teaching. First, the approach will not work well for young children because of their limited cognitive ability. Second, it may not work for students who do not benefit from cognitive analysis due to their learning styles. Third, the approach should be used cautiously with students of low language proficiency. For these students, raw corpus data should be avoided. Instead, the teacher can select, from the raw data, examples that suit the students' level and ability. Fourth, the level of complexity of cognitive analysis in collocation learning can vary substantially from one collocation to another, thus presenting different levels of challenges. For example, the reason for the use of the preposition *between* in the collocation "*a gulf between a and b*" may be somewhat easier to understand than the reason for the use of *on* in the collocation "*be on the phone.*" This is because while it is the literal meaning of the preposition *between* that is used in the "*gulf between*" collocation, it is not the case with the use of *on* in *on the phone*, as explained earlier. Because of the difference in the complexity of cognitive analyses involved in collocation learning, a teacher should be prepared to provide appropriate assistance to the students based on the level of the difficulty of the collocations being learned. Visual aids including diagrams are an especially useful tool. For example, to help students understand why we use *between* instead of *in* or any other prepositions in the "*gulf between*" collocation, we can draw a picture with a gulf (lake/river) in the middle and the A person/thing on one side of the gulf and the B person/thing on the other side. Viewing this picture, students can see clearly the reason for using *between*, rather than one of the other prepositions. Similarly, a diagram can be drawn to help illustrate the semantic difference between the *high* and *tall* collocations. Finally, not all the collocations are clearly motivated, for sometimes the historical reason(s) for the motivation may have been lost (an issue that will be discussed in Chapter 14 on idioms). So, teachers and students should be prepared for the fact that sometimes a search for the motivation(s) for a collocation may fail. Yet despite the failed attempt, the cognitive exploration process that the students went through should still be beneficial because of the additional opportunity for processing the collocation and the extra attention the students paid to its composition. The exploration process should raise students' consciousness of the collocation, which should in turn result in better retention.

## Suggested teaching activities

1.  *Figuring out collocations that appear strange.* Ask students each to give at least five English verb–noun collocations that they find strange and explain why they consider them so. Then they should try to see whether they can find any motivations for these collocations from the perspective of English. Students may do this first in pairs and then share their work with the class.

2.  *Understanding the contexts in which the collocations are typically used.* Give students a list of collocations and have them do a corpus query to decide whether each is used more frequently in speaking or academic writing. Here are a few examples of collocations for the activity:

    *good/great/optimal/splendid/performance*
    *get/obtain/reap good results*
    *give/make/exert/expend effort*

3.  *Error correction.* Give students a list of sentences that contain collocational errors that resulted either from L1 interference or from over-generalization. Then ask students to correct any errors and explain the problems. Here are a few examples from actual students' writing:

    After this activity, the teacher finalized the class.

    Convicted murderers should be sentenced to death because murder is a great crime.

    Could you please help me solve the question?

    They decided to make business with this small company.

    We have to exercise and eat healthy food in order to omit the risk of heart disease.

    The decision had an affirmative impact on public education in the U.S.

4. *Motivations of collocations.* Give students a few related collocations (e.g., *draw* vs. *reach a conclusion*) and have them explore their motivations. The teacher can first have students examine a list of sentences involving the collocations with the two verbs, such as the following:

We've <u>reached</u> a conclusion.

We can't really <u>draw</u> a conclusion based upon just one set of data.

Ask the students whether the verbs *draw* and *reach* are fully interchangeable and why. A close examination and discussion should lead to an understanding that the two verbs are generally interchangeable when collocated with *a conclusion*, but they reflect two different angles from which to view the conclusion drawing/reaching process. When we say *draw a conclusion*, it emphasizes the process of analyzing the evidence/information about an issue and having a decision based on the information analyzed. On the other hand, when we say *reach a conclusion*, we view the conclusion as an endpoint at which we arrive after analyzing all the evidence/information. So the process is not the focus. Hence, when we are only interested in the result, we usually say "Have you/they reached a conclusion?" instead of "Have you drawn a conclusion?"

5. *Grouping collocations semantically.* Have students do a query of the adjective or verb collocations of a noun. Then have them examine the concordance results and then group the listed collocations by meaning. For an example, the results of a corpus query of verbs used with *ability* will include, among others, *acquire, demonstrate, develop, show, measure,* and *under/overrate the ability.* Semantically, *acquire* and *develop* form one group; *demonstrate* and *show* belong to the same group; *measure* and *under/overrate* form another group.

## Note

1 This chapter draws heavily from the author's (Liu 2010a) article on collocation learning and teaching.

# 14

# MULTI-WORD EXPRESSIONS

## Idioms, phrasal verbs, and formulae/lexical bundles

As mentioned in Chapter 5, language is composed of an enormous number of prefabricated and semi-prefabricated expressions. Many different terms have been used to refer to such expressions, including *idioms*, *fixed expressions*, **formulae** (or *formulaic sequences*), **lexical bundles**, **phrasemes** (**phraseology**), and *word clusters*. While many of the terms are often used interchangeably, some of them do refer to different types of multi-word units. This chapter will focus on three important ones for language learning purposes: *idioms*, *phrasal verbs*, and *formulae/lexical bundles*.[1] First, each type will be defined and its functions described. Then a discussion will follow on effective ways to explain and teach them.

## 14.1 Describing idioms/phrasal verbs/lexical bundles and their functions

### 14.1.1 Idioms

Semantic opaqueness and structural fixedness are two key criteria used in idiom definition. Yet, as Liu (2007) shows, both criteria are often gradable rather than binary; as a result, existing idiom definitions vary considerably. A few definitions (e.g., Moon, 1998) are extremely rigid in the application of the criteria and are hence narrow in meaning, limiting idioms to a small number of expressions that are completely opaque in meaning and entirely fixed in structure. In contrast, a few others (e.g., Fernando, 1996) are quite lax and broad in meaning, including as idioms even some semantically transparent or literal expressions. However, a majority of definitions adopt a more balanced position which defines idioms as multi-word expressions that are opaque or semi-opaque in meaning and invariant or variance-restricted in structure. Such a definition would include many figurative expressions that are not entirely opaque in meaning or fixed in structure, e.g., *drop/fumble the ball* and *tie up (all) the loose ends*. It is also important to note that such a definition is especially sensible from L2 learners' perspective. This is because even semi-opaque and variance-restricted expressions often present great challenges for these learners. It is also necessary to note that, based on such a definition, a phrasal verb is also an idiom (Liu, 2007) because phrasal verbs are often idiomatic in meaning and fixed in structure. Phrasal verbs will be discuss in a separate section below due to their high frequency and their uniqueness in structure.

Idioms can be divided into several sub-categories based on semantic motivation and structural form. Semantically, idioms fall mainly into two types: figurative (e.g., *drop the ball* and *play with fire*) and non-figurative (or semantically-unmotivated, e.g., *happy go lucky* and *so long*). However, an overwhelming majority of idioms are figurative. In fact, if we could uncover the lost historical reasons, even many of those idioms now considered non-figurative would become figurative. *By and large*, which is often considered non-figurative, offers a good example. Quinion (2011) has shown that, based on information in an eighteenth-century marine dictionary, the phrase was originally a sailing term. It means "all possible points of sailing," a meaning that has evolved metaphorically into the current general sense of "all things being considered" or simply "in general." With regard to structural form, idioms may be grouped largely into three types: (1) two-word (mostly adjective–noun) units, such as *fat chance* and *red herring*; (2) three-word or longer (mostly verb–noun) phrases, such as *jump the gun* and *pull someone's leg*; (3) complete clauses (including proverbs), such as *What's up?* and *The early bird gets the worm*.

One important point about the forms of idioms is that although idioms are generally quite fixed, corpus research (Liu, 2003; Moon 1998) has shown they do allow certain variations, including a few systematic variations, due to, among other things, the creative nature of language. According to Moon (1998), systematic variations include *lexical variation* (e.g., *jump on/join the bandwagon* and *start/set the ball rolling*) and *truncation* or *abbreviation* (e.g., *a bird in hand* with *is worth two in the bush* omitted). Non-systematic variations are often creative impromptu uses of idioms that speakers/writers make for dramatic effect, such as *burn the candle at five ends* (rather than *at two ends*) and *pull a highway* (rather than *a rabbit*) *out of the hat*. Creative uses of idioms are actually quite common based on corpus research (Langlotz, 2006; Liu, 2007; Moon, 1998). Of course, such creative use of idioms requires a solid command of the language and good imagination.

Idioms can perform a variety of functions, which can be grouped into three main categories based on Halliday's theory, previously explained in Chapter 3: ideational (to convey information), interpersonal (to help effectively interact in interpersonal exchanges), and textual (to provide cohesion and coherence). Each main function also includes a few sub-functions. The following are corpus examples taken mostly from my book (2007, pp. 30–32) to help illustrate the point (a few phrasal verbs are included):

*Ideational*
a) Informational:
  - Mayor Bloomberg [of New York City] is trying to get New Jersey and neighboring states to go ahead and *jump on this bandwagon*.

- Since [Japanese] Prime Minster Hosokawa left, we have not heard back from the Japanese government on the framework talks. *The ball is in their court.*

b) Evaluative:
- … they're *in the driver's seat* in these negotiations.
- The Navy Seals *chickened* out on this.

*Interpersonal*

a) Interactions:
- Mike, let me *jump in* for a moment quickly. And we need to begin to *wrap this up.* But can you *put a little bit of bones on* the references I made earlier …
- *Knock it off*, will ya? You're *drowning out my big drum solo* [*drowning out my big drum solo* is also an idiom but its function is ideational, not interpersonal].

b) Modality or adverbial adjuncts of qualifications:
- Our soldiers? Well, our soldiers are not in the line of fire, *so to speak*, over in the region. They are not at risk in the State of Israel, if that's what you are suggesting.
- But, *by and large*, he still commands the authority of the military.

*Textual*
- The two teenagers have pleaded not guilty to the koala caper … *By the way*, koalas are not bears at all … OK, well, listen, you know what? I want to *switch gears* for a second and go from America to the Middle East.
- Let's *call it a day here.* We can continue on this tomorrow.

Of course, sometimes, an idiom may perform multiple functions simultaneously. For example, the above example "The Navy Seals *chickened out*" is both informative and evaluative (Liu, 2007). Also worth noting regarding the functions of idioms is that these multi-word expressions help make language more specific and vivid (Fernando, 1996). However, idioms are attitudinal and, as such, they are used much more often to express negative emotions and evaluations than to express the positive (Fernando, 1996; Liu, 2007). Because of these unique semantic functions of idioms, it is very important for learners to learn when and where to use them as well as when and where to avoid them. This issue will be explored below in the section on teaching idioms. Finally, corpus studies (Biber et al., 1999; Liu, 2003; Moon, 1998) have also shown that while there are many idioms in English, most of them register a very low frequency. Thus, knowing which idioms are frequently used is very important. Some corpus studies (Biber, et al., 1999; Grant, 2005; Grant & Nation, 2006; Liu, 2003) have provided useful lists of the most common idioms in specific registers.

## *14.1.2 Phrasal verbs*

As mentioned above, phrasal verbs are a type of idiom. In terms of form, a phrasal verb consists of a verb plus one of the following three forms: a particle (e.g., *give up*/*take over*), a preposition (e.g., *look after*/*run into*), or a particle together with a preposition (e.g., *put up with*). Because many particles are prepositions in origin (e.g., *on* in *take on something*), sometimes it is difficult to determine whether the non-verb form/word in a phrasal verb is a particle or a preposition. The most effective way to determine the issue is to ascertain whether the word can be placed after the object. While a particle can be placed either before or after the object, a preposition cannot, as shown below:

1a.  He decided to take <u>on</u> the task.  1b.  He decided to take it (the task) <u>on</u>.
2a.  He is looking <u>after</u> his mom.  2b.  *He is looking her (his mom) <u>after</u>.

It is important to note that there are two subtypes in the *verb + particle* phrasal verbs: intransitive (e.g., *give in*/*show up*) and transitive (e.g., *take over*/*turn down* a job). Some phrasal verbs can function either intransitively or transitively (e.g., *break up* used intransitively in "The couple *broke up*" and transitively in "They plan to *break up* the company"). However, in many cases, the intransitive and transitive uses of a phrasal verb may differ significantly in meaning, e.g., *turn in* intransitively = go to sleep, but *turn in* transitively = submit, as in *turn in one's homework*.

A phrasal verb is believed to be largely opaque or non-literal in meaning, i.e., its meaning is not compositional or cannot be derived from its individual parts. Based on this criterion, verb phrases whose meanings are derivable from their individual parts are not phrasal verbs, e.g., *come in, go out, listen to,* and *look at*. However, as mentioned above, semantic opaqueness/non-literalness is often a gradable rather than a binary issue. Therefore, this meaning criterion may not always be straightforwardly applied. Then, how can we accurately differentiate phrasal verbs from those verb phrases that also contain an adverb or preposition, such as the aforementioned *come/go in/out*? There are actually two effective rules or tests we can use for this purpose (Celce-Murcia & Larsen-Freeman, 1999; Liu, 2007). The first is that an adverb cannot be inserted between a verb and its particle or preposition in a phrasal verb, but it can be inserted in a non-phrasal verb phrase. For example, we cannot say *\*take quickly over the job* or *\*gave completely in*, but we can say *listen carefully to someone* or *look closely at an issue*. Second, while a particle in a phrasal verb cannot be placed at the front of a sentence (e.g., *\*In he gave* or *\*Up they broke*), an adverbial in a non-phrasal verb phrase can (e.g., *Out he went* and *In she came*). These two rules can help us easily decide whether a verb phrase is a phrasal verb when the meaning test fails.

In terms of use and function, phrasal verbs are ubiquitous in English, especially in speaking and informal context, and they perform mainly ideational (informational) functions. They help convey to us, in informal context what one-word formal verbs would do in formal context, what happened, e.g., "John *turned in* (*submitted* in formal context) his resignation"/"They finally *put out* (*extinguished*) the fire." The use of phrasal verbs is a hallmark of everyday English. An adequate and proper use of phrasal verbs is thus a good indicator of a person's English proficiency and idiomaticity. It is also important to note that while phrasal verbs are generally informal, corpus research (Biber et al., 1999; Liu, 2011b) has shown that some of them are actually used most often in formal contexts, including academic writing, such as *bring about, carry out*, and *point out*. Furthermore, the use and functions of phrasal verbs are a complex issue because many phrasal verbs are polysemous. For example, *make up* can mean, among others, *compose* ("Five members *make up* the committee"), *compensate* ("I need to *make up* for the time lost"), *fabricate* ("He *made up* the story"), and *apply cosmetics* ("She seldom *makes herself up*"). Fortunately, many of the meanings of the phrasal verbs are actually motivated, largely determined by the meanings of the verbs and the particles, an issue that will be explored below. Added to the problem of the polysemous nature of phrasal verbs is the enormous number of phrasal verbs in the English language. According to Gardner and Davies (2007) and Liu (2011b), there are over 10,000 phrasal verbs in English. The good news is that most of them are of low frequency. Only about 100 to 150 of them are frequently used and they account for approximately 65 percent of all the occurrences of phrasal verbs (Liu, 2011b). Furthermore, these most frequent phrasal verbs are all composed of common verbs, such as *come/get/ go/make* and common particles like *down/up/in/out*.

### 14.1.3 Formulae/lexical bundles

Formulae or/lexical bundles "are recurring expressions, regardless of their idiomaticity, and regardless of their structural status" (Biber et al., 1999, p. 990). They are identified automatically based solely on frequency, with the use of a corpus and a computer search program. In other words, formulae (e.g., *for the purpose of* and *it is likely that*) are identified entirely by the high frequency with which the words in each of them co-occur. Defined and identified in such a manner, formulae differ from idioms in that they are in general "semantically transparent and formally regular" (Hyland, 2008, p. 6). The minimum frequency adopted for identifying formulae has varied from 10 to 40 tokens per million words (PMWs), with 20 or 30 PMWs being the norm (Liu, 2012a). Formulae may also vary in length ranging from three to six words, with four-word bundles being the most common.

It is very important to note that due to the automatic identifying method used, many lexical bundles so identified are incomplete phrases, such as *as well as the* and *to do with the*. Such structurally incomplete bundles may not be psychologically salient and therefore may not be of much value for language students to learn (Simpson-Vlach & Ells, 2010). Hence, Simpson-Vlach and Ellis (2010) developed an empirically-derived "measure of utility, called 'formula teaching worth' (FTW)'" for screening and identifying useful formulae. While the measure can significantly reduce the number of incomplete psychologically non-salient formulae, it cannot completely screen them out. As an alternative to solving the problem, Liu (2012a) suggests turning these incomplete formulae into complete meaningful schematic constructions. For example, we can present the incomplete *as well as the* and *to do with the* bundles in the form of *as well as (NP)* and *to do with (NP)*. By changing *the* into NP, we make clear to students that any noun phrase can follow *as well as/to do with*. This practice not only broadens the structure of lexical items that can follow the two said phrases but also more accurately describe their use because each phrase can indeed take noun phrases that do not begin with *the*, e.g., *as well as Smith/students*. More importantly, based on Cognitive Linguistic research, acquiring such schematic constructions constitutes a major part of language acquisition (Liu, 2012a).

In terms of use and function, formulae are register-specific. For example, *research results indicate that* and *it is the purpose of this/the paper* are formulae found in academic journal articles, but they are rarely used in other registers. Used frequently in a given register, formulae serve as building blocks for the speech and writing texts in that register and they help create fluent and coherent discourse (Biber, Conrad, & Cortes, 2004, Hyland, 2008; Wray, 2002, 2008). The ability to use such expressions is a strong indicator of a person's language proficiency (Wray, 2002, 2008). Semantically, these formulae are found to perform functions across all of the three major semantic function categories: ideational, interpersonal, and textual. More importantly, corpus research (Biber, Conrad, & Cortes, 2004; Liu, 2012a) has shown that while some formulae can perform multi-functions, many are used mainly to perform certain specific ones. For example, some prepositional phrases (e.g., *as a result/on the contrary/in summary*) are used exclusively for textual functions, i.e., for providing discourse cohesion. In contrast, some other prepositional phrases (e.g., *as a whole* and *in general*) are used mainly as qualifiers in the ideational function. Also, some frequently used partial-clause formulae (e.g., *if you want to/we're going to do/it is important/necessary to*) are typically used to express attitude/modality stances in interactions. Many full-clause formulae (e.g., *What can I do for you?/You're welcome*) perform speech act/pragmatic functions of offering help, requesting information/help, etc. Such semantic and usage information about formulae is very useful for language teachers and learners alike. It may help teachers and material writers to better select and present formulae that best meet their students' needs. For learners, the information may enable them to use formulae appropriately.

## 14.2 Explaining/teaching idioms and phrasal verbs with new insights

Explaining/teaching of idioms and phrasal verbs are discussed together here because both types of expressions are often idiomatic in meaning.

### 14.2.1 Teaching the right idioms with noticing/retrieval/ generating activities

First, given the enormous number of idioms and phrasal verbs and the fact that many of them are of low frequency, it is important to teach those that are of high frequency and of the most use to students. The teacher may consult the corpus-research-based lists of the most frequent idioms and phrasal verbs in various registers, such as those provided by Biber et al. (1999), Grant (2005, 2007), and Liu (2003, 2011b). Most existing idiom/phrasal verb dictionaries are not very helpful, however, because they include many low-frequency items and they do not provide frequency information. The teacher may also consult corpora themselves on this issue. There are several points that need to be considered in selecting which idioms and phrasal verbs to teach. First, while an item's general frequency is an important criterion, we should also look at its frequency in specific registers. This is because many items (especially those in phrasal verbs) are register-specific. For example, *carry out* and *point out* are very common in academic English. Hence they should be taught in academic writing classes. Second, many phrasal verbs are polysemous and their various meanings and functions are also register-sensitive (Liu, 2012b). For example, *make up* used in academic writing typically means "compose," but its use in speech often means "fabricate" or "compensate." Hence, polysemous phrasal verbs should be the focus of instruction. Attention should be paid especially to the register-specific meanings/functions of such phrasal verbs. The WordNet provided by Princeton University (previously mentioned in Chapter 12) is an especially useful tool for this teaching purpose. One can type in any phrasal verb and find all of its possible meanings illustrated with examples.

As with any other lexical items, idioms may be acquired more effectively by direct learning/teaching. It is imperative that teachers create ample opportunities and use many activities to help learners notice, retrieve, and generate target expressions because, according to Nation (2001), noticing (encountering and recognizing a new item), retrieving (recalling its meaning and/or using it), and generating (using it in a different context) are three essential steps or conditions for successful learning of lexical items. A focus on the right idioms assisted with such essential helpful learning activities should significantly enhance idiom acquisition.

### 14.2.2 Exploring semantic (especially metaphorical) motivations

Because of the unique semantic and structural features of idioms and phrasal verbs, defining/explaining the meaning of an idiom and drawing students' attention to its form are crucial in teaching these unique multi-word expressions. Teachers should make sure that idioms are presented and defined in meaningful context. For instance, in explaining the "look good/positive" meaning of *look up*, the teacher should use contextualized examples such as "Both Tom and Mary have now found a job. Things are *looking up* for the family." Given that most idioms and many phrasal verbs are motivated either by conceptual metaphors or historical reasons, it would behoove us to go beyond simple definitions by exploring the motivations of the expressions. Such explorations can help learners more effectively grasp the idioms and phrasal verbs being learned, as recent research has shown strong positive effects of such cognitive explorations. In an experimental study, Kövecses and Szabó (1996) taught two groups of EFL students phrasal verbs made up of the particle *up* and *down* (e.g., *move up, go up, cut down, die down*). The students in the experimental group were made aware of the conceptual metaphors that motivate the phrasal verbs, such as "More is up" and "Less is down." The students in the control group learned the phrasal verbs without exploring the motivating conceptual metaphors. The results indicate that the experimental group significantly outperformed the control group on the achievement test. Boers (2000) reports similar findings in an experimental study that involved phrasal verbs as well as other types of idioms. The usefulness of the exploration of conceptual metaphors is twofold. First, conceptual metaphors are generally universal (Kövecses, 2002). Second, understanding the conceptual metaphor motivation behind many specific idioms enables learners to more easily and effectively understand these idioms.

### 14.2.3 Studying culture-specific motivations: comparison and contrast

While it is very useful to examine universal conceptual metaphors behind idioms and phrasal verbs, teachers should also help learners understand the culture-specific motivations behind many of the L2 idioms (Kövecses, 2002; Liu, 2007). For example, as Liu (2002) demonstrates, due to the extreme importance of sports, business, and automobiles in America, many American English idioms are based on American sports (e.g., *drop the ball/hit a homerun/strike out/touch base with*), business (*cash in/live up to the billing/get shortchanged*), and driving (*in the driver's seat/spinning the wheels/switch gears*). Research has shown that cross-cultural differences often cause difficulty in L2 idiom comprehension (Boers & Demecheleer, 2001; Boers, Demecheleer, & Eyckmans, 2004). To help learners grasp culture-specific idioms, the teacher can lead students in exploring not only the major conceptual metaphors behind the idioms (e.g., life is essentially competition/sports) but also the specific cultural activities that many individual idioms are based on, such as baseball, boxing, and American football in the case of American English. If learners know that life is viewed as competition in America, and if they also understand how baseball and American football are played, they can better understand why *drop the ball* and *strike out* mean failures while *run with the ball* and *hit a homerun* suggest success. Similarly, if learners know that life is viewed as business in the West and if they also understand the basic concepts of business including the stock market, it would enable them to understand that *the bottom line* is the most important thing; *bargaining chips* are leverages in negotiation; and *put stock in something* means "place belief/trust in something." To help learners gain the necessary cultural knowledge for understanding culture-specific idioms, the teacher may use video clips, movies, and other visuals or games that show or simulate the cultural activities or artifacts, such as a baseball game and a business accounting spreadsheet.

In teaching students of a homogeneous L1, exploring similarities and differences between L1 and L2 idioms and their culture-specific motivations can be very useful. For example, as Liu (2002) shows, due to cultural and historical reasons, many of the meanings expressed by sports-based idioms in American English are often conveyed by eating-based idioms in Chinese, e.g., *dropped the ball>broke the cooking pot* (Chinese) and *letting someone off when you had the person on the ropes>letting a cooked duck fly away* (Chinese). As another example, in English, the brain or the mind is the place for thinking while the heart is the place for emotions. However, in Chinese, the heart is also a place for thinking. Without knowing this, ESL/EFL learners and teachers alike may be confused by expressions motivated by the different cultural beliefs. One American instructor in our school's first-year writing class was bewildered to read the following sentence in a Chinese student's composition: "I complained loudly in my heart" (meaning the student did not complain audibly). Knowing the cultural differences can help L2 learners better understand and use idioms. An important related point to note is that idioms that are similar in form in both L1 and L2 but different in metaphorical conceptualization and meaning are especially difficult for learners. Here is an example of such idioms: the English idiom *One bit off more than s/he can chew* is quite similar in form to the Chinese idiom *One cannot finish eating the food that s/he grabbed and therefore has to hold it in his/her lap while walking.* Yet the two idioms differ completely in meaning, with the former meaning taking on something that is beyond one's ability and the latter meaning getting oneself into trouble by being greedy and too clever (a meaning similar to the English business-based idiom *got more than one bargained for*). Teachers and learners should pay special attention to such idioms.

### 14.2.4 Learning the origins of idioms and sorting idioms by source

Explorations of the motivations of idioms often lead to the uncovering of the origins of idioms. For example, in exploring the motivations of the idiom *ballpark figures* (which means approximate estimates of the number of something), one is likely to find baseball as its origin, although there are two different stories regarding the issue. One story says that in old days, for lack of an accurate counting method, the report of the number of attendants at a baseball game was estimation; the second story is that historically the dimensions of baseball parks have often varied from one to another, hence *ballpark* (or estimated) *figures* (Liu,

2002). Teachers should help learners explore the origins of idioms whenever possible because research results (Boers, 2001; Boers & Lindstromberg, 2008) indicate that learning the origins of idioms can also significantly enhance the grasp and retention of idioms. A useful practice related to the exploration of the origins of idioms is to have students sort idioms by source. For example, they may sort idioms by the following source categories: animals (*a big fish in a small pond/let the cat out of the bag*); body parts (*be all ears/has a big mouth/pull someone's leg*); food (*bit off more than one could chew/it's a cakewalk/a piece of cake*). Sorting idioms in this manner may enable learners to more systematically explore the conceptual metaphorical motivations the idioms in each group share, which will in turn help learners more effectively grasp the idioms. Of course, there are many other useful ways to sort and organize idioms (Liu, 2007), such as by the motivating conceptual metaphor (e.g., "anger is pent up steam": *having steam coming out one's ears* and *blow off steam*), by topic on which the idiom is used to comment (e.g., "difficulty/problem": *a pain in the neck* and *a hard nut to crack*), and by key words (e.g., "ball": *dropped the ball, have a ball*, and *the ball is in your court*).

### 14.2.5 Encouraging appropriate and also creative use of idioms/idioms

L2 learners generally have trouble with the use of idioms and phrasal verbs: they seldom use these multi-word expressions, but when they do, they often use them inappropriately. For instance, on the one hand, they tend to use one-word formal verbs instead of a phrasal verb in daily conversation, e.g., saying to the library circulation desk staff, "I need to *borrow* (rather than *check out*) these books." On the other hand, they may use informal expressions in formal writing, e.g., writing in a research paper, "The added procedure *got rid of* (rather than *eliminated*) this side effect." Thus, teachers face a double challenge: to encourage learners to not just use more idioms and phrasal verbs but also to use them appropriately. To confront the challenge, we should first understand and let students know when and where idioms and phrasal verbs are generally used and, more importantly, when and where they should not be used, as well as the functions and effects of using idioms. Generally, idioms and phrasal verbs should not be used in formal and serious social contexts (with the exceptions of some specific items). For example, in a court report about a fire incident, one should say "The fire was *extinguished* (not *put out*) at 2:30 pm"; also one should not use *kick the bucket* to refer to the death of a friend or colleague and should not tell a colleague at work to *shake a leg* (i.e., to move and act quickly). However, in most informal contexts, phrasal verbs can and should be used, and so should idioms especially if one wants to create a dramatic effect.

For more advanced learners, teachers can also encourage creative use of idioms, e.g., *a small fish in a big pond* (based on *a big fish in a small pond*) and the aforementioned *burn the candle at five ends* and *pull a highway out of the hat*. It is important to give these students examples of creative use in context so they can learn how and when idioms may be used creatively. Intermediate and advanced learners should also be encouraged to note and learn permissible varied forms of idioms, such as permissible lexical substitutions and abbreviations mentioned above.

## 14.3 Explaining and teaching formulae/lexical bundles with new insights

As explained earlier, formulae are generally non-idiomatic in meaning. Thus, some of the practices used to teach idioms (such as the exploration for conceptual metaphors and historical reasons) will not work for teaching formulae. Also, some scholars (Coxhead, 2008; Wray, 2000, 2008) find the teaching of formulae especially challenging because the idea of using formulae as unanalyzed chunks runs against the typical classroom teaching practice of analyzing and finding rules/patterns for language learning. Despite the challenges, researchers and teachers have developed some useful strategies.

### 14.3.1 Direct, focused learning/teaching

Given the nature of formulae/lexical bundles and based on research on lexical learning, many experts (Coxhead, 2008; Jones & Haywood, 2004; Wray, 2008) recommend direct learning/teaching of these lexical units and suggest some useful activities, such as reading texts with formulae highlighted, analyzing formulae in context, memorizing target formulae, filling in missing formulaic parts, and using learned formulae in actual speaking and writing. Hill, Lewis, and Lewis (2000) also recommend having students translate formulae back into their L1 so as to draw their attention to L1 and L2 differences in such multi-word units. It is clear that these activities all help with one or more of the aforementioned three essential steps (*noticing/retrieving/generating*) in lexical learning put forward by Nation (2001). Ample empirical research (Bardovi-Harlig & Vellenga, 2012; Bishop, 2004; Jones & Haywood, 2004; Schmitt, Dörnyei, Adolphs, & Durow, 2004; Soler 2005) has shown such direct learning including various conscious strategies helps learners develop both receptive and productive knowledge of formulae. A specific research-proven effective and interesting noticing/ memorizing strategy worth mentioning is the noticing of alliterations in many formulae, e.g., *friend and foe/mind over matter* (Boers & Lindstromberg, 2005; Linstromberg & Boers, 2008).

However, it is worth noting that sometimes conscious learning does not always ensure accurate grasp (i.e., the correct wording) of a formulaic sequence (Cortes, 2004; Coxhead, 2008; Jones & Haywood, 2004). Learners sometimes memorize an expression incorrectly (often with one or two incorrect words in it), e.g., "a danger phenomenon" for "a dangerous phenomenon" (Coxhead, 2008, p. 157). Therefore, it is extremely important to draw learners' attention to the exact wording of a formulaic sequence and to make sure they memorize it correctly. Having students frequently double-check sources for the correct wordings of formulae and do filling-in the missing words should help.

## 14.3.2 Focusing on use and functions

Because formulae often perform specific semantic functions, it is helpful for learners to understand and learn lexical bundles along with their functions. Some studies (e.g., Bardovi-Harlig, 2009; Biber, Conrad, & Cortes, 2004; Liu 2012a) have produced lists of lexical bundles with their functions classified. To help learners understand the functions of lexical bundles, the teacher can use such lists as a guide to introduce students to the topic. Then the teacher should create various opportunities for students to encounter and use the formulae in meaningful contexts (Bardovi-Harlig, 2009; Meunier & Granger, 2008; Nattinger & DeCarrico, 1992). One type of activity is to have students read passages with the target formulae marked (or unmarked) and ask them to pay special attention to these items and their functions.

Another is to "frontload the learner with functional form–meaning pairings" (Wray, 2008, p. 232), i.e., to present to students formulae together with their functions clearly marked, as shown in the following example taken from Nattinger & DeCarrico (1992, pp. 171–172) for teaching formulae used in the argumentation essay:

| | |
|---|---|
| Opening | It has been often asserted that … The purpose of this paper is to … and to maintain that … The paper will show that … by comparing … and contrasting … |
| Body | |
| first paragraph | It can be said that … lend support to the argument that … |
| second paragraph | … does not support the argument that |
| third paragraph | Both … and … are similar in that … is unlike… with respect to |
| Closing | In conclusion, one can generalize that … |

In this example, the functions are general in nature and tied to the organization of the paper. In other contexts, the functions can be topic/situation specific (especially in conversation), such as *asking the teacher for permission to …/ greeting a colleague*. Of course, learners need to have ample opportunity to use the learned expressions in meaningful contexts, such as simulated real-life exchanges that would call for the use of certain specific formulae (e.g., those used in advising sessions between a student and an academic advisor). For learning written academic formulae, students will need to engage in various writing tasks in which they must practice using the formulae they have learned or are learning.

In short, at the risk of repetition, formulae must be learned via repeated focused encounters in meaning contexts.

### 14.3.3 Using helpful authentic sources

Providing learners with a variety of useful authentic materials is instrumental for successful learning of formulae (Coxhead, 2008; Simpson-Vlach & Ellis, 2010). Sound files and corpora, especially situation/discipline-specific ones, are particularly helpful. Students can listen to/read the materials for repeated input. More importantly, they can query the data for the frequency of and the typical context in which a given lexical bundle is used. Such activities enable students to have ample meaningful encounters with the target formulae. The reason for using situation/discipline-specific corpora is that, like idioms and phrasal verbs, formulae are large in number and are register/discipline specific. It is thus very important to choose for instruction only those items useful for students in a given program or field of study. Of course, teachers can also consult or use those aforementioned register-specific lists researchers have produced as well as those presented in Francis, Huston, and Manning's (1996, 1998) two corpus-based pattern grammar books.

### Suggested teaching activities

(Activities 1, 2, and 4 are adapted from those in Liu, 2007.)

1.  *Guessing the idiom (A charade game).* Either the teacher or a student acts out an idiom. Then ask students to guess the idiom based on the charade and explain its meaning. Examples of idioms suitable for this activity include *a lame duck, cutting corners, drop the ball, play with fire,* and *tie up loose ends.*
2.  *What does it mean?* Give students a series of sentences with each containing an idiom and ask students to guess its meaning from context by looking for and using clues, such as *cause–effect, contrast,* and *explanation/definition.* Here are a few examples.
    1.  Tom was laid off and his girlfriend had left him so he really *felt down in the dumps.*
    2.  He said he was going to confront the boss about the issue at the meeting, but he *chickened out* at the last minute.
    3.  Tom is *full of hot air.* He likes to think he knows everything and is eager to tell other people what is right and what is wrong.
3.  *Exploring the different meanings of a phrasal verb and their motivations.* Give students a list of sentences with a phrasal verb used in different meanings as shown below with *look up.* Ask them for the meaning of the phrasal verb in each sentence. Then have them explore the motivations behind the

meanings, paying special attention to the possible conceptual metaphors. Finally, ask students to make sentences by using each meaning of the phrasal verb.

1. Because he's a winner, people really *look up* to him.
2. She *looked up* the word in the dictionary.
3. The economy is *looking up* right now.

4. *Identify the origins/sources of idioms.* Give students a list of idioms and ask them to identify their origins/sources and explain how the origin/source of each may help understand its meaning. Here are some examples: *give the green light, take the bull by the horns, jump on the bandwagon,* and *jump the gun.*

5. *The formulaic sequence notebook.* Ask students to have a notebook (either in hardcopy or electronic version) for recording useful formulae. Students should collect and record in the notebook one expression a day. The entry should also specify the register/context in which it is used and the function it performs. Every week, each student should share with the class the formulae s/he has collected that week as well as the usage and function information of the formulae.

## Note

1 The two terms are placed together with a slash because they are often used interchangeably to refer to the same thing (see Simpson-Vlach & Ellis, 2010). For the sake of simplicity, only one term (mostly *formulae*) will be used each time in most cases hereafter.

# ANNOTATED LIST OF FREE ONLINE RESOURCES FOR GRAMMAR/ VOCABULARY LEARNING/TEACHING

## Free online corpora

British National Corpus (BNC) via Brigham Young University's (Mark Davies's) web interface, http://corpus.byu.edu/bnc/
> Composed of language data produced between the mid 1970s and the early 1990s, this 100 million-word British English corpus contains seven major registers, including spoken, fiction, newspaper, and academic written English. The BYU interface for the corpus is user-friendly with many useful query functions. The corpus is a very useful source for studying British English. The corpus can also be accessed via other portals.

Corpus of American Soap Operas, http://corpus2.byu.edu/soap/
> This 100 million-word corpus contains transcripts of ten American soap operas from 2001 and 2012. It can be used as a source for studying contemporary colloquial American English.

Corpus of Contemporary American English (COCA), http://corpus2.byu.edu/coca/
> This corpus consists of five major registers. It currently has 450 million words with language data gathered from 1990 to 2012, but it is still growing. Each year, 20 million words of language data from the year are added to the corpus. The search functions are the same as the BYU–BNC interface; hence it is user-friendly. It is an excellent source for studying contemporary American English. One thing to note is that the spoken English in COCA is from TV/radio broadcasting programs. In other words, it is not conversational English.

Corpus of Historical American English (COHA), http://corpus.byu.edu/coha/
> This corpus contains American English from 1810 to 2009. It is an excellent source for studying historical American English and for examining changes in American English. Its query functions are essentially the same as COCA.

Michigan Corpus of Academic Spoken English (MICASE), http://quod.lib.umich.edu/cgi/c/corpus/corpus?c=micase;page=simple
> This two million-word corpus contains academic spoken English in various forms such as lecture, discussion, and advising. It is useful for learning American academic spoken English.

Michigan Corpus of Upper Level Student Papers (MICUSP), http://search-micusp.elicorpora.info/simple/
> This 2.6 million-word corpus contains upper-level student papers in 16 disciplines. It may be queried by paper types (seven) and textual features (eight). It is a helpful source for learning academic written English in various disciplines.

## Free useful websites for grammar and vocabulary learning/teaching

Complete Lexical Tutor, www.lextutor.ca/
> This website has three sections, one for language learners, one for researchers, and one for teachers. It offers a variety of learning, teaching, and research information and functions. More importantly, although the site is called "Complete Lexical Tutor," it actually also offers information on grammar learning and teaching.

English Grammar: Grammar lessons, exercises, and rules for everyday use, www.englishgrammar.org/
> This site offers a quite comprehensive coverage of most grammatical rules and usage issues, as well as useful grammar lessons and exercises.

English4today: Online English grammar resources, www.english4today.com/englishgrammar/grammar/index.php
> This site offers a variety of information and learning activities/exercises on English grammar/vocabulary. Its free membership enables you to track your improvement, test yourself, keep your scores, communicate with other members, and post questions to its teachers.

GameZone, www.english-online.org.uk/games/gamezone2.htm
> This site offers many interesting and engaging grammar and vocabulary learning games for learners of various levels.

The Academic Word List, www.victoria.ac.nz/lals/resources/academicwordlist/
> This site (provided by Victoria University of Wellington, New Zealand) offers not only all of the 570 most common academic word families but also many other relevant and useful information about the use and learning of academic words.

Using English: References, www.usingenglish.com/reference/
    This is a section of the Using English website. This section offers definition of grammatical terms and lists of useful English idioms and phrasal verbs.
Vocabulary Resources, www.victoria.ac.nz/lals/resources/vocrefs
    This site (also provided by Victoria University of Wellington, New Zealand) offers various types of very useful information about vocabulary learning and teaching.
WordNet Search, http://wordnetweb.princeton.edu/perl/webwn
    This site offers a very comprehensive coverage of the meanings of lexical items. A query of a single word or a phrase (such as a phrasal verb) will yield all of the possible meanings of the lexical item illustrated with examples.

# GLOSSARY

**Argument structure:** The semantic and syntactic structure of a verb, i.e., the number of arguments (noun phrases) a verb may have and the semantic roles the nouns play in relation to the verb. For example, intransitive verbs like *smile* each have only one argument and the typical role of the argument (the subject) is *agent* or *theme* as shown in *Mary smiled/The mail arrived*, whereas the transitive verbs each need to have two or more arguments fulfilling the semantic roles of *agent, theme, recipient*, etc.

**Base:** The conceptual structure that offers the contextual information/knowledge needed for the understanding of a profiled concept. For example, to understand the profiled concept (word) *radius*, one has to understand its base: a *circle* because *radius* refers to a line segment that joins the center of a circle.

**Bounded/boundedness:** The notion used in Cognitive grammar to mean a region or a concept that is enclosed with closely interconnected entities.

**Cognitive grammar:** A grammar or linguistic theory developed by Ronald Langacker; it considers language to be conceptual in nature and its basic units to be symbolic pairings of form and meaning.

**Colligation:** The collocation of a lexical item with a particular grammatical structure or the syntactic pattern of a word. For example, while *surprising, amazing*, and *astonishing* are synonyms, only *surprising* typically is used in the negative sentence structure, e.g., *It's not surprising*.

**Collocation:** Either the tendency for certain words to co-occur more than by chance or an established combination or co-occurrence of words, e.g., *heavy rain*.

**Collostruction:** A term coined by Anatol Stefanowitsch and Stefan Gries; it blends *collocation* and *construction* to refer to the tendency of certain words to appear in a construction.

**Communicative competence:** A term coined by Dell Hymes to refer to the ability to use language appropriately and effectively.

**Conceptual metaphor:** A metaphor in which one conceptual domain is understood in terms of another, e.g., *life is a journey*.

**Concordancing:** A corpus query method which generates a list of all of the contexts in which the word appears and all of the key words in context (KWIC).

**Construal:** The process/way in which an event/issue is viewed and structured by a speaker/writer. Often, an event/issue can be construed in different ways.

**Construction:** A stored form and meaning pairing established through language experience; a construction can be **filled**, **partially-filled**, or **unfilled** (*see* their entries respectively).

**Construction grammar:** A grammar that treats language as a system composed of patterns or constructions that combine form and meaning in conventionalized or partially non-compositional ways.

**Corpus linguistics:** The study of language through the examination of a collection of real language data. Corpora today are mainly in electronic form and the analysis is carried out using computer search programs.

**Culturally-loaded word:** A word which as a special connotation in one language/culture but not in another language, e.g., *individualism*, which has a positive connotation in American English but a negative one in many Asian languages.

**Discourse grammar:** A grammatical approach which focuses on the role of discourse in the use of grammar.

**Figure:** Used along with the term *ground* to show the relationship in a scene; the meaning of the pair is essentially the same as that of *trajectory* and *landmark*, with *figure/trajectory* being the more prominent (the focus) and *ground/landmark* being the less prominent (the background), e.g., *the book* (figure/trajectory) *on the table* (ground/landmark).

**Finite clause:** A clause with a finite or tensed verb, e.g., *Tom smiles a lot.*

**Filled-construction:** a fixed expression/idiom such as *by and large* and *kick the bucket.*

**Formula/formulaic sequence:** A frequently occurring multi-word expression.

**Frame:** The way a person looks at an issue or the background knowledge that shapes a person's understanding of it. See also *construal.*

**Generative grammar/linguistics/generativism:** A grammar/linguistic approach developed by Noam Chomsky; it strives to offer a set of rules that would generate all the grammatical sentences in a language.

**Ground:** *See* **figure.**

**Homonymy:** A term referring to words which are spelt the same but have different, unrelated meanings, e.g., *bear* the animal and *bear* the verb.

**Immediate constituent (IC) analysis:** The sentence structural analysis method used in structural grammar that breaks down a sentence into immediate constituents/parts until it reaches the smallest meaningful constituents.

**Interlanguage:** The language produced by an L2 learner and the language knowledge that an L2 learner possesses.

**Landmark:** *See* **figure.**

**Language description:** The analysis and description of how a language works, i.e., how its lexical, morphological and syntactical components, among others, combine to convey meanings.

**Lexical bundle/cluster:** *See* **formulaic sequence.**

**Lexical category:** A term for part of speech.

**Lexicogrammar:** A grammatical approach that rejects the traditional linguistics treatment of lexis and grammar as two rigid separate domains and instead views them as the two ends of one continuum.

**Metonymy:** A figure of speech by which one thing is referred to via the mention of something closely related to it, e.g., *the White House* for the U.S. government.

**Nonfinite clause:** A clause with a non-finite or non-tensed verb, such as an infinitive or a participle, e.g., *for him to go.*

**Partially-filled construction:** A partially-fixed expression/idiom such as *bring <someone> up to speed* and *jog <someone's> brain.*

**Pattern grammar:** A lexicogrammar that describes the typical structural patterns in which given nouns and verbs are used.

**Pedagogical grammar:** A description of the grammar of a language intended to help language learning and teaching.

**Pedagogical language description:** *See* **pedagogical grammar.**

**Phraseme/phraseology:** A multi-word unit/the study of multi-word units.

**Polysemy:** A term referring to words which have different but related meanings, e.g., *bright,* which can mean *shining/cheerful/intelligent.*

**Pragmatic failure:** A communication breakdown due to the transfer of a pragmatic rule from a learner's L1. *See* also **sociolinguistic transfer.**

**Pragmatics:** The study of how interlocutors understand and communicate their intended meanings in context.

**Prescriptive grammar/prescriptivism:** A grammar that offers rules about what usages are acceptable or most correct; the rules are often based on the grammarian's view rather than actual usages.

**Pro-drop language:** A language which allows extensive omission of the subject and/or object of a verb/sentence.

**Profile:** *See* **base.**

**Prototype:** The most representative form of a construction, e.g., *give someone something* is the prototype of the Cause to Receive construction.

**Register:** A style of language used in a given social/situational context. There are formal and informal registers as well as various professional registers such as legal and academic writing.

**Schematic construction:** An abstract, unfilled construction like the ditransitive Cause to Receive construction.

**Schematicity:** The status of being schematic or abstract.

**Semantic prosody:** The unique connotative meaning that a word or phrase acquires as a result of its co-occurrence with a given word or phrase.

**Semelfactive verb:** A verb which expresses momentary actions, e.g., *blink/knock.*

**Sociolinguistic transfer:** The use of an L1 sociolinguistic/pragmatic rule in L2, e.g., asking an acquaintance in America "Where are you going?" (a form of greeting in Chinese). *See* also **pragmatic failure.**

**Speech Act theory:** A theory developed by John L. Austin to explain how speakers use language to accomplish intended actions and how hearers interpret the intended meaning form the utterances they hear.

**Structural grammar/linguistics/structuralism:** A grammar/linguistic approach which treats language as a system of interrelated hierarchical structures; it focuses on analyzing and contrasting formal structures of language, such as phonemes, morphemes, and phrases.

**Structure dependence:** The UG principle that language is composed of structured segments, not just a string of words, and that the movement of sentence parts is based on structure (e.g., NP) rather than on single words or word sequences.

**Subcategorization:** The variation of lexical items (usually verbs) in the number and type of syntactic arguments they require in order to be a complete lexical structure. *See* **argument structure.**

**Subset/Superset:** The UG concept/principle which posits that a grammatical usage/ rule may be set up differently between different types of language, with one type permitting more varied or uncommon forms than the other. The type with more varied forms has the superset concerning the rule whereas the one with only the common forms has the subset, e.g., regarding the provision/omission of the subject of a sentence, Spanish has the superset because it allows both while English has the subset since it does not permit broad subject omission. The principle also postulates that learners from a subset language need only positive evidence to acquire the superset language rule while learners from a superset language will need negative evidence (correction) to acquire the subset language rule because these learners tend to assume that the subset language also allows the uncommon form found in their superset L1.

**Symbolic unit:** A conventionalized pairing of form and meaning; it may vary in length and complexity, e.g., a morpheme, and a clause-length idiom.

**Synonymy:** A term referring to words which have essentially the same meaning, e.g., *big/large*.

**Syntactic category:** A term referring to both part of speech and phrase category such as *noun phrase* and *verb phrase*.

**Syntagmatics:** The structural relationship between the linguistic items or structures at various levels in an utterance.

**Systemic functional grammar/linguistics:** A linguistic approach developed by Michael Halliday; it treats language as a social semiotic system or a resource used for making meaning in communication rather than a set of formal rules.

**Token:** An instance or occurrence of a linguistic item (a word, phrase, etc.) in a text/ corpus.

**Token frequency:** The number of times a linguistic item appears in a text/corpus.

**Trajector:** *See* **figure**.

**Type:** One of the different forms of a linguistic item/structure, e.g., for the ditransitive Cause to Receive construction, *give someone something* and *cook someone something* are two types of the same construction; similarly, *happiness* and *quickness* are two different types for the noun-forming morpheme *ness*.

**Type frequency:** The number of times different forms of a linguistic item appear in a text/corpus.

**Unfilled construction:** An abstract or schematic pairing of form, such as the ditransitive Cause to Receive construction.

**Universal Grammar (UG):** An innate system of grammatical rules and constraints assumed to exist in all human languages, a theory developed by Noam Chomsky.

**Word class:** Part of speech.

# REFERENCES

Aijmer, K. (2009). *Corpora and language teaching.* Amsterdam: Benjamins.

Alejo, R., Piquer, A., & Reveriego, G. (2010). Phrasal verbs in EFL course books. In S. De Knop, F. Boers & A. De Rycker (Eds.), *Fostering language teaching efficiency through cognitive linguistics* (pp. 59–78). Berlin: De Gruyter.

Andrews, S. (2007). *Teacher language awareness.* Cambridge: Cambridge University Press.

Aston, G. (2001). *Learning with corpora.* Houston, TX: Athelstan.

Austin, J. L. (1962). *How to do things with words.* Cambridge, MA: Harvard University Press.

Azar, B. S., & Hagen, S. A. (2009). *Understanding and using English grammar* (4th Ed.). White Plains, NY: Pearson/Longman.

Azar, B. S., & Hagen, S. A. (2011). *Fundamentals of English grammar* (4th Ed.). White Plains, NY: Pearson/Longman.

Bardovi-Harlig, K. (1998). Narrative structure and lexical aspect: Conspiring factors in second language acquisition of tense-aspect morphology. *Studies in Second Language Acquisition, 20,* 471–508.

Bardovi-Harlig, K. (1999). From morpheme studies to temporal semantics: Tense–aspect research in SLA. State of the art article. *Studies in Second Language Acquisition, 21,* 341–382.

Bardovi-Harlig, K. (2009). Conventional expressions as a pragmalinguistic resource: recognition and production of conventional expressions in L2 pragmatics. *Language Learning, 59,* 755–795.

Bardovi-Harlig, K., & Vellenga, H. E. (2012). The effect of instruction on conventional expressions in L2 pragmatics. *System, 40,* 77–89.

Barnlund, D., & Araki, S. (1985). Intercultural encounters: The management of compliments by Japanese and Americans. *Journal of Cross-Cultural Psychology, 16,* 9–26.

Beebe, L. (1980). Sociolinguistic variation and style shifting in second language acquisition. *Language Learning, 30,* 433–441.

Benson, M. (1989). The structure of the collocational dictionary. *International Journal of Lexicography, 2,* 1–14.

Berns, M. S. (1984). Functional approaches to language and language teaching: Another look. In S. Savignon & M. S. Berns (Eds.), *Initiatives in communicative language teaching. A book of readings* (pp. 3–21). Reading, PA: Addison-Wesley.

Biber, D., & Conrad, S. (1999). Lexical bundles in conversation and academic prose. In H. Hasselgard & S. Oksfjell (Eds.), *Out of corpora: Studies in honor of Stig Johansson* (pp. 181–190). Amsterdam: Rodopi.

Biber, D., Conrad, S., & Cortes, V. (2004). If you look at ...: Lexical bundles in university teaching and textbooks. *Applied Linguistics, 25*, 371–405.

Biber, D., Conrad, S., & Reppen, R. (1998). *Corpus linguistics: Investigating language structure and use.* Cambridge: Cambridge University Press.

Biber, D., Johansson, S., Leech, G., Conrad, S., & Finegan, E. (1999). *Longman grammar of spoken and written English.* London: Longman.

Bishop, H. (2004). The effect of typographic salience on the look up and comprehension of unknown formulaic sequences. In N. Schmitt (Ed.), *Formulaic sequences* (pp. 227–247). Amsterdam: Benjamins.

Bley-Vroman, R. (1989). What is the logical problem of foreign language learning?. In S. Gass & J. Schachter (Eds.), *Linguistic perspectives on second language acquisition* (pp. 41–68). Cambridge: Cambridge University Press.

Bloomfield, L. (1933). *Language.* New York: Henry Holt.

Blum-Kulka, S., House, J., & Kasper, G. (Eds.), (1989). *Cross-cultural pragmatics: Requests and apologies.* Norwood, NJ: Ablex.

Boers, F. (2000). Metaphor awareness and vocabulary retention. *Applied linguistics, 21*, 553–571.

Boers, F. (2001). Remembering figurative idioms by hypothesizing about their origin. *Prospect, 16*(3), 35–43.

Boers, F., & Demecheleer, M. (2001). Measuring the impact of cross-cultural difference on learners' comprehension of imaginable idioms. *ELT Journal, 55*, 255–262.

Boers, F., Demecheleer, M., & Eyckmans, J. (2004). Cross-cultural variation as a variable in comprehending and remembering figurative idioms. *European Journal of English Studies, 8*, 375–388.

Boers, F., & Lindstromberg, S. (2005). Finding ways to make phrase learning feasible: The mnemonic effect of alliteration. *System, 33*, 225–238.

Boers, F., & Lindstromberg, S. (2008). How cognitive linguistics can foster effective vocabulary teaching. In F. Boers & S. Lindstromberg (Eds.), *Cognitive linguistic approaches to teaching vocabulary and phraseology* (pp. 1–61). Berlin: Mouton de Gruyter.

Bouton, L. (1994). Conversational implicature in the second language: learned slowly when not deliberately taught. *Journal of Pragmatics, 22*, 157–167.

Brown, H. D. (2007). *Teaching by principles: An interactive approach to language pedagogy* (3rd Ed.). London: Longman.

Brown, R. (1973). *A first language: The early stages.* Cambridge, MA: Harvard University Press.

Burnard, L., & McEnery, T. (Eds.). (2000). *Rethinking language pedagogy from a corpus perspective.* Berlin: Peter Lang.

Burt, M. (1975). Error analysis in the adult EFL classroom. *TESOL Quarterly, 9*, 53–63.

Bybee, J. (2008). Usage-based grammar and second language acquisition. In P. Robinson & N. C. Ellis (Eds.), *Handbook of cognitive linguistics and second language acquisition* (pp. 216–236). New York/London: Routledge.

Byrd, P., & Benson, B. (1992). *Applied English grammar.* Boston: Heinle & Heinle.

Campbell, A., & Tomasello, M. (2001). The acquisition of English dative constructions. *Applied Psycholinguistics, 22,* 253–267.

Canale, M. (1983). From communicative competence to communicative language pedagogy. In J. Richards & R. Schmidt (Eds.), *Language and communication* (pp. 2–27). London: Longman.

Canale, M., & Swain, M. (1980). Theoretical bases of communicative approaches to second language teaching and testing. *Applied Linguistics, 1,* 1–47.

Carter, R., & McCarthy, M. (1997). *Exploring spoken English grammar.* Cambridge: Cambridge University Press.

Carter, R., & McCarthy, M. (2006). *Cambridge grammar of English.* Cambridge: Cambridge University Press.

Casenhiser, D., & Goldberg, A. (2005). Fast mapping of a phrasal form and meaning. *Developmental Science, 8,* 500–508.

Celce-Murcia, M. (1991). Discourse analysis and grammar instruction. *Annual Review of Applied Linguistics, 11,* 135–151.

Celce-Murcia, M., & Larsen-Freeman, D. (1999). *The grammar book: An ESL/EFL teacher's course* (2nd Ed.). Boston: Heinle & Heinle.

Celce-Murcia, M., & Olshtain, E. (2000). *Discourse and context in language teaching.* Cambridge: Cambridge University Press.

Celce-Murcia, M., & Sokolik, M. E. (Eds.). (2007–2009). *Grammar connection (5 books).* Boston: Heinle & Heinle.

Chan, T., & Liou, H. (2005). Effects of web-based concordancing instruction on EFL students' learning of verb–noun collocations. *Computer Assisted Language Learning, 18,* 231–250.

Cho, K. (2010). Fostering the acquisition of English prepositions by Japanese learners with networks and prototypes. In S. D. Knop, F. Boers & A. D. Rycker (Eds.), *Fostering language teaching efficiency through cognitive linguistics* (pp. 259–275). Berlin: Mouton de Gruyter.

Chomsky, N. (1957). *Syntactic structures.* The Hague: Mouton.

Chomsky, N. (1965). *Aspects of the theory of syntax.* Cambridge, MA: MIT Press.

Chomsky, N. (1995). *The minimalist program.* Cambridge, MA: MIT Press.

Church, K. W., & Mercer, R. L. (1993). Introduction. In S. Armstrong (Ed.), *Using large corpora* (pp. 1–24). Cambridge, MA: MIT Press.

*Collins COBUILD English language dictionary.* (1987). Glasgow: HarperCollins.

*Collins COBUILD learner's dictionary.* (1996). Glasgow: HarperCollins.

Comrie, B. (1976). *Aspect: An introduction to the study of verbal aspect and related problems.* Cambridge: Cambridge University Press.

Conrad, S. (2004). Corpus linguistics, language variation, and language teaching. In J. Sinclair (Ed.), *How to use corpora in language teaching* (pp. 67–85). Amsterdam: Benjamins.

Conrad, S., & Biber, D. (2009). *Real grammar: A corpus-based approach to English.* White Plains, NY: Pearson/Longman.

Cortes, V. (2004). Lexical bundles in published and student disciplinary writing: Examples from history and biology. *English for Specific Purposes, 23,* 397–423.

Coxhead, A. (2000). A new academic word list. *TESOL Quarterly, 34,* 213–238.

Coxhead, A. (2008). Phraseology and English for academic purposes. In F. Meunier & S. Granger (Eds.), *Phraseology in foreign language learning and teaching* (pp. 149–161). Amsterdam: Benjamins.

Croft, W., & Cruse, D. A. (2004). *Cognitive linguistics*. Cambridge: Cambridge University Press.

Culicover, P. (1997). *Principles and parameters: An introduction to syntactic theory*. Oxford: Oxford University Press.

Davies, M. (2011). *The corpus of contemporary American English*. Provo, UT: Brigham Young University. Available at: <www.americancorpus.org/>.

Davies, M., & Gardner, D. (2010). *A frequency dictionary of contemporary American English: Word sketches, collocates, and thematic lists*. London: Routledge.

Dik, S. C. (1980). *Studies in Functional Grammar*. London: Academic.

Dik, S. C. (1989). The Theory of functional grammar: *Part 1: The structure of the clause*. Dordrecht: Foris.

Dik, S. C. (1997). In K. Hengeveld (Ed.), *The theory of functional grammar. Part 2: Complex and derived constructions*. Berlin: Mouton de Gruyter.

Dirven, R. (2001). English phrasal verbs: Theory and didactic application. In M. Pütz, S. Niemeier & R. Dirven (Eds.), *Applied cognitive linguistics II: Language pedagogy* (pp. 3–27). Berlin: Mouton de Gruyter.

Elbaum, S. N. (1996). *Grammar in context (3 books)* (2nd Ed.). Boston: Heinle & Heinle.

Ellis, R. (1995). Interpretation tasks for grammar teaching. *TESOL Quarterly, 29*, 87–105.

Ellis, R. (2006). Current issues in the teaching of grammar: An SLA perspective. *TESOL Quarterly, 40*, 83–107.

Evans, V., & Green, M. (2006). *Cognitive linguistics: An introduction*. Mahwah, NJ: Lawrence Erlbaum.

Fernando, C. (1996). *Idioms and idiomaticity*. Oxford: Oxford University Press.

Fillmore, C. J. (1968). The case for case. In E. Bach & R. Harms (Eds.), *Universals in linguistic theory* (pp. 1–88). New York: Holt.

Fillmore, C. J. (1985). Syntactic intrusions and the notion of grammatical construction. *BLS, 11*, 73–86.

Fillmore, C. J. (1988). The mechanisms of "Construction Grammar.". *BLS, 14*, 35–55.

Firth, J. R. (1957). *Papers in Linguistics, 1931–1951*. New York: Oxford University Press.

Francis, G. (1993). A corpus-driven approach to grammar: Principles, methods, and examples. In M. Baker, G. Francis & E. Tognini-Bonelli (Eds.), *Text and technology*. Amsterdam: Banjamins.

Francis, G., Hunston, S., & Manning, E. (1996). *Grammar patterns 1: Verbs*. London: HarperCollins.

Francis, G., Hunston, S., & Manning, E. (1998). *Grammar patterns 2: Nouns and adjectives*. London: HarperCollins.

Fuches, M., & Bonner, M. (1995). *Focus on grammar: A higher-intermediate course*. Reading, MA: Addison-Wesley Longman.

Gardner, D., & Davies, M. (2007). Pointing out frequent phrasal verbs: A corpus based analysis. *TESOL Quarterly, 41*, 339–359.

Gass, S., & Neu, J. (Eds.). (1995). *Speech acts across cultures: Challenges to communication in a second language*. New York: Mouton de Gruyter.

Gass, S., & Selinker, L. (2008). *Second language acquisition: An introduction*. New York: Routledge.

Givón, T. (1984). *Syntax: A functional-typological introduction* (Vol. 1). Amsterdam: Benjamins.

Goldberg, A. E. (1995). *Constructions: A construction grammar approach to argument structure*. Chicago: Chicago University Press.

Goldberg, A. E. (2005). Argument realization: The role of constructions, lexical semantics and discourse factors. In J. Östman & M. Fried (Eds.), *Construction grammars: Cognitive grounding and theoretical extensions*. Amsterdam: Benjamins.

Goldberg, A. E. (2006). *Constructions at work*. Oxford: Oxford University Press.

Goldberg, A. E., Casenhiser, D., & Sethuraman, N. (2004). Learning argument structure generalizations. *Cognitive Linguistics, 15*, 289–316.

Granger, S., Dagneaux, E., & Meunier, F. (Eds.), (2002). *The international corpus of learner English: Handbook and CD-ROM*. Louvain-la-Neuve: UCL Presses.

Grant, L. E. (2005). Frequency of "core idioms' in the British national corpus (BNC). *International Journal of Corpus Linguistics, 10*, 429–541.

Grant, L. E. (2007). In a manner of speaking: Assessing frequent spoken figurative idioms to assist ESL/EFL teachers. *System, 35*, 169–181.

Grant, L. E., & Nation, P. (2006). How many idioms are there in English? *ITL International Journal of Applied Linguistics, 151*, 1–14.

Gregg, K. R. (1984). Krashen's Monitor and Occam's razor. *Applied Linguistics, 5*, 79–100.

Gries, S. Th. (2001). A corpus linguistic analysis of English *-ic* vs *-ical* adjectives. *ICAME Journal, 25*, 65–108.

Gries, S. Th. (2008). Corpus-based methods in analyses of second language acquisition data. In P. Robinson & N. Ellis (Eds.), *Handbook of cognitive linguistics and second language acquisition* (pp. 406–432). London: Routledge.

Gries, S. Th., & Otani, N. (2010). Behavioral profiles: A corpus-based perspective on synonymy and antonymy. *ICAME Journal, 34*, 121–150.

Gries, S. Th., & Stefanowitsch, A. (2004). Extending collostructional analysis: A corpus-based perspective on 'alternations'. *International Journal of Corpus Linguistics, 9*, 97–129.

Gunpowder [web page]. (2012). Retrieved from: <http://en.wikipedia.org/wiki/Gunpowder/>.

Hall, E. T. (1976). *Beyond culture*. New York: Doubleday.

Halliday, M. A. K. (1973). *Explorations in the functions of language*. London: Edward Arnold.

Halliday, M. A. K. (1994). *An introduction to functional grammar* (2nd Ed.). London: Edward Arnold.

Halliday, M. A. K., & Hasan, R. (1976). *Cohesion in English*. London: Longman.

Hanks, P. (1996). Contextual dependency and lexical sets. *International Journal of Corpus Linguistics, 1*, 75–98.

Hawkins, J. (1978). *Definiteness and indefiniteness*. London: Croom Helm.

Hill, J., Lewis, M., & Lewis, M. (2000). Classroom strategies, activities and exercises. In M. Lewis (Ed.), *Teaching collocation: Further developments in the lexical approach* (pp. 86–117). Boston: Heinle & Heinle.

Hilles, S. (1986). Interlanguage in the pro-drop parameter. *Second Language Research, 2*, 33–52.

Hinkel, E., & Fotos, S. (Eds.). (2002). *New perspectives on grammar teaching in second language classrooms*. Mahwah, NJ: Erlbaum.

Hoey, M. (1991). *Patterns of lexis in text*. Cambridge: Cambridge University Press.

Hoey, M. (2005). *Lexical priming: A new theory of words and language*. London: Routledge.

Holme, R. (2009). *Cognitive linguistics and language teaching*. New York: Palgrave Macmillan.

Holme, R. (2012). Cognitive linguistics and the second language classroom. *TESOL Quarterly, 46*, 6–29.

Hopper, P. J. (1987). Emergent grammar. *BLS, 13*, 139–157.

Hudson, R. (2001). Grammar teaching and writing skills: The research evidence. *Syntax in the Schools, 17*, 1–6.

Hughes, R., & McCarthy, M. (1998). From sentences to discourse: Discourse grammar and English language teaching. *TESOL Quarterly, 32*, 263–287.

Hunston, S., & Francis, G. (1998). Verbs observed: A corpus-driven pedagogical grammar. *Applied Linguistics, 19*, 45–72.

Hunston, S., & Francis, G. (2000). *Pattern grammar: A corpus-driven approach to the lexical grammar of English.* Amsterdam: Benjamins.

Hyland, K. (2008). As can be seen: Lexical bundles and disciplinary variation. *English for Specific Purposes, 27,* 4–21.

Hymes, D. (1962). The ethnography of speaking. In T. Gladwin & W. C. Sturtevant (Eds.), *Anthropology and human behavior* (pp. 13–53). Washington, DC: The Anthropology Society of Washington.

Hymes, D. (1964). Introduction: Toward ethnographies of communication. *American Anthropologist, 66*(6), 1–34.

Hymes, D. (1966). Two types of linguistic relativity. In W. Bright (Ed.), *Sociolinguistics* (pp. 114–158). The Hague: Mouton.

Hymes, D. (1971). *On communicative competence.* Philadelphia: University of Pennsylvania Press.

Hymes, D. (1982). Prague functionalism. *American Anthropologist, 84,* 398–399.

Imai, M., & Gentner, D. (1997). A cross-linguistic study of early word meaning: Universal ontology and linguistic influences. *Cognition, 62,* 169–200.

Ionin, T., & Montrul, S. (2010). The role of L1-transfer in the interpretation of articles with definite plurals in L2-English. *Language Learning, 60,* 877–925.

Ionin, T., Montrul, S., Kim, J., & Philippov, V. (2011). Genericity distinctions and the interpretation of determiners in L2 acquisition. *Language Acquisition, 18,* 242–280.

Ishihara, N., & Cohen, A. (2010). *Teaching and learning pragmatics: Where language and culture meet.* White Plains, NY: Pearson Longman.

Jones, M., & Haywood, S. (2004). Facilitating the acquisition of formulaic sequences: An exploratory study in an EAP context. In N. Schmitt (Ed.), *Formulaic sequences* (pp. 269–291). Amsterdam: Benjamins.

Keith, F. S. (2010). *Clear grammar: Keys to grammar for English language learners (2 books)* (2nd Ed.). Ann Arbor, MI: University of Michigan Press.

Keshavarz, M. H., & Salimi, H. (2007). Collocational competence and cloze test performance: A study of Iranian EFL Learners. *International Journal of Applied Linguistics, 17,* 81–92.

Kettemann, B., & Marko, G. (Eds.). (2002). *Teaching and learning by doing corpus analysis.* Amsterdam: Rodopi.

Koike, D. A., & Pearson, L. (2005). The effect of instruction and feedback in the development of pragmatic competence. *System, 33,* 481–501.

Kövecses, Z. (2002). *Metaphor: A practical guide.* Oxford: Oxford University Press.

Kövecses, Z. (2006). *Language, mind, and culture.* Oxford: Oxford University Press.

Kövecses, Z., & Szabó, P. (1996). Idioms: A view from cognitive linguistics. *Applied Linguistics, 17,* 326–355.

Krashen, S. (1981). *Second language acquisition and second language learning.* Oxford: Pergamon Press.

Lado, R. (1972). Patterns of difficulty in vocabulary. In H. B. Allen & R. N. Campbell (Eds.), *Teaching English as a second language* (pp. 275–288). New York: McGraw-Hill.

Lakoff, G. (1987). *Women, fire, and dangerous things: What categories reveal about the mind.* Chicago: University of Chicago.

Lakoff, G., & Johnson, M. (1980). *Metaphors we live by.* Chicago: University of Chicago Press.

Langacker, R. W. (1987). *Foundations of cognitive grammar: Theoretical prerequisites.* Stanford, CA: Stanford University Press.

Langacker, R. W. (1991). *Foundations of cognitive grammar: Descriptive application.* Stanford, CA: Stanford University Press.

Langacker, R. W. (1999). *Grammar and Conceptualization*. Berlin: Mouton de Gruyter.

Langacker, R. W. (2001). Cognitive linguistics, language pedagogy, and the English present tense. In M. Pütz, S. Niemeier & R. Dirven (Eds.), *Applied cognitive linguistics I: Theory and language acquisition* (pp. 5–39). Berlin: Mouton de Gruyter.

Langacker, R. W. (2008a). *Cognitive grammar: A basic introduction*. Oxford: Oxford University Press.

Langacker, R. W. (2008b). Cognitive grammar as a basis for language instruction. In P. Roberson & N. Ellis (Eds.), *Handbook of cognitive linguistics and second language acquisition* (pp. 66–88). New York/London: Routledge.

Langlotz, A. (2006). *Idiomatic creativity: A cognitive-linguistic model of idiom-representation and idiom-variation in English*. Amsterdam: Benjamins.

Larsen-Freeman, D. (Series Ed./Dir.) (1993). *Grammar dimensions: Form, meaning, and use (4 books)*. Boston: Heinle & Heinle.

Larsen-Freeman, D. (2003). *Teaching language: From grammar to grammaring*. Boston: Heinle & Heinle.

Larsen-Freeman, D., & Cameron, L. (2008). *Complex systems and applied linguistics*. Oxford: Oxford University Press.

Laufer, B. (1997). What's in a word that makes it hard or easy: some intralexical factors that affects the learning of words. In N. Schmitt & M. McCarthy (Eds.), *Vocabulary description, acquisition, and pedagogy* (pp. 140–154). Cambridge: Cambridge University Press.

Lee, D. (2001). *Cognitive linguistics: An introduction*. Oxford: Oxford University.

Leech, G. (1992). Corpora and theories of linguistic performance. In J. Svartvik (Ed.), *Directions in corpus linguistics: Proceedings of Nobel symposium 82* (pp. 125–148). Berlin: Mouton de Gruyter.

Leech, G. (2000). Grammars of spoken English: New implications of corpus-oriented research. *Language Learning, 50*, 675–724.

Lester, M. (1990). *Grammar in the classroom*. New York: Macmillan.

Lewis, M. (2000). *Teaching collocation: Further developments in the lexical approach*. Boston: Heinle & Heinle.

Lindquist, H. (2009). *Corpus linguistics and the description of English*. Edinburgh: Edinburgh University Press.

Lindstromberg, S., & Boers, F. (2008). The mnemonic effect of noticing alliteration in lexical chunks. *Applied Linguistics, 29*, 200–222.

Liu, D. (1995). Sociocultural transfer and its effect on second language speakers' communication. *International Journal of Intercultural Relations, 19*, 253–265.

Liu, D. (2002). *Metaphor, culture, and worldview: The case of American English and the Chinese language*. Lanham, MD: University Press of America.

Liu, D. (2003). The most frequently used idioms in American spoken English: A corpus analysis and its implications. *TESOL Quarterly, 37*, 671–700.

Liu, D. (2007). *Idioms: Description, comprehension, acquisition, and pedagogy*. New York: Routledge.

Liu, D. (2008a). Intransitive or object deleting: Classifying English verbs used without an object. *Journal of English Linguistics, 36*, 289–313.

Liu, D. (2008b). Adequate language description in L2 research/teaching: The case of pro-drop language speakers learning English. *International Journal of Applied Linguistics, 18*, 274–293.

Liu, D. (2008c). Linking adverbials: An across-register study and its implications. *International Journal of Corpus Linguistics, 13*, 491–518.

Liu, D. (2010a). Going beyond patterns: Involving cognitive analysis in the learning of collocations. *TESOL Quarterly, 44,* 4–30.

Liu, D. (2010b). Is it a *chief, main, major, primary,* or *principal* concern: A corpus-based behavioral profile study of the near-synonyms. *International Journal of Corpus Linguistics, 15,* 56–87.

Liu, D. (2010c). Using Corpora for language learning, teaching, and research. In A. Mahboob (Ed.), *NNEST Lens: Nonnative English Speakers in TESOL* (pp. 305–324). Newcastle upon Tyne: Cambridge Scholars Publishing.

Liu, D. (2011a). Making grammar instruction more empowering: An exploratory case study of corpus use in the learning/teaching of grammar. *Research in the Teaching of English, 45,* 353–377.

Liu, D. (2011b). The most-frequently used English phrasal verbs in American and British English: A multi-corpus examination. *TESOL Quarterly, 45,* 661–688.

Liu, D. (2012a). The most frequently-used multi-word constructions in academic written English: A multi-corpus study. *English for Specific Purposes, 31,* 25–35.

Liu, D. (2012b). Teaching grammar. In C. A. Chapelle (Ed.), *Encyclopedia of applied linguistics* (pp. 5572–5578). Oxford: Wiley-Blackwell. doi: 10.1002/978140519843.

Liu, D. (2013). Salience and construal in the use of synonymy: A study of two sets of near-synonymous nouns. *Cognitive Linguistics, 24,* 67–113.

Liu, D., Ahn, G., Baek, K., & Han, N. (2004). South Korean high school English teachers' code switching: Questions and challenges in the drive for maximal use of English in teaching. *TESOL Quarterly, 38,* 605–638.

Liu, D., & Espino, M. (2012). *Actually, genuinely, really,* and *truly*: A corpus-based Behavioral Profile study of near-synonymous adverbs. *International Journal of Corpus Linguistics, 17,* 198–228.

Liu, D., & Gleason, J. (2002). The acquisition of the article *the* by nonnative speakers of English: An analysis of four nongeneric uses. *Studies in Second language Acquisition, 24,* 1–26.

Liu, D., & Jiang, P. (2009). Using a corpus-based lexicogrammatical approach to grammar instruction in EFL and ESL contexts. *Modern Language Journal, 93,* 61–78.

Liu, D., & Master, P. (Eds.). (2003). *Grammar teaching in teacher education.* Alexandria, VA: TESOL Inc.

Liu, D., & Zhong, S. (1999). Acquisition of culturally-loaded words in EFL. *Foreign Language Annuals, 32,* 177–187.

*Longman Corpus Network.* (2003). London: Longman.

Louw, B. (1993). Irony in the text or insincerity in the writer? The diagnostic potential of semantic Prosodies. In M. Baker, G. Francis & E. Tognini- Bonelli (Eds.), *Text and technology* (pp. 157–176). Amsterdam: Benjamins.

Lowth, R. (1763). *A short introduction to English grammar, with critical notes.* London: A. Millar, R. and J. Dodsley.

Lyster, R. (1994). The effect of functional-analytic teaching on aspects of French immersion students' sociolinguistic competence. *Applied Linguistics, 15,* 263–287.

Master, P. (1997). The English article system: Acquisition, function, and pedagogy. *System, 25,* 215–232.

Maurer, J. (1995). *Focus on grammar: An advanced course for reference and practice.* Reading, MA: Addison-Wesley Longman.

Mayntz, M. (2012). Wild turkey history [web site]. Retrieved from: <http://birding.about.com/od/Bird-Trivia/a/Wild-Turkey-History.htm/>.

McCarthy, M. J., & Carter, R. A. (1994). *Language as discourse: Perspectives for language teaching.* London: Longman.

McCarthy, M., & O'Dell, F. (2005). *English collocations in use: Intermediate*. Cambridge: Cambridge University Press.

McLaughlin, B. (1978). The monitor model: Some methodological considerations. *Language Learning, 28,* 309–332.

*Merriam-Webster's dictionary of English usage* (2nd Ed.). (1994). Springfield, MA: Merriam-Webster.

Meunier, F., & Granger, S. (Eds.). (2008). *Phraseology in foreign language learning and teaching.* Amsterdam: John Benjamins.

Michigan corpus of academic spoken English. (2002). Ann Arbor, MI: The Regents of the University of Michigan.

Moon, R. (1998). *Fixed expressions and idioms in English: A corpus-based approach*. Oxford: Clarendon Press.

Nation, P. (2001). *Learning vocabulary in another language*. Cambridge: Cambridge University Press.

Nattinger, J., & DeCarrico, J. (1992). *Lexical phrases and language teaching*. Oxford: Oxford University Press.

Nesselhauf, N. (2003). The use of collocations by advanced learners of English and some implications for teaching. *Applied Linguistics, 24,* 223–242.

O'Dell, F., & McCarthy, M. (2008). *English collocations in use: Advanced*. Cambridge: Cambridge University Press.

*OED (Oxford English Dictionary) online.* (2012). Institution-paid submission at <http://dictionary.oed.com>.

O'keeffe, A., McCarthy, M., & Carter, R. (2007). *OED (Oxford English Dictionary OED (Oxford English Dictionary) online.* (2012). Institution-paid submission at <http://dictionary.oed.com> *From corpus to classroom*. Cambridge: Cambridge University Press.

Palmer, F. R. (1971). *Grammar*. Harmondsworth: Penguin.

Palmer, H. E. (1933). *Second interim report on English collocations.* Tokyo: Kaitakusha.

Parrott, M. (2000). *Grammar for English language teachers*. Cambridge: Cambridge University Press.

Pawley, A., & Syder, F. H. (1983). Two puzzles for linguistic theory: Nativelike selection and nativelike fluency. In J. C. Richards & R. W. Schmidt (Eds.), *Language and communication* (pp. 191–226). New York: Longman.

Pütz, M., Niemeier, S., & Dirven, R. (Eds.), (2001). *Applied cognitive linguistics I: Theory and language acquisition*. Berlin: Mouton de Gruyter.

Quinion, M. (2011). By and large [web page]. Retrieved from: <www.worldwidewords.org/qa/qa-bya1.htm/>.

Quirk, R., Greenbaum, S., Leech, G., & Svartvik, J. (1989). *A Comprehensive grammar of the English language* (2nd Ed.). New York: Longman.

Reed, A., & Kellogg, B. (1887). *Higher lessons in English*. New York: Clark & Maynard. (Delmar, NY: Scholars' Facsimiles and Reprints, 1987).

Reppen, R. (2010). *Using corpora in the language classroom*. Cambridge: Cambridge University Press.

Richards, J. C., & Rodgers, T. S. (2001). *Approaches and methods in language teaching* (2nd ed.). Cambridge: Cambridge University Press.

Rivers, W. M. (1981). *Teaching foreign-language skills* (2nd ed.). Chicago: University of Chicago Press.

Robinson, P., & Ellis, N. (2008). Conclusion: Cognitive linguistics, second language acquisition and L2 instruction—issues for research. In P. Robinson & N. Ellis (Eds.), *Handbook of cognitive linguistics and second language acquisition* (pp. 489–545). New York/London: Routledge.

Rose, K. R. (2005). On the effects of instruction in second language pragmatics. *System*, *33*, 383–399.

Roulet, E. (1975). *Linguistic theory, linguistic description, and language teaching*. London: Longman.

Rudman, J. (1981). *Rudman's questions and answers on the TOEFL*. Plainview, NY: NLC.

Sanchez-Stockhammer, C. (2010). Improving word learn-ability with lexical decomposition strategies. In S. D. Knop, F. Boers & A. D. Rycker (Eds.), *Fostering language teaching efficiency through cognitive linguistics* (pp. 337–356). Berlin: Mouton de Gruyter.

Saussure, F. (1916).. In C. Bally & A. Sechehaye (Eds.), *Course de linguistique*. New York: Philosophical Library. (trans. as *Course in general linguistics* by W. Baskin, 1959).

Schachter, J. (1988). Second language acquisition and its relationship to Universal Grammar. *Applied Linguistics*, *9*, 219–235.

Schmitt, N. (1998). Tracking the incremental acquisition of second language vocabulary: A longitudinal study. *Language Learning*, *48*, 281–317.

Schmitt, N., Dörnyer, Z., Adolphs, S., & Durow, V. (2004). Knowledge and acquisition of formulaic sequences: A longitudinal study. In N. Schmitt (Ed.), *Formulaic sequences* (pp. 55–86). Amsterdam: Benjamins.

Schwartz, B., & Sprouse, R. (1996). L2 cognitive states and the full transfer/full access model. *Second Language Research*, *12*, 40–72.

Searle, J. (1969). *Speech Acts*. Cambridge: Cambridge University Press.

Simpson-Vlach, R., & Ellis, N. (2010). An academic formulas list: New methods in phraseology research. *Applied Linguistics*, *31*, 487–512.

Sinclair, J. M. (1987). Collocation: A progress report. In R. Steele & T. Thomas (Eds.), *Language topics: Essays in honor of Michael Halliday II* (pp. 319–331). Amsterdam: Benjamins.

Sinclair, J. M. (1991). *Corpus, concordance, collocation*. Oxford: Oxford University Press.

Sinclair, J. (2004). *Trust the text: Language, corpus and discourse*. London: Routledge.

Skinner, B. F. (1957). *Verbal behavior*. Acton, MA: Copley Publishing Group.

Smadja, F., & McKeown, K. (1991). Using collocations for language generation. *Computational Intelligence*, *7*, 229–239.

Soler, E. A. (2005). Does instruction work for learning pragmatics in the EFL context? *System*, *33*, 417–435.

Stageberg, N. C. (1981). *An introductory English grammar* (4th Ed.). Fort Worth, TX: Holt, Rinehart, & Winston.

Stefanowitsch, A., & Gries, S. Th. (2003). Collostructions: Investigating the interaction between words and constructions. *International Journal of Corpus Linguistics*, *8*, 209–243.

Stewart, D. (2009). *Semantic prosody: A critical evaluation*. London: Routledge.

Stubbs, M. (1995). Corpus evidence for norms of lexical collocating. In G. Cook & B. Seidlhofer (Eds.), *Principle and practice in applied linguistics* (pp. 245–256). Oxford: Oxford University Press.

Stubbs, M. (2001). *Words and phrases: Corpus studies of lexical semantics*. Oxford: Blackwell.

Sun, Y., & Wang, L. (2003). Concordancers in the EFL classroom: Cognitive approaches and collocation difficulty. *Computer Assisted Language Learning*, *16*, 83–94.

Swan, M. (1994). Design criteria for pedagogic language rules. In M. Bygate, A. Tonkyn & E. Williams (Eds.), *Grammar and the language teacher* (pp. 45–55). New York: Prentice Hall.

Takahashi, S. (2005). Noticing in task performance and learning outcomes: A qualitative analysis of instructional effects in interlanguage pragmatics. *System*, *33*, 437–461.

Talmy, L. (1988). Force dynamics in language and cognition. *Cognitive Science*, *12*, 49–100.

Talmy, L. (1991). Path to realization: A typology of event conflation. *Berkeley Working Papers in Linguistics*, 480–519.

Talmy, L. (2000). *Toward a cognitive semantics. (Volume I: Concept structuring system. Volume 2: Typology and process in concept structuring.)*. Cambridge, MA: MIT Press.

Taylor, J. R. (2002). *Cognitive grammar*. Oxford: Oxford University Press.

Thomas, J. (1983). Cross-cultural pragmatic failure. *Applied Linguistics*, *4*, 91–109.

Tomasello, M. (2000). First steps toward a usage-based theory of language acquisition. *Cognitive Linguistics*, *11*, 61–82.

Tomasello, M. (2003). *Constructing a language: A usage-based theory of language*. Cambridge, MA: Harvard University Press.

Tomasello, M., & Brooks, P. J. (1998). Young children's earliest transitive and intransitive constructions. *Cognitive Linguistics*, *9*, 379–395.

Towell, R., & Hawkins, R. (1994). *Approaches to second language acquisition*. Clevedon: Multilingual Matters.

Tsui, A. (2004). What teachers have always wanted to know – and how corpora can help. In J. Sinclair (Ed.), *How to use corpora in language teaching* (pp. 39–61). Amsterdam: Benjamins.

Tyler, A. (2008). Cognitive linguistics and second language instruction. In P. Robinson & N. Ellis (Eds.), *Handbook of cognitive linguistics and second language acquisition* (pp. 456–488). New York/London: Routledge.

Tyler, A. (2012). *Cognitive linguistics and second language learning: Theoretical basics and experimental evidence*. New York/London: Routledge.

Tyler, A., & Evans, V. (2003). *The semantics of English prepositions: Spatial senses, embodied meaning and cognition*. Cambridge: Cambridge University Press.

Vendler, Z. (1957). Verbs and times. *The Philosophical Review*, *66*, 143–160.

Walker, C. P. (2011). A corpus-based study of the linguistic features and processes which influence the way collocations are formed. *TESOL Quarterly*, *45*, 291–312.

White, L. (1985). The "pro-drop" parameter in adult second language learning. *Language Learning*, *35*, 47–62.

White, L. (1989). *Universal grammar and second language acquisition*. Amsterdam: Benjamins.

Wilkins, D. A. (1976). *National syllabus*. London: Oxford University Press.

Williams, J. D. (2005). *The teachers' grammar book* (2nd Ed.). Mahwah, NJ: Lawrence Earlbaum.

Willis, D. (2003). *Rules, patterns, and words: Grammar and lexis in English language teaching*. Cambridge: Cambridge University Press.

Wolfson, N. (1981). Compliments in cross-cultural perspective. *TESOL Quarterly*, *15*, 117–124.

Wolfson, N. (1989). *Perspectives: Sociolinguistics and TESOL*. Rowley, MA: Newbury House.

Wray, A. (2000). Formulaic sequences in second language teaching: Principle and practice. *Applied Linguistics*, *21*, 463–489.

Wray, A. (2002). *Formulaic language and the lexicon*. Cambridge: Cambridge University Press.

Wray, A. (2008). *Formulaic language: Pushing the boundaries*. Oxford: Oxford University Press.

Yoon, H., & Hirvela, A. (2004). ESL student attitudes toward corpus use in L2 writing. *Journal of Second Language Writing*, *13*, 257–283.

Yuan, B. (1997). Asymmetry of null subjects and null objects in Chinese speakers' L2 English. *Studies in Second Language Acquisition*, *19*, 467–497.

Yule, G. (1998). *Explaining English grammar*. Oxford: Oxford University Press.

Zimmerman, C. B. (2009). *Word knowledge: A vocabulary teacher's guide*. Oxford: Oxford University Press.

# AUTHOR INDEX

# SUBJECT INDEX

Note: References in **bold** are to the glossary